MARIJUANA NATION

MARIJUANA NATION

One Man's Chronicle of America Getting High:
From Vietnam to Legalization

ROGER ROFFMAN

PEGASUS BOOKS
NEW YORK LONDON

MARIJUANA NATION

Pegasus Books LLC
80 Broad Street, 5th Floor
New York, NY 10004

Copyright © 2014 by Roger Roffman

First Pegasus Books edition April 2014

Interior design by Maria Fernandez

The quote on page 195 from the article "The Importance of Being Stoned in Vietnam" by John Steinbeck IV originally appeared in a 1968 issue of *The Washingtonian* magazine. Reprinted with permission from *The Washingtonian* and Nancy Steinbeck, co-author of *The Other Side of Eden* with John Steinbeck IV. Because he died clean and sober at the age of 44, due to the effects of a life-long struggle with drugs and alcohol, John would warn against romanticizing marijuana use, especially during a senseless war that damaged so many vets. He often said "When you accept Life on Life's terms, sobriety is the strongest dope on earth."

The quote on page 87-88 is from the book *Achilles in Vietnam: Combat Trauma and the Undoing of Character* by Jonathan Shay, Simon & Schuster, 1994. Reprinted with permission.

Library of Congress Cataloging-in-Publication Data is available.

ISBN: 978-1-60598-546-6

10 9 8 7 6 5 4 3 2 1

Printed in the United States of America
Distributed by W. W. Norton & Company

For Cheryl

Fortune is guiding our affairs better than we ourselves could have wished. Do you see over yonder, friend Sancho, thirty or forty hulking giants? I intend to do battle with them and slay them. With their spoils we shall begin to be rich for this is a righteous war . . .

—Miguel de Cervantes Saavedra
The Ingenious Hidalgo Don Quixote of La Mancha

CONTENTS

PART 3. ACTIVISM

PART 4. DEPENDENCE

PART 5. ACTIVISM RENEWED

AUTHOR'S NOTE

While reconstructing events, the earliest of which took place more than forty-five years ago, I benefited from a wealth of resource materials. The stack of letters I wrote to my parents from Vietnam, my journal, files packed with Army orders and correspondence, and many rolls of snapshots and slides all contributed. A number of books, articles, and websites focusing on such topics as military psychiatry, court martial procedures, and the Army's stockade at Long Binh were also helpful.

Binders that I filled with twelve years worth of newspaper and magazine clippings about illicit drugs, beginning in the late 1960s, were a treasure trove, as were boxes of records from my stint in the 1970s as a NORML activist. I made use of verbatim transcripts and audio recordings of legislative hearings and floor debates, entries in *The Congressional Record*, and numerous publications on the history of marijuana policy reform.

I was able to check the accuracy of my memory with many of the people who appear in the book, a number of whom generously reviewed chapter drafts and helped fill in missing dates as well as details about key events. I must add a caveat, however. While the events that appear as scenes in this book took place, and the people portrayed in them are represented as I remember them, the dialogue, of necessity, is the product of artistic license. Throughout, I have striven for honesty in how I've presented my perceptions, motivations, feelings, and actions, as well as the actions of others.

Some names have been altered, either at an individual's request or when I believed it would be in their interest to protect their privacy. Certain descriptions of individuals were changed for the same purpose.

In most of the text, as well as in the title, marijuana is spelled with a "j." The few exceptions, however, are when I've cited a document in which an earlier spelling, "marihuana," was used.

PROLOGUE

have been involved with marijuana for more than 45 years and it has changed me.

Since the dawn of the twentieth century, both truths and myths about marijuana have vied for believers and their contest endures to this day.

Marijuana first piqued my interest when I served as an Army officer in Vietnam. Later, as a researcher, a scholar of the drug, a therapist, an activist, a casual and then compulsive user, marijuana has retained its fascination.

Ever since America's young first marched in opposition to the war in Vietnam, pot's popularity has periodically ebbed and surged. Calls for greater, fewer, or no marijuana penalties also have swung on their own pendulum.

Along the way, my ideas and beliefs about marijuana have evolved. They continue to do so. At times, the cacophony of views, passionately expressed by those who hold diametrically opposing perspectives about the drug, causes me to wonder if I'm somehow misunderstanding, just not getting it, and downright wrong in what I believe.

Seven years ago my retirement from the University of Washington faculty loomed, and the prospect of writing a book about marijuana, a kind of summing up of the focus of my career, seemed a good idea. When I first imagined writing this memoir, its central theme eluded me.

Then, early in the autumn of 2007, my wife and I explored English Camp, a historic military installation that is now a national park on San Juan Island, part of a magnificent Puget Sound archipelago about 80 miles northwest of Seattle. With the exception of a hawk on the hunt, Cheryl and I, along with our Australian Shepherd, Teddy, had the park to ourselves, most of the summer tourists having given back the island to its permanent residents just after Labor Day.

In the late afternoon we tromped along the expansive beach of another former military post known as American Camp on San Juan Island's southern tip. Our guidebook described a British–American conflict that almost led to war in this place 150 years earlier.

As we talked about this piece of history, my thoughts drifted to the quandaries I was trying to resolve about the book. That day I found the theme.

But first, let me tell you the story about what nearly happened at the spot where we were standing. Something historians call "The Pig War."

On this island on June 15, 1859, Lyman Cutlar, an American, shot a pig owned by Charles Griffin, a Brit. A minor flap, one would think. But an 1846 treaty had put the ownership of this and several nearby islands in Puget Sound in dispute. Both Britain and the United States laid claim to them. Peaceful relations were maintained while the ownership remained in question. The shooting of the pig rapidly set the two countries on a collision course.

When British authorities threatened to arrest Cutlar for discharging a firearm in what was that era's version of a de-militarized zone, the Americans called for military protection. Soon, 66 soldiers of the 9th Infantry had been deployed to San Juan Island. Shortly thereafter, three British warships arrived. Within two months, 461 American servicemen with 14 cannons faced off with 2,140 marines aboard five British warships mounting 70 guns. The battle most certainly would have been joined had not Britain's Admiral Robert Baynes refused to carry out an order to attack, deciding that "two great nations in a war over a squabble about a pig" was irrational. Ultimately, the tensions defused and the war was called off.

Walking down the American Camp beach on that sunny autumn afternoon, Teddy joyfully retrieved a stick we took turns throwing into the surf, eagerly waiting each time for the game to be repeated. Cheryl roamed off in search of artfully shaped pieces of driftwood, and I sat on a log and thought about wars.

A war over a pig . . . a war over marijuana.

War had been averted on San Juan Island, we'd learned, because Admiral Baynes knew that once combat began, other options for resolving the dispute would be severely curtailed. How unfortunate, I thought, that his style of reasoned analysis was nowhere to be found as marijuana's popularity exploded during the 1960s and 1970s and a war concerning marijuana and marijuana laws commenced. It was, and continues to be, a tumultuous period rife with political and cultural conflict, as well as its own casualties.

For decades the combatants on one side have included federal drug abuse agencies and community groups marching behind the banner of zero tolerance. On the other side are advocacy groups rallying for liberalized marijuana laws and demanding civil liberties.

Each side strives for hegemony in shaping the public's attitudes about marijuana. On one hand, policy reform groups emphasize the harms to those otherwise law-abiding citizens who, having been convicted of possessing marijuana, carry the burden of a lifelong criminal record. But they usually leave some facts out. They rarely acknowledge the very real adverse health and behavioral consequences that some marijuana smokers face.

On the other hand, those favoring prohibition commonly warn of marijuana's dangers. But they, too, leave out important truths. They ignore the considerable evidence that most adult occasional users are not harmed.

Both sides acknowledge the huge criminal network that has sprung up, the murderous cartels in Mexico, and the billions in illicit profits that fuel their operations and feed their greed. For the prohibitionists, this is a matter of collateral damage, a regrettable cost of a justified policy. For the reformers, it's an egregious aberration that must be abolished.

A war is underway and it has been difficult to find common ground. In 1994 during the Clinton administration, Surgeon General Jocelyn Elders, in what turned out to be a futile and personally costly effort, called for dialogue about drug policy alternatives, the distribution of condoms in schools, and encouraging masturbation as a means of preventing pregnancy and sexually transmitted diseases in teens. In a firestorm of protest, she was quickly forced to resign. I think of her as a modern-day Admiral Baynes, a reasoning person who saw meager success in our national response to drugs and risky sex, and looked for smarter answers.

In the midst of this war of half-truths and myths, the public pays the price for being misinformed. Users, potential users, parents, teachers, and the friends and family members of pot smokers need and are entitled to more accurate and balanced information to support their own decision-making.

With one foot on each side of the fence, at times feeling at odds with both camps, this journey has meant more to me than forty

years of tilting at myths. I have been on a quest to challenge those who insist we think of marijuana as a weapon of mass destruction as well as those who would have us see it as a harmless source of pleasure and relief.

One of the attractions of myths, I suspect, is their simplicity. I'm sometimes asked if marijuana is "good" or "bad," as if hardly anything in this world could easily be distilled down to such polar absolutes. Usually the questioner is looking for a certain and short answer to what, in their mind, ought to be a black or white issue. It is just not that simple, and when I try to respond with a nuanced explanation of what I believe and why, their eyes often glaze over.

These four-plus decades of tilting at marijuana myths while seeking common ground have generated many stories. I believe it's time to tell them. Perhaps they'll be useful for readers finding themselves on a similar quest.

Roger Roffman

Seattle

April, 2014

MARIJUANA NATION

PART 1

VIETNAM

We all lit up and by and by
The whole platoon was flying high.
With a beautiful smile on the captain's face
He smelled like midnight on St. Mark's Place.
Cleaning his weapon, chanting the Hare Krishna.

> —*Talking Vietnam Potluck Blues*
> Words and music by Tom Paxton

1

PLEA

A t two A.M. he lay awake in a tent in a part of the compound reserved for those who had yet to face trial. From his cot, the sound of a Huey helicopter landing at the nearby hospital, the heavy whump-whump of its rotors pummeling the tropical night air, and the sight of flares illuminating the horizon at the base's southern perimeter seemed familiar. Sights and sounds no different here than back at his unit, less than a mile away on the sprawling Long Binh Army base.

Yet at this moment nothing else felt the same. The double chain link fences topped with barbed wire coils, the guard towers, and the sweeping arc of the powerful flood lights reminded him of that stark reality at every turn. After the MPs delivered him to the stockade and removed the handcuffs, he was assigned a number, photographed and fingerprinted, strip searched, ordered to shower, and issued prisoner garb that told neither his rank nor the unit to which he belonged. Not even his name.

He still felt in shock as he sat alone in the mess hall with his tray of food, none of it touched. Looking around at the hundreds of others held in this compound, he assured himself that he was not like them. He'd avoided speaking to anyone since being processed in hours earlier and felt relieved that no one had harassed him since.

He pictured what the guys in his unit had been doing that day, the 1st Sergeant's weekly inspection and a goodbye party for Olson. Did any of them know where he was? He smiled when he thought about his buddy Rudy who would surely roar with laughter, eager to rib him mercilessly for getting into such hot water. That smile vanished, however, when he thought about being called in by his CO, who wouldn't have seen any humor whatsoever in the day's events.

Would they have told his parents? He pictured his folks reading an official letter about his arrest. Would his 11-year-old brother find out? He felt the tears welling up and quickly suppressed any sounds of the sobs that racked his chest in case anyone else in the tent was awake and might hear.

In those initial hours he realized the likelihood that he'd spend months in a place just like this after being convicted. He urgently wanted to regain what had been, to put back the pieces of a life that so unexpectedly had been yanked away. He was eager to tell them he was deeply sorry, that it would never happen again. Would they please give him another chance?

But at that hour no one was there to listen.

2

COPING

U.S. Army Specialist Michael Gordon, a 24-year-old transportation mechanic from Columbus, Ohio, rose to his feet and stood at rigid attention at the front of the courtroom. His crisply ironed khaki uniform displayed numerous ribbons and awards above his left shirt pocket. With all of those medals, I thought, this sandy-haired athletically built fellow could have been a poster boy for Army recruitment. Instead, he was facing the possibility of a six-month prison sentence. I was one of six officers appointed to serve on a board that would determine his guilt or innocence.

That morning I too had dressed in a khaki uniform and smartly shined shoes, more formal than the olive drab jungle fatigues and combat boots I typically wore while on duty as the 9th Infantry Division's Social Work Officer. I walked to division headquarters and entered the two-story prefab building. The offices had doors and were furnished with the same kinds of desks and chairs that might be found in any office building back home. Quite a contrast, I thought, with the hundreds of sandbag-encased tents throughout most of the Camp.

The commanding general's jeep was parked outside the building entrance, and military policemen flanked the door. Inside the first floor courtroom, a United States flag was placed to the left of the long table where the board members would be seated. To the right, the 9th Division's flag and campaign streamers were displayed. I had the sense that this imposing setting was intended to remind all present of the full force and authority of the U.S. Government and of the gravity of what lay ahead.

Major Richard Evans, serving as president of the court due to his seniority, sat in the middle seat. At 6'6" he towered over the rest of us at that table, yet he was surprisingly soft-spoken and his speech carefully measured. A second major, three captains, and I, the junior member, sat to his right and left, our positions determined by rank. A table on the left was assigned to the two officers serving on the defense team, with the accused seated between them. The two prosecutors were seated at a table to the right. A table for witnesses was placed in the room's center. Each of us had been issued a Defense Department book titled *Manual for Courts Martial* that would guide us through the arraignment, trial, and—if the defendant was convicted—the sentencing.

I was the last to be sworn. Captain Earl Junker, an African-American infantry officer whose rows of medals gave evidence of his extensive combat experience, served as the lead trial counsel. He instructed me to stand and raise my right hand.

As he read the lengthy oath my thoughts drifted and his words ran together. The droning of two large fans in the room accomplished little except keeping the dust from settling and somewhat buffering the noise of truck traffic. I was grateful when I finally heard "So help you God," and quickly replied, "I do."

Captain Junker then proceeded with the arraignment.

"The charges have been properly referred to this court for trial, and with their specifications, are as follows: Charge I: Violation of the Uniform Code of Military Justice, Article 134. Specification: In that Specialist Michael Gordon did, on or about February 2, 1967, wrongfully have in his possession one-quarter ounce, more or less, of marijuana. Specialist Gordon, how do you plead?"

"Not guilty," Specialist Gordon replied, his voice clear and assertive, and the trial got underway.

It was pot.

As I learned for the first time the charge against this guy, I felt a growing sense of discomfort. I had never smoked marijuana and didn't think I knew anyone who had. I didn't question there being justification for its being illegal, but should guys like Gordon be sent to prison for possessing it? Was it that serious? I had heard the term *reefer* and associated it with Harlem jazz and beat generation poets, hardly images of crime and violence.

I looked over at him, thinking that somehow I'd be able to spot something in his appearance or demeanor that would fit with my image of a criminal. Before entering the service, I had worked as a caseworker for the Federal Bureau of Prisons. Did he look like any of the inmates at the U.S. Reformatory at Chillicothe, Ohio?

He didn't. He looked more like the classmates I went to school with, where the troublemaker was a kid who stole from his parents' liquor cabinet or shoplifted a pack of cigarettes.

Captain Junker called Sgt. Galen Hennings, a military policeman, to the witness table and swore him in. Hennings took his seat, looking unfazed by the proceedings, and opened a folder containing a sheaf of papers.

I guessed he was in his late twenties. His head was shaved and he wore a black armband on his left arm with MP in white letters. A whistle on a lanyard was threaded through the button hole on his shirt collar and a holstered pistol hung from his web utility belt. He set aside his helmet and waited for Captain Junker to begin the questioning.

"Sgt. Hennings, tell the court the circumstances which led to Specialist Gordon being charged."

"Sirs, on February 2nd, at about 1600 hours, I was called to the scene of an accident on the road between Camp Bearcat and Long Binh. Specialist Gordon was the driver of a jeep that had collided with a moped driven by a Vietnamese civilian."

Glancing at his clipboard, Junker asked, "What happened when you arrived at the scene?"

"As I walked in Specialist Gordon's direction he flipped something behind his back into a nearby ditch. I ordered him to stay where he was and retrieved the item which turned out to be a Marlboro cigarette package."

"Did you examine the contents of the package, Sgt. Hennings?"

"Yes, sir, I did. He clearly wanted to get rid of it when he saw me coming so I suspected it was marijuana. It turned out that was correct. There were ten joints in the package."

Marijuana, grown in the mountains of Vietnam, Laos, and Cambodia, had become widely available to American troops. Vietnamese entrepreneurs carefully unsealed the cellophane wrapping on American commercial brand cigarette packages. Then they removed the twenty tobacco cigarettes and replaced them with nineteen rolled joints. The cellophane was then resealed and the package looked untouched.

The MP was excused and left the courtroom. Then Captain Ben Collier, the lead Defense Counsel, called Specialist Gordon to the witness table. Collier was an ordnance officer, but with his pencil-thin moustache, thinning hair, and slouching posture, he struck me as looking more like an accountant.

"Specialist Gordon, did you have marijuana in your possession?"

"Yes, sir, I did."

"Tell the court how you obtained it."

"Sir, I found what I thought was a package of regular cigarettes on the back seat of a jeep I checked out of the motor pool. Marlboros are my brand so I felt lucky."

Captain Collier, pacing back and forth in front of the witness table, asked the defendant to continue. "When did you realize what the package actually contained?"

"Sir, just before leaving for Long Binh, I opened the package and discovered that it contained joints, not tobacco cigarettes. I decided I'd turn it in to the MPs after I got back to Bearcat, but then the accident happened. It's true that I tried to throw it away when Sgt. Hennings walked up to me, but I did that only because I didn't think he'd believe me if I told him the truth."

On cross examination, the lead trial counsel challenged this version of the events. With more than a hint of sarcasm he asked Specialist Gordon to explain why he hadn't immediately disposed of the package once he discovered what it contained. He also asked what had happened to the missing joints. Specialist Gordon repeated that he had intended to turn it in, that he didn't smoke pot, and that it had only contained ten joints when opened.

Captain Collier stood and addressed the board. "Sirs, the fact of the matter is that Specialist Gordon did possess 10 joints. But it was the result of a mistake. By holding on to it with the intention of turning it over to an MP, he possessed it in the performance of his duty, his duty being to uphold the Uniform Code of Military Justice by delivering contraband to law enforcement authorities."

He looked intently at each of us on the board for a moment and when our eyes met, I almost nodded, wanting to somehow let him know I was in his client's corner. Instead, I looked away, remembering I was expected to remain neutral until the board had arrived at a verdict.

There were no other witnesses, and the trial moved to the next phase. Major Evans ordered that the court be closed so that the members of the board could deliberate the verdict. All others left the room.

Almost immediately, Major Oscar Henley set the tone for what would follow. His thick neck, barrel chest, shaved head, ramrod straight posture, and near-bellowing voice added up to a considerably intimidating presence. "I've heard some tall tales, but this guy is a pro. He says he intended to turn it in to the MPs, but when that opportunity presented itself, he ditched the pot. And if there were only ten joints in the pack when he opened it, this jerk let himself get cheated." His voice dripped with contempt. "He's a lousy liar to boot, even if he's managed to convince his defense counsel that it was all some gosh darn terrible mistake. I'm ready to vote." He shook his head with a look of disgust.

I felt my pulse quicken. Specialist Gordon's version of the facts was plausible, I thought, but several others had nodded in apparent agreement as Major Henley spoke. I kept silent and the moment in which any difference of opinion might be voiced soon passed.

The vote was taken by secret ballot. Five had voted to convict and there was one lone vote to acquit—mine. The rules required a two-thirds majority, not unanimity.

The court was called back into session and Major Evans, the *Manual* in his right hand, asked the defendant to stand. "Specialist Michael Gordon, it is my duty as president of this court to inform you that the court, in closed session and upon secret written ballot, finds you, of the Specification and Charge, guilty."

I wondered how Specialist Gordon reacted as the verdict was announced, but I avoided eye contact with him. He'd surely know at this point that jail time was inevitable. I didn't want to see the implications of that stark reality reflected on his face.

The next step involved a pre-sentence procedure. First, the trial counsel reported that the defendant had no prior convictions. Then Captain Collier, the lead defense counsel whom I had pegged as an accountant, rose to speak on Specialist Gordon's behalf. As I listened to him, it seemed as if he genuinely believed his client.

"Sirs, Specialist Gordon did, in fact, possess ten marijuana joints. The issue about which there is less certainty is his intent. I ask you once again, while determining the sentence, to consider the possibility that Specialist Gordon's offense truly was unintentional."

I glanced at Specialist Gordon, hoping that something in his expression would shore up my courage to try to slow down what was feeling like a runaway train. All I could detect with any assurance was that this fellow was scared. Perspiration had stained the armpits of his uniform, and his eyes were wary as he briefly glanced at the members of the board.

Captain Collier continued, talking calmly as he walked slowly back and forth in front of our table. "Specialist Gordon has told us the following." He ticked his points off one by one. "He doesn't smoke marijuana. He intended to turn the package over to authorities. There were never more than ten joints inside."

Where was this leading? It soon became evident. He'd test our empathy.

"I suspect that if you or I had mistakenly bought or maybe found a cigarette package that contained joints, we'd have gotten rid of it immediately."

Captain Collier paused, and then scratched his chin as if to appear in doubt. "But then again, might we have held on to it with a plan to turn it over to an MP? A noble plan but, my God, what a risk we'd be taking!" Captain Collier looked over at Specialist Gordon, who smiled for the first time that morning and nodded his enthusiastic agreement.

Man, that argument convinced me. But would it sway any of the others?

Following Captain Collier's statement, the president announced that the court again would be closed. All but the six board members left the room and the sentencing deliberations began.

Major Henley, who had so quickly voiced his skepticism earlier, again spoke first. "If the defendant had owned up to what he had done, I could be convinced that some leniency is called for, particularly since he doesn't have a record. But that's not what has been presented to this court."

One of the captains added, "I agree, sir. If we only give him a slap on the wrist, it'll send a message that using narcotics is tolerated. We can't do that unless we're willing to see our fighting force seriously impaired by drug abuse."

Owned up to what he had done? I repeated to myself. Wait, wasn't it the task of the prosecutor to prove guilt? We seemed headed again to a rapid decision and I couldn't stay silent. I motioned to speak and was recognized by Major Evans.

"Sirs, will sending Specialist Gordon to prison be in anybody's best interest? He's got a clean record and has an important job that he's apparently doing well. I think his explanation could be true, but even if he has smoked pot, I'm not so sure that he's any different than those of us who have a few drinks when we're off duty. Why not just sentence him to pay a fine?"

From their body language, none of the senior officers seemed to have even heard what I'd said, and only Captain Carlos Ramirez, a member of my unit, made eye contact with me. Might he join me in arguing for a lenient sentence?

I felt relieved when I heard what he had to say. "I agree. We're not talking about assault or theft, or anything remotely close to that degree of seriousness. This defendant didn't go AWOL, he wasn't derelict in the performance of duty, and he didn't disobey a direct order. Let's not waste all of the training he's had by sending him to jail. A stiff fine will get the message across that he screwed up."

The president's scowl conveyed his disagreement with what Carlos and I had said, an unexpected reaction given how neutral he had been up to this point. "Remember, gentlemen," Major Evans said, "that the convening authority will review whatever sentence we give, and may see fit to reduce it. I don't want us to tie the colonel's hands by limiting his latitude to offer or not offer leniency." He looked at his watch and then quickly glanced at Major Henley before calling for a recess. "I suggest we take a break for a few minutes."

As I headed for the door, I was aware that Major Henley, the board member who used intimidation at every turn, had followed me outside. We both lit cigarettes, and after a pause he quietly, but with a steely edge to his voice, offered some advice.

"Look, lieutenant, I don't know whether you're considering a career in the Army, but let me tell you that if you are, you're not doing yourself any favors. Listen to what Major Evans said. The convening authority will probably reduce the sentence, but our job is to give him that chance rather than to box him in with a slap-on-the-wrist punishment."

Much later I realized that Major Henley was violating the Code himself by pressuring me in this way. At the time, however, I was very much aware of the contradiction in what he wanted me to think was a desire to help out a junior officer.

We were called back to order and the deliberations continued for nearly an hour. Carlos and I reiterated our reasoning for a lenient sentence and the bullish Major Henley led the opposition by countering each point.

Carlos asked how soldiers in a war zone could be expected to cope with constant danger without some ways of reducing the stress, usually by getting drunk, sometimes getting laid by a bar girl, or maybe even getting high. Major Henley would have none of this. If there's a law on the books, he argued, violation of that law requires punishment. Otherwise, military discipline suffers and soldiers without discipline get themselves and others killed.

I found myself wondering how his rigid black and white thinking went over with his wife and kids, if indeed they existed. I pictured a family that experienced a lot of fear.

This back and forth reminded me of a criminal law course I had taken at the University of Michigan three years earlier. Ninety first-year law students and two of us from the school of social work were enrolled, and the course was co-taught by professors of law and psychiatry. When the professors wanted to illustrate competing values in the operation of the criminal justice system, the other social work student and I would often find ourselves on the hot seat as they played us off against the law students who tended to be uncompromising.

What should the penalty be for theft, for example, of an item worth $25? Easy enough, perhaps, but what if the theft is of a loaf of bread and a package of cheese by someone who is homeless and hungry? Homeless, hungry, and the parent of two children who are living in their car?

What should the penalty be for committing murder? And what if it's a consensual act by the spouse of a terminally ill person who pleads for help in dying? Or an act of abject desperation by a woman whose husband has been brutally abusive?

The debates inevitably led to a discussion of context and were stimulating. They helped all of us to question our underlying assumptions about right and wrong, human nature, and the function of criminal law. They led us to wonder what social justice meant.

The debate today, however, was hardly an academic exercise. There were no professors there to help us understand the perspectives and beliefs contributing to the widely opposing positions we were taking.

This court martial occurred in February of 1967. Back home, the "summer of love," a bursting into the public's consciousness of the hippie counterculture movement, was about to happen. An estimated 100,000 young people were finding their way to San Francisco's Haight-Ashbury neighborhood and forming a community united by cultural and political rebellion. If this movement had had an emblem other than the peace symbol, it might well have been a marijuana leaf. Getting high served as a kind of glue that bound the movement's diverse members together.

For some, pot smoking represented a looming threat, an unraveling of moral standards vital to civilized society. For others it was part and parcel of a shared activism aimed at ending racial oppression, defending women's rights, questioning traditional authority, and redefining sexual mores. Ultimately, these vividly opposing interpretations of the motivation for getting high would have even more of an influence on what people thought about the drug, far more than actual facts about the consequences of its use.

Were the other officers on the panel aware of what was happening in the States? It never came up in the proceedings, but I later wondered if the counter-culture's challenge to the values held tight by those making a career of the military might have played a part in determining Specialist Gordon's fate.

The president instructed us to vote, reminding us that determining a sentence required only a two-thirds majority, four or more concurring votes in this case as there were six members. I was heartened that there weren't enough to send Specialist Gordon to prison for six months.

The debate resumed and we covered much of the same ground. I hoped at least one other member would be swayed by the points Carlos and I had argued. But before long another vote was held. Someone indeed had changed his mind, but in favor of jail, albeit a shorter term. I felt hopeless.

Captain Collier was speaking quietly to Specialist Gordon as they re-entered the room, and the Captain's hand on Gordon's shoulder appeared as if it was intended to help him prepare for bad news. Gordon looked frightened.

Major Evans called the court to order and instructed Specialist Gordon to stand. Once again, following the template in the *Manual*, he sentenced Gordon to confinement at hard labor for four months.

It was over and I left the room quickly. This pot smoker, if indeed he was one, was 24 years old and had otherwise played by the rules. We were the same age. He hadn't hurt anyone. Remembering the ever-present risk of explosive violence in the Chillicothe Reformatory where I had once worked, I was troubled at the thought of how dramatically different Specialist Gordon's life was about to become as he served his sentence in a U.S. military prison.

This waste of human potential was difficult to accept, all the more so since some commanders, knowing their troops were getting high, simply looked the other way. Drunk, high, whatever. As long as the GI was in shape when he was needed, it was all good. Ultimately the guy's fate turned out to be the luck of the draw, and Specialist Gordon had lost. I had lost as well because of the instrumental role I had played in producing what I considered an unjust punishment.

However, the polarized positions taken by different board members helped open my eyes. I began to understand the reasoning that shaped the very different conclusions people were drawing, both in military and civilian societies, about the justness of jail terms for marijuana possession. Those reasons, it seemed to me, had a great deal to do with symbolism, a perception that the act of smoking pot was a threatening challenge to the conventions that were perceived as making it all work, keeping us all safe.

Ironically, there was an unspoken assumption that soldiers in the combat zone could make reasonable decisions about drinking, when it was safe to cut loose, even to get dead drunk. And if their decisions were sometimes untimely, so be it. It was war and the troops, as well as their commanders, had needs.

Getting high was different.

3

SUICIDE ATTEMPT?

ABOARD THE USNS *UPSHUR*, VUNG TAU HARBOR, SOUTH VIETNAM
2 JANUARY 1967

Six weeks earlier, the sun had been rising as the USNS *Upshur*, an American President Lines cruise ship converted for military transport, dropped anchor in Vung Tau Harbor. We had flown from Kansas to California and then embarked from Oakland, passing under the Golden Gate Bridge, a last vestige of a normal world as a trip of 6,000 miles and a transition from peace to war began.

A band had played as we'd boarded the buses at Ft. Riley, Kansas, and a general shook each of our hands, specifically instructing the senior sergeants to "take care of our boys." Now, after 22 days at sea we were not yet in the war, but the flares that lit up the horizon that night as we lay at anchor, and the thump-thump of intermittent mortars, made me wonder if that general, even as he wished us Godspeed, had calculated his own estimate of how severe our casualty rate would be.

The *Upshur* was one of about 50 ships awaiting dockside space to unload, and its passengers included 1,587 9th Infantry Division enlisted men, non-coms, and officers. We were one part of the continuing build-up of American military in Vietnam, an escalation matched in its intensity by the increasingly fervent anti-war sentiments back home. It would be another three days before the *Upshur* docked and a convoy of trucks, protected by helicopter gunships and armored personnel carriers, transported us 40 miles inland to Camp Martin Cox, better known as Bearcat, the base camp for the U.S. Army's 9th Infantry Division.

But even before any of us stepped foot on Vietnamese soil, one soldier already had come close to death. Calvin Phelps, a 19-year-old Private First Class from Nebraska had smuggled pills aboard ship, partied with his buddies on Christmas Eve, and overdosed on alcohol and Darvon. His friends had been unable to rouse him the next morning and carried him to sickbay.

Calvin's condition was critical. We were to reach Okinawa for refueling in just one more day, but the physicians determined that medications unavailable on the ship were needed immediately to treat his failing urinary system and dangerously low blood pressure. An air-drop of medicines from Okinawa was requested.

At about 4:00 P.M. as the plane approached, the *Upshur*'s captain slowed the engines to a near stop and turned the bow into the wind. We crowded the decks and watched the plane circling the ship while six sailors were lowered in one of the lifeboats, a maneuver made all the more dangerous due to the heavy swells. Once the boat had been launched, a bright yellow package was dropped from a rear door of the plane. Retrieving the container took more than an hour because it had quickly drifted away from the ship. The task of re-fastening the boat to the hoist was also dicey due to the rapid rising and falling of the ship in the waves that slammed against the hull. The sailors looked exhausted as they were knocked about in the lifeboat. When both hooks were finally attached and the hoist motors started, the ship rolled in a particularly strong swell, nearly throwing several of the men into the sea. But at last the retrieval operation succeeded and the sailors were greeted with rebel shouts and pats on the back as they stepped over the ship's rails onto the deck with their life-saving cargo.

Calvin responded well to his treatment, and the crisis soon passed. But the physicians had to tend to a remaining issue that was of grave concern in Vietnam-bound GIs. Had he intended to overdose?

Captain Ron Davis, a surgeon who headed my unit, the 9th Medical Battalion's Headquarters Company, had a decision to make. "Roger, will you check out Phelps and give me your opinion? If he tried to kill himself, we'll need to consider evacuating him from the ship while we're refueling in Okinawa. If not, his medical condition is improving enough so that I think we'll be able to keep him with us."

Each Army infantry division, a unit of about 16,000 soldiers, had both a psychiatrist and a professional social worker in its medical battalion. Our division psychiatrist had remained at Ft. Riley and would join us some weeks later in Vietnam. Therefore, it was my task to advise Captain Davis on Calvin's psychological state.

I had been commissioned as a 2nd Lieutenant a year earlier, several months after completing studies for the masters degree in social work at the University of Michigan. I was 24 years old and wet behind the ears, my clinical experience being limited to six months working with a street gang in Detroit, about eighteen months with inmates in federal prisons, and less than a year with soldiers at Ft.

Riley. At any one moment I felt either reasonably competent or deeply anxious about how much damage I might cause.

Over the next several hours, just before disembarking for a 10-hour leave in Okinawa's port city of Naha, I talked twice with Calvin in the ship's infirmary, taking a history to learn how he had responded to earlier emotional difficulties in his life. I particularly wanted to know what he thought about the overdose.

Calvin was a lanky teenager with a blond buzz cut, blue eyes, and a patriotic American eagle tattoo on his left arm, likely acquired while on pass in a town with a shady reputation a few miles down the road from Ft. Riley. There was no shortage of tattoo and massage parlors, taverns, hookers, and pawn brokers in Junction City, all catering to the thousands of young soldiers stationed at the Army base.

"Lieutenant," he told me, sitting up in bed, "I really need you to understand that I wasn't depressed and I didn't want to hurt myself. Suicide was never even in my mind. It couldn't have been. I've got too much to live for back home and that's not the kind of person I am. Sir, I . . ."

He began to choke up and I sat with him quietly and waited.

"Sir, I don't want to tell you their names, but please trust me that the four guys I was with were just trying to have a good time. We pooled our booze and pills, and I guess for me it just got out of hand. I was dumb, but believe me, it was an accident."

Alcohol-related accidents were no rarity in the Army and the prevalence of alcoholism, particularly in the upper enlisted and non-commissioned officer ranks, was also a significant health concern. Yet these consequences were accepted, and in the combat zone opportunities to drink were considered every bit as essential as food and ammunition.

As he answered questions about his family, experiences in school, and friendships, Calvin showed me photos of his parents and sister, his girlfriend, and several of his high school baseball team. He had enlisted along with two friends from school, one of whom was also aboard ship.

In his descriptions, his affect as he talked, and his demeanor, there was no hint that Calvin's overdose was suicidal. There seemed to be an unambiguous conclusion, but I still worried about the possibility of being wrong. Perhaps he had intended to commit suicide, but now that his attempt had failed, he was relieved and regretted what he had tried to do. It was one of many possible options that I still had to explore as I spoke with him.

I gave him another chance to let me know how he felt about going to war. "Calvin, some guys would grab the free ticket home you could get at this point. What about it?"

"Not me, sir. It was a damn stupid mistake, I know, but I'd let my buddies down if I took that ticket."

He looked at me with a pleading expression on his face. "Please, don't make me go home."

I was now convinced, and shared my evaluation with Captain Davis. He agreed. With the refueling completed, we left at midnight on December 28th for the last leg of our trip.

But within hours the situation had changed. Calvin's recovery unexpectedly nose dived when he became partially paralyzed a day after the *Upshur* departed from Naha. The physicians, now suspecting a brain hemorrhage, decided that his medical evacuation from the ship was urgent. I asked to see him, but was told he was too ill.

The ship changed course and we headed for Formosa.

As we approached the harbor and came to a stop, a small Navy boat came alongside. While Calvin's stretcher was being lowered, I heard jeers from soldiers lining the rails. At first, it was unclear what had stimulated their antagonism, and then I understood. Because it would no longer be possible for the ship to be within 100 miles of

Vietnam's shores by midnight on December 31st, none of us would receive the war zone combat pay supplement of $65 for December or a $500 tax deduction for 1966. Despite being seriously ill, Calvin was getting the brunt of their anger.

The conversation among eight of us that evening became contentious.

"Look, he knew the rules about bringing booze or pills on board. We all did. This fellow apparently made a decision they didn't apply to him." George Strong, one of the Medical Battalion docs sounded indignant as we sat at dinner in the Officers Mess. "Maybe it's harsh, but I don't blame the guys who think he should pay for this. We're going to miss the tax deadline and it's going to cost each of us a lot of money."

He looked around the table to see if any were agreeing, and when he saw some nods he continued with his rant. "Yeah, and then there's the expense to the government for the airdrop and medical evacuation. He should have known better, and I'm angry. When he recovers, the CO should submit papers for a court martial. Hell, I'll testify for the prosecution."

Ron Davis, our Company CO, disagreed. A few years later when the television program *M*A*S*H* was in its prime, Alan Alda's character "Hawkeye" Pierce brought back memories of Ron, solid competence and unabashed irreverence. "I'm not so sure we should pillory this guy. If he goes down for what he did, some of us at this table probably ought to go down with him." Ron looked my way and winked.

I smiled, knowing that Ron was thinking about how several of us (not including George) had spent Christmas Eve. Fueled by a whoppingly powerful punch concocted with 180 proof grain alcohol appropriated from our medical stores, six of us had had our own party, singing carols to the notes I picked out on the chaplain's field organ, and even making a piñata shaped like a monstrous mouse and filling it with candy, cookies, and fruit for Carlos Ramirez who was born in Mexico. Ron had then had the idea, a notion that seemed inspired at the time, for us to go down to the enlisted quarters and sing carols with the men. Bad idea! A half-dozen inebriated officers did not succeed in bringing Christmas cheer to the very sober and quite somber enlisted men who were enduring the packed confines of the ship's holds on this lonely holiday far from home. Our visit to their compartment was short.

A few days later in Vung Tau Harbor as we waited to disembark, I thought about George's anger and his adamant conviction that Calvin should be court-martialed for having done something with his buddies that to me seemed normal, given the circumstances, but had exercised bad judgment by surpassing his limits. Even the dockside scene as the *Upshur* had prepared to leave Naha after refueling, as bizarre as it was, had seemed normal given the context. Many men had returned to the ship from that 10-hour leave drunk or high, quite a few having been injured in fights. One guy had walked up the gangplank stark naked.

A lot of steam had been let off, and yet every one of those men was back onboard. Was it just to prosecute someone like Calvin, or for that matter any of these guys, for trying to hold it together while on their way to a war?

There would be no court martial. We learned a few weeks later that Calvin, while being treated in the Philippines, had died of a previously undiagnosed brain injury. Apparently, when his friends aboard the *Upshur* found him unconscious on Christmas Day, they had tried to sober him up with a cold shower. But he had slipped from their grasp and hit his head on the shower stall floor causing a subdural hematoma to form. Initially undetected, it was that injury that eventually took Calvin's life.

In coping with the war's hardships, drinking was nearly universal and even encouraged through the role-modeling of more experienced GIs and the ready availability of cheap alcohol. This socialization process was hardly an abstraction for me, as I'd watched myself falling right into line, drinking more often, valuing the camaraderie of partying as an act of solidarity with guys that held in common the inherent fears of what lay ahead, feeling the safety of membership in a tight group.

When the official standards for military personnel were examined in parallel with what people actually did, the incongruity was unmistakable. The formal norms were in writing and taught during training sessions on military comportment, and the informal norms—far more influential in day-to-day life—were taught after hours in the clubs. It didn't take long for any of us to learn how far the limits could be pushed, even the implicit reinforcement, the "he's one of us" acceptance, from participating in the many occasions, promotion parties as an example, in which excesses were expected. Chest-thumping and an unspoken dose of hypocrisy, particularly in light of the disciplinary authority held by officers, all rolled into one cultural theme. Remembering that aborted Christmas caroling episode aboard ship still brings a shudder.

Over time, as I began to learn how getting high fit into the picture, two truths became evident. First, getting drunk and getting stoned fulfilled a common purpose for soldiers, acts of solidarity that enhanced group cohesion and a resulting sense of safety. Second, when it came to pot, for most in military officialdom, particularly those for whom military service was a career, there was no parallel set of informal norms that permitted, even encouraged, getting stoned. In their eyes, marijuana was perceived as alcohol had once been at a time when puritanical values prevailed: immoral and forbidden. The experience of America's youth fighting the war in Vietnam illuminated a vast cultural divide.

4

FELLINI FILM

CAMP BEARCAT
5 JANUARY 1967

After waiting at anchor for three days in Vung Tau Harbor, space at the dock opened up and we were able to disembark. Vietnam and the war, both abstractions until now, became very concrete. Wearing flak jackets and helmets and carrying live ammunition for our M16s, we sweated as a convoy of trucks, jeeps, and armored personnel carriers sped us through the Vietnamese countryside for three hours, not slowing down even one iota as we passed through crowded villages on our way to Camp Bearcat.

As we rode in the cargo beds of 2½ ton trucks, our first views of inland Vietnam were of broad expanses of rice paddies being worked by stooped women and men wearing conical hats, and water buffaloes hitched to plows in the fields. In the villages, the fronts of the tiny shops were filled with colorful displays of clothing, cookware, and baskets that spilled out onto the sidewalk. Sampans and junks traversed muddy rivers lined with shacks on pilings. Mopeds, some carrying passengers and others used as small carts, clogged the streets and clouded the air with their exhaust. Throughout this journey, the convoy and accompanying helicopter gunships were seemingly ignored by all except the youngest children. Were the adults that accustomed to soldiers moving through their villages? Or might they have feared appearing to be welcoming of the Americans if Viet Cong were observing? For that matter, were they themselves Viet Cong?

Camp Bearcat was still being carved out of the jungle. Over the weeks ahead, bulldozers, backhoes, and road graders busily cleared trees, leveled the land, mounded earth into defensive berms, and dug trenches. Rows, streets, and then blocks of army tents were erected and quickly encased by head high banks of sandbags. Trucks and helicopters delivered construction supplies, artillery pieces were set in place, bunkers, latrines, and mess halls were built, and—over those early weeks—a small city was created, complete with PXs, civilian laundry concessions, and clubs for officers, noncoms, and enlisted men.

Six of us shared a tent that at first was pretty bleak: six Army cots, each with its own mosquito netting, and our foot lockers. But bartering between units was commonplace, and we soon learned how to scrounge, usually with the expert guidance of senior sergeants who knew the ropes of off-the-books wheeling and dealing and thus were quickly able to spruce up our living quarters.

We got creative in making our tent more livable. At first we hung blankets from clotheslines to give each person a bit of privacy. Later, as we explored the markets in nearby villages, colorful straw mats, beaded curtains, and even some local artwork lessened the harsh barracks-like feel of the tent.

Another challenge was finding a place to work. The Army's Table of Organization and Equipment hadn't made provision for a separate mental health facility, but it seemed to me privacy required one. Before long I had bargained for a 16' x 32' GP Medium tent to house the Mental Hygiene Clinic and lumber and screens for its floor and walls. I even managed to trade 15 cases of C-rations with someone in the Air Force for a water cooler—a difference maker in that tropical climate.

Empty ammunition crates provided the lumber to build partitions and cabinets. No longer usable parachutes made for great tent liners, helping to keep down both heat and dust. I obtained bamboo mats, beaded curtains for the entrances to each of the Clinic's small offices and reception area, as well as lawn chairs and tables. All of these could be purchased cheaply from the local shops.

When it was all set up, a small reception area gave patients a place to wait at the front of the Clinic, and a passageway separated two small offices in the middle. The rear of the tent had one larger office that the Division's psychiatrist would use once he arrived from Ft. Riley. In those early weeks, making our living and work-spaces more comfortable and personalized buoyed our morale and helped stave off the reality of warfare, at least for some of the time.

But it was not to last. About three weeks after arriving, I was urgently summoned to see a new patient who, I was told, was non-communicative. As I entered the hospital triage area, I saw a soldier lying on a cot in a fetal position with his fatigue jacket covering his face. I quietly sat down beside him.

"I'm Lt. Roffman. What's your name?"

No answer. I waited for a few moments.

"Okay. Just so you know, you've been brought to the medical clinic at Camp Bearcat and that's a good thing, because there are people here who can help."

Still nothing.

"Will you tell me what's happened?" I paused for a moment. "I'd like to understand."

I hoped that if I spoke quietly and gave him time, I'd eventually get a response. But I suddenly had the sense that something else was wrong. I glanced over my shoulder and saw a physician and two medics watching the scene with huge grins on their faces.

Seeing my confusion, they laughed, and then the patient abruptly sat up and complimented me on my therapeutic style. The 9th Infantry Division's psychiatrist, Captain William Baker, had arrived.

I was more than happy to have been the brunt of that joke. Bill and I had worked well together the preceding year at Ft. Riley's outpatient mental health clinic where, as we finished our work, he'd often facetiously ask if I'd cured anyone that day.

Skinny, about 5'10" tall, with heavy black eyeglass frames that seemed three sizes too large for his face, Bill had grown up in rural Oklahoma admiring Marlin Perkins, director of the Chicago Zoo and host of the popular television program *Wild Kingdom*. Bill had planned to become a veterinarian, but his career path changed when as an undergraduate he was assigned to write a paper on neurotransmitters and became excited about the workings of the brain. Soon after completing a psychiatry residency, Bill was drafted.

Bill and I became close colleagues. As I passed his open door one morning at Ft. Riley, I saw him gazing out the window at the rolling Kansas landscape in back of the clinic and stopped to chat.

"Bill, you look like you're a thousand miles away."

He chuckled and said, "No, I'm actually up on the top of that hill, right where those two boulders are leaning against each other."

He waited until I joined him at the window, and then pointed out the exact spot. "You know, I like to imagine what might be on the other side of that hill, and I've given some serious thought to climbing up there to find out."

"Gonna do it?" I asked.

"Nah, I'd rather hold on to my fantasies. Gives me someplace to flee to in my mind when this place gets to be too much."

I learned something that day about this man's imaginative adaptability.

It was a relief to no longer be the sole mental health specialist at Bearcat. As we moved Bill's gear into his hooch (Army lingo for personal living space) and helped him get settled, he asked what life had been like since I'd left Ft. Riley.

"Some situations have been really puzzling, Bill," I said, eager to talk, "and it's taken a while to figure out just what's happened. For example, about a week after our ship left Oakland, the chaplain's assistant was carried to the ship's sickbay in an agitated state. When the doctor asked him questions, he seemed to understand, but replied in a language that no one could identify, and that only served to increase his distress. I was asked to see him, but was baffled."

Bill scratched his head. "Maybe an aphasia. Curious!"

"Someone then wondered if any of his shipmates knew where he had grown up. The chaplain arrived and told us he was probably speaking Maltese. A call was then put out to see if anyone aboard ship spoke that language. Someone who did came to the infirmary and hearing his native language being spoken immediately calmed the patient. We learned through our translator that this fellow had been extremely seasick and believed he was about to die. The doctor gave him I.V. fluids and a dose of chlorpromazine, and the next morning the patient had regained the ability to speak English and quickly recovered."

"Good sleuthing! What other kinds of patients have you seen?"

I told Bill about Calvin's alcohol and Darvon overdose aboard ship and subsequent death, and about Stan, a soldier who had been flown in from the field in a state of extreme despair. He had seen a buddy get killed right next to him and had become grief-stricken.

Bill's attentive way of listening must have triggered a need to unload because I talked non-stop. I told him about Tom, a newly arrived young physician with whom I had sat awake throughout the night because he was panicking yet refused medication to help him calm down. I talked about the manic-depressive patient who had tried to deck me, and several men who had attempted suicide, one after a friend was accidentally electrocuted while trying to repair a generator. I described the glassy, unblinking eyes and rigid muscles of a 20-year-old apparently catatonic soldier and how frightening it was to imagine what he might be experiencing.

Then I turned to an aspect of my functioning as a mental health specialist about which I alternately felt intense anger and hopeless despair. Military psychiatry protocol called for sending traumatized soldiers, men like Stan who had watched his buddy die right next to him, back to their units after a few days of rest. First they were to be reassured that they'd get through this very normal reaction to a very tragic experience. Then they were given medication to help them sleep and the chance the next day to talk about what had happened, but with the understanding that they'd soon be ready to return to duty. They'd remain in uniform and be assigned some tasks on the hospital grounds.

In training prior to deployment, professionals in the mental health disciplines had been taught that inducting soldiers who had been exposed to trauma like this into the status of psychiatric patient was harmful. By medically evacuating them with the expectation of a prolonged period of disability, the likelihood of long-lasting mental illness increased.

While being trained at Ft. Sam Houston, this protocol made sense. Once in the war zone, however, it was an entirely different matter for me. Listening to a boy sob uncontrollably about the horrific injuries he had seen happen to buddies, the friend whose mangled body he had zipped into a body bag, or the terror he so vividly felt about the certainty that he'd never see his mom and dad again, tore into my soul.

"Dear God, Bill," I said, "if there were any justice, any mercy in this life, boys who've gone through horrors like that would be told they'd done enough and be sent home, not as patients, but as having paid their dues." I looked at him, pleading for his agreement, but he knew to wait.

I ranted about contrasts that seemed incomprehensible in a war zone, maybe even obscene. American kids were losing limbs when stepping on land mines, being impaled on stakes in punji pits, and being decimated in ambushes. Yet many of us frequently dined in superb riverfront French restaurants in Bien Hoa, spent hours at an officers' swimming pool, and enjoyed "happy hour" in Saigon's Rex Hotel roof-top bar.

"Bill, it's as if we're all characters in a Fellini film, and at times it feels grotesque."

He looked at me for a moment and smiled compassionately. "Sounds like you've been through a lot, Rog. So, how're you really doing? I want to know."

Without having seen it coming, I choked up and couldn't answer him. He passed a box of tissues and sat with me quietly. I let go and the tears came.

Man, I was glad he was there.

5

NO REDEMPTION

CAMP BEARCAT
JANUARY–MARCH 1967

Gradually a routine set in, with a somewhat predictable rhythm to our days and the nights. We acclimated to the humid climate and to the recurrent torrential downpours that began and ended in just minutes during monsoon season. Somehow, even the thunderous swarming of helicopter gunships, the barrage of outbound artillery fire, and the extraordinary visual contrasts between the lush rural Vietnamese countryside and the massive American machinery of war receded from the front page of our attention.

Over time, Bill and I learned what textbooks couldn't teach us about the impact of war on soldiers' mental health. Competent unit leadership was all important, we came to realize. Spiking rates of AWOLs, fights between soldiers, court-martial trials for disobeying orders, and mental health appointments were good signs that one

ROGER ROFFMAN

or more of a unit's leaders were not functioning well. Moreover, each of us had to adjust to being in Vietnam ourselves. Decades later, Bill is still tormented by the memory of a sniper's bullet just missing his head while on the road between Bearcat and Long Binh.

Not all of our work was entirely bleak, however. For that matter, some difficult circumstances were also funny in a dark and perverse way. One day Bill was asked by the Medical Battalion CO to talk with an anesthesiologist who had been drinking heavily and acting belligerently. This doc insisted to Bill that he did his job well, and if he drank off duty, it was nobody's business. Bill warned him that he was a candidate for an attack of delirium tremens due to the amount of booze he admitted drinking, making sure that he understood what the symptoms would be if the DTs set in. One symptom could be intense hallucinations.

A few days after their conversation, Bill awoke in the middle of the night to see the anesthesiologist standing by his cot with a .45 caliber pistol in his hand. Bill laughed as he told what happened next. "His gun wasn't pointed at me, thank God. He said he wanted me to step outside with him, and I did. We looked together at the fence and he asked if I saw any VC climbing over. I said, 'There are no people climbing the fence.' 'Well then,' he said, 'I must be having those DTs you told me about.' So we walked together to the ward, where he was admitted. I think the experience scared him sober, at least for a while."

But learning to care for severely traumatized patients and maintaining some semblance of personal mental health was another challenge entirely. I still remember the turbulent mixture of anger and helplessness I felt when I met PFC Edward Wilson, who had made a fateful decision. It was non-negotiable. He was done.

Wilson's squad had been ambushed and, with a relatively minor wound to his left arm, he was one of the few survivors. When Ron

Davis talked with him after surgery and told him he'd be discharged back to his unit in about a week, the patient asked if he could speak with a lawyer and explained that he intended to refuse any further involvement in the war. Suspecting combat stress, Ron referred him to the Mental Hygiene Clinic.

Wilson was a tall 23-year-old blond fellow from Portsmouth, New Hampshire, whose muscular and hefty appearance suggested he might well have played fullback. Having dropped out of college during his junior year, he had been drafted after losing the educational deferment.

I introduced myself and explained that he had been referred for an assessment. In my first few minutes observing him, it occurred to me that if he were actually experiencing a temporary combat stress reaction, PFC Wilson was not at all typical. He seemed calm, with no signs of anxiety.

"Private Wilson, you've been through a terrible ordeal. You've lost a number of friends. I'm sorry. Would you like to talk about it?"

"No, sir." PFC Wilson returned my eye contact and patiently waited.

Wondering what he was thinking, I asked, "Is there something else you might want to discuss?"

"Sir, I'm going to jail. There's nothing for me to say." He bit a fingernail and looked at his watch. It seemed he wanted this to end quickly.

"You're going to jail? Why? What happened?"

Wilson paused for a moment, and then apparently decided he'd talk with me. "I told Dr. Davis that I was going to refuse to fight anymore, and I guess he thinks I'm a psych case."

"Maybe he thought you could use a chance to talk this through with someone. How about it?"

"Won't do any good."

"Let's decide about that later. Tell me about it."

Wilson took a deep breath, exhaled, and looked down at the floor, slowly shaking his head. After a minute, he went on. "When I got my draft notice, I should've taken off for Canada. I thought about it, and one of the guys from my school wanted us to go there together. I almost did it, but then I chickened out. I knew my dad would be pissed off at me if I went, and my mom would have been hysterical that I'd never be able to come back home."

"You had a tough decision to make. What happened just recently?"

"Sir, when my squad got beat up, it was the last straw for me. This war is wrong and I won't be part of it anymore. You need to know I'm not quitting 'cause I'm scared. I mean, I am scared, of course. All the guys are. But I'm quitting because this war is just a ginned-up excuse for U.S. imperialism. None of my friends think that McNamara's domino theory is true. We think it's just propaganda."

Secretary of Defense Robert McNamara believed that if communism took hold in Vietnam, other countries in Southeast Asia would soon follow. This "domino theory" strengthened the justification for the U.S. being involved in Vietnam.

PFC Wilson stopped and looked at me, probably expecting me to spout the party line. I kept quiet and waited for him to continue.

He glanced away and quietly said, "I'm gonna be court-martialed."

"What was it like? I'd like to know what happened to you two days ago."

He stood and walked toward the entrance to my cubicle where he paused. Just when I thought he was going to leave, he turned toward me and with a look of anguish on his face began to answer. "Pete . . ." His voice broke and he struggled to continue. "Pete was the first to get hit, and he was right next to me." He pointed to his left. "One minute he was talking about some glare he saw in the trees, and we both looked over there, and . . . and he . . ." Wilson started to sob.

"One minute we were talking and the next minute half of his head had been blown off." As he cried, Wilson held his hands out, cupping his fingers as if trying to hold on to the spilled brain and pieces of his friend's scalp. The haunted look on his face and the tears flowing from his eyes conveyed the despair he had felt in realizing that he could do nothing at all for his friend.

I knew that he needed me to hear him, so I stopped myself from giving in to the deep sadness I felt and directed all my attention back to him.

He struggled to pull himself together and again took a seat next to my desk. "He was dead." His voice cracked as he spoke, a jolting reminder that this warrior still had one foot in adolescence. "Pete was dead and all I could do for him was help pick up the pieces of his head to go into the body bag."

As he described it, I felt as if I were there. I saw him experiencing the shock of what had just happened. I felt sick to my stomach.

Wilson was quiet again and then, taking a deep breath, looked me in the eyes and brought us both back to his original agenda. "Lieutenant, I'll answer your questions about the firefight, and I'll even tell you about my childhood if you want me to, but none of that will make a difference. I know what I've gotta do."

"Okay," I responded, "tell me more about what you've decided. I'd like to know."

"This is a mistake," PFC Wilson said, "and I've got to stop being a cog in the war machine. A lot more Petes are gonna get killed, but I'm not willing to play any part in this anymore, no matter what it costs me."

He paused again, looking to me for a response.

As he talked, I felt myself becoming even more uncomfortable. I knew from their letters that some of my friends thought as he did, and I had largely avoided conversations about what the U.S. was doing. I knew criticisms were being voiced and I just turned off the volume. I had plenty of anger, but for me it was about what was happening to those sent to war, a horrible waste of human life. Perhaps not thinking about the legitimacy of the war itself was my way of coping with the inherent conflict between the choice I had made to serve in the military and the compelling arguments urging resistance being expressed by those active in the anti-war movement.

As I thought about it, I realized that the topic came up only very rarely in conversations in my unit. Was questioning the war, even acknowledging that many were doing just that back home, too risky a topic, somewhat akin to avoiding religion or politics at the dinner table?

I also was aware that I had stopped thinking of this fellow as someone needing mental health care. Rather, he came across as courageous, principled, and resolved.

"Sir?" Wilson had noticed my silence.

"I'm wondering if you're prepared for what you're going to face by making this decision. It's not a pretty picture, Ed. You'll face years in prison, and in the inmate hierarchy you'll be at the bottom of the heap because of what you're doing. I'm feeling sad for you."

It was his turn to be silent for a few moments, and then he looked up at me, tears again flowing down his face. "Thank you, sir. You're the first person I've talked to who hasn't tried to talk me out of it or been angry."

But I did not feel like I was doing anything particularly admirable at that moment. In meeting him, I was confronted by my own compromises. I was one of the cogs in the machine that PFC Wilson was now opting out of, and talking with him brought me face to face with that choice.

Following the interview, I felt torn. I began writing the formal assessment, knowing the boilerplate language I was expected to use, but feeling sickened by the huge chasm between how this fellow would appear on paper and how I actually perceived him.

I needed to talk. I gave Bill a brief description of Wilson's circumstances and then asked if he'd hear me out about what I was feeling.

He saw the look on my face and read me accurately. "Let's go for a walk, Rog." We left the clinic and I lit a cigarette. "Rant away," Bill said. "From what you've told me, it's easy to understand why you're troubled."

"Look," I said, pacing back and forth, "this guy is one of the most emotionally put-together people I've ever met. He's gone through a gruesome tragedy, lost everyone close to him, and is unbelievably strong in how he's holding it together. And they're going to put him in a fucking prison."

Bill listened.

"On the one hand, I want you to find some pathology in this guy so he can be medically discharged. On the other hand the idea of doing that feels not only fraudulent, but enormously disrespectful to this guy's incredible integrity. If there were any justice, this guy would be honored, not vilified. What about giving him conscientious objector status? Can't we do something, Bill?"

He paused, undoubtedly anticipating that his answer wouldn't really satisfy either of us. "We play the cards we've been dealt, Rog. There's no redemption here. He'll be just one more casualty in a god-awful war."

Sensing Bill's unspoken sorrow helped me gradually calm down, although the feeling of despair about PFC Wilson stayed with me for months. It readily returns even today, more than forty years later, when I wonder if he ended up serving that long prison term. Hopefully, he would have benefited from the amnesty policies eventually adopted by our government for those who'd fled the country to avoid the draft.

—⁂—

Bill and I had also learned that not all commanders were going to be receptive to our recommendations about how to help a soldier in crisis. Neither of us anticipated, however, that our own Medical Battalion Commander, a career Army physician, would undermine our work. But that is indeed what happened one day when an angry voice at the reception desk in the Mental Hygiene Clinic tent let me know something was awry.

"Specialist Mackean, I want to see Captain Baker immediately. Is he here?"

The commanding officer was nearly shouting, and the venom in his voice was unmistakable. Before the Social Work Tech could answer, the colonel barged past him, saw that Bill wasn't at his desk, and charged into my cubicle.

"Lieutenant, where is Captain Baker?"

I jumped to my feet. "Sir, he left an hour ago by chopper to visit battalion surgeons with the 3rd Brigade. Is there something I can help with?"

"Yes, you can. There's a soldier standing at the front entrance who is to be discharged from my hospital immediately and returned to duty. See to it. Now!"

Even before he finished speaking, the colonel had turned away and walked rapidly out of the tent. When he was gone, we asked the obviously frightened soldier to come in and tell us what had happened.

His name was PFC Ted Hampton. He had been medevac'd in the previous day. After his unit had been on three days of reconnaissance and had incurred several casualties from snipers, he had become hyper-anxious, repeatedly hyperventilated, and began shaking violently, certain that the next Viet Cong bullet would be aimed at him. When he threatened to look for a mine to step on, the medic with his infantry company sent him to us. Hampton had talked with Bill, who administered a sedative and admitted him. Bill expected he'd be ready to go back to his unit in a few days.

And that would have been the end of the story if Hampton hadn't had the misjudgment, while on a one-hour pass the next morning, of ducking into a bunker to take a leak rather than finding a latrine, and the misfortune of being interrupted mid-stream when the Medical Battalion CO, who happened to own that bunker, walked in. The colonel blew his stack and, upon learning that Hampton was a psych patient, came up with his own treatment plan, that is, the immediate hospital discharge that I had been ordered to arrange.

I had Hampton wait with Specialist Mackean in the clinic and went looking for Ron Davis, the doc who served as our company commander. After telling him Bill was in the field and about the order I had been given, Ron interceded and mollified the colonel by assuring him that we'd do a better job in supervising our patients. PFC Hampton remained in the hospital for two more days and then was ready to return to his unit.

Later, in debriefing this dustup, Bill and I joked that we seemed to have our very own George Patton clone. In a well known WWII incident, Patton, a highly decorated tank commander, was ordered by General Eisenhower to apologize to the troops after slapping a hospitalized GI whom he thought was malingering.

While many commanders had a more enlightened perspective about the potential adverse effects of combat on mental health, I found myself conjecturing about the images commonly found on Army recruitment posters. Typically they portrayed a strapping youth in a crisply starched uniform bedecked with medals, posed with flags and shiny weaponry. Did those images implicitly reinforce a myth that the well-trained soldier is impervious to being harmed psychologically by war?

Was that myth further reinforced by the beliefs of soldiers in earlier wars, beliefs that those who had become psychiatrically impaired were somehow at fault? Beliefs held by those affected that to talk about what had happened to them was shameful?

The staggeringly high rates of post-traumatic stress disorder in the years following the war's end were obviously unanticipated. It's estimated that one million of the 3.14 million Americans who served in Vietnam experienced PTSD at some point.

It seems clear to me that a collective denial of the prevalence of mental health casualties from combat sustains a fantasy, a fantasy that makes it more likely that young people will enlist, their parents' generation will approve, and Americans will support their government as it wages war.

The doctor who served as Medical Battalion CO ought to have known better, but he was by no means unique in his thinking. When our advice was rebuffed by a psychiatrically impaired soldier's commander who had what I came to think of as a recruitment poster perspective, it was discouraging. And it was a reminder of the power and authority of command, sometimes arbitrarily exercised, and where the mental health professions stood in the pecking order.

Many years later, I laughed when a psychiatrist told me about an interaction he had with General George Patton's son when we were in Vietnam. After one of his infantry troops had become impaired by anxiety, the younger Patton, a colonel, had responded with compassion, saying "Okay, I'll take him off the line and make him my driver for a while. We'll see if that helps." From my perspective, that story removed some of the tarnish from the Patton legacy, and perhaps is a small indicator of how military culture evolved in its understanding of how mental health and combat are inextricably linked.

Combat casualties are generally reported as the numbers killed or wounded, but this definition of casualty is far too narrow. That began to become clear as I interacted with soldiers such as PFC Hampton and PFC Wilson and became all the more evident as the actual toll of the Vietnam War was revealed through the PTSD statistics in the years following its end.

I was angered by arrogant commanders who chose to dismiss the impact of combat-related psychological trauma. It saddened me that PFC Wilson was going to spend years in prison, a terrible waste of this principled man's life. And, when it came to waste, realizing, in the midst of the alcohol-saturated combat zone culture, that a number of GIs, along with Specialist Gordon whose court martial I had participated in, were going to prison for smoking pot was yet another example.

What do they expect happens to people when they're sent into combat? It was a question I kept returning to, never to find an acceptable answer.

And if I'd been able to reconcile each of these conundrums, I suspect it would have been as easy to leave Vietnam psychologically as it had been to leave it physically at the end of my tour. But in truth I had mixed thoughts, not easily resolved, about much of the work I was doing.

In my journal I railed against how abjectly inhumane it was to make a boy into a warrior. Even the word *warrior*, so obviously a glorifying of the role of soldier by using a John Wayne-like Hollywood image, rankled me. The fact that it worked so well with so many, a lemming-like acquiescence as I saw it in my darker moments, was disturbing, all the more so when I realized some soldiers were volunteering for second, third, or even more tours in Vietnam.

Then I heard in my imagination the counter argument. Did I want these guys to have a chance of surviving? If so, I'd better recognize what it took to form cohesive fighting units in which the individualism of civilian culture was replaced by discipline, readiness to unquestioningly follow orders in the midst of battle, and a keen loyalty to the group in which membership had, quite purposefully, been hard won.

I wrote Bill's words, "There's no redemption here," in my journal. The war was happening and boys, hundreds of thousands of them, were in it. Period. I would do what I could in my current situation to help, as I was involved in it now, too, no matter how conflicted I was inside.

My friend Evi, from my undergraduate days at Boston University, wrote and asked what it was like to be there while so much protesting was occurring at home. As students, we had talked about our evolving career interests and she had listened as I weighed the pros and cons of choosing social work as my profession. She understood my values, perhaps more clearly than I did.

Her question was not at all easy to answer and it took weeks before I was ready to reply. Did I even know what I thought?

I eventually found a way to respond. "Evi, your question caught me off guard. My first reaction was to be defensive, to argue that while others can debate the war's pros and cons, doctors, and nurses, and psychiatrists, and social workers, and lots of other health professionals have to be here for the guy who gets shot or experiences acute psychological trauma or has a toothache. But I think the truth of the matter is that I get by simply by putting one foot in front of the other and not thinking much about the journey. Writing letters and reading books sent from home, listening to taped music on a fancy tape deck I bought while on an R&R in Japan, and watching movies or going to USO shows keep me going. And perhaps they also keep many of us distracted from the larger questions you raise. It's just one day at a time, Ev."

Recently, I was reminded yet again of my still-festering misgivings when a colleague's 12-year-old daughter, having overheard me talk about being in the Army in Vietnam long before she was born, looked up at me with a questioning expression and said, "My mom was against that war."

"Yeah, I know," I said with deep sadness.

6

DINKY DOW SMOKE

ROAD TO LONG BINH
MARCH 1967

The boy asked, "Hey, đại uý, you wan numa wun dinky dow smoke? You fey 300 p, I gib you."

I was sitting alone in my jeep in a dusty clearing just outside the entrance to Camp Bearcat waiting for a convoy to assemble. Because the Viet Cong occasionally fired on U.S. military vehicles on the 11-mile road I was about to drive to Long Binh, the Army required drivers to wait until several vehicles headed to the same destination had arrived. Then the trip could begin.

The teen-aged entrepreneur who had walked up to my jeep, barely 5' tall and wearing shorts and flip flops, was offering a pack of joints for 300 piasters, the equivalent of about $2.00. After quickly glancing around to see who might be watching, he also showed me some pornographic photos, eagerly asking "You like?"

I wasn't in the market for dirty pictures, but on this day, only a few weeks after Specialist Gordon's court martial, I took the risk that I had been mulling over since the first time I had had such an easy opportunity to buy pot. When I heard hospital techs joking about getting high as an "instant R&R," I was curious. I handed over the 300 p, quickly hiding the pack under my seat. If stopped by an MP, I thought I'd be credible in denying knowing it was there since the jeep was one of hundreds checked in and out of the motor pool every day. I wouldn't make the mistake Specialist Gordon made by throwing it into a ditch.

I returned to Bearcat about 4:00 that afternoon and, after checking to see that I didn't have any responsibilities at the clinic, made preparations for my first experience smoking pot—an experiment that I planned to carefully document. Maybe it'd be a good idea to do this with someone else, I thought. My friend Turk might be a candidate, but I quickly dismissed that idea when I remembered he was considering making the Army his career. He had too much to lose. Come to think of it, I'd have tried to dissuade him if he had come up with the idea. I was on my own.

I placed a notebook and pen on my cot, and then left the tent and walked along a road toward the motor pool, taking care to stay downwind of anyone who might smell the smoke. Was anyone watching? I noticed my heart was beating faster and made an attempt to scan the environment while not conspicuously drawing attention to myself. It seemed the coast was clear.

I lit the joint, inhaled, and immediately had an unpleasant bout of reflexive coughing. After a few more puffs, I made my way back to my hooch where I intended to record my experiences. Fortunately, I had the tent to myself.

Sitting on the cot, I tried to discern any changes in sensation, however subtle. I thought of myself as emulating the Swiss scientist

Albert Hofmann whom I had read about in a college course. Hofmann had first synthesized LSD-25 in 1938 and carefully documented his self-experiments with the drug in the early 1940s.

The minutes passed and nothing at all was happening. No weird changes in the shapes of objects, no suddenly vibrant colors, no fuzzy feelings in my head, no great insights about the interconnectedness of all mankind, nothing. Except that after thinking it would be more comfortable to lie down, I quickly fell asleep.

My opportunity to record data was lost. I was more confused than ever. And then I wondered if I'd been ripped off by the guy who sold me the pot. Maybe what he gave me was really just some weeds rolled in cigarette paper. Literally weeds.

I woke about an hour later. Greatly relieved that I hadn't been caught, I dropped the rest of the pack of joints into a trash can along the way to the mess hall.

Ah, there was a difference. I was starving.

What being high felt like was still a mystery. Was it really more than deep relaxation? What had they meant when people said it gave them an "instant R&R?" My only reference point involved the feelings I experienced with alcohol, and I wondered if getting high was maybe a quicker or slower, happier or mellower version of getting a buzz on with scotch. And if it was just a variation of being tipsy, how could it possibly have been worth the jail term that Specialist Gordon and so many others had apparently been willing to risk?

I eventually got the hang of what being "high" meant as a sensation, but not until I was out of the Army and attending school at Berkeley, a considerably more conducive setting for altering one's consciousness with pot. As the sociologist Howard Becker pointed out in a classic 1950s paper titled *Becoming a Marihuana User*, there's some learning involved, like the importance of inhaling deeply and holding the smoke in the lungs, and connecting the ensuing sensations with marijuana and perceiving them as pleasurable. It helps when friends with experience can show the way and when the setting is a good deal more mellow than it was at Camp Bearcat that hot afternoon in March of 1967.

Without question, I had been among the greenest of greenhorns. Telling friends later about my furtive experiment was always guaranteed to bring laughter at my naïveté. A stoner I was not, at least not at this point, and—in current day lingo—I'd have been more accurately described as straight and uptight.

It would have been an entirely different story if I'd been caught. I wasn't, of course, yet within a short period I'd be in jail and pot would have a lot to do with it.

7

LONG BINH JAIL

93RD EVACUATION HOSPITAL, LONG BINH
6 APRIL 1967

t was moving day. After three months at Bearcat, I packed my foot locker, completed a pile of paperwork, and said goodbye to Bill, Ron, and other friends, many of whom I'd first met at Ft. Riley a year earlier. I had been reassigned from the 9th Infantry Division to the 935th Medical Detachment, the mental health department of the 93rd Evacuation Hospital in Long Binh.

Located eleven miles north of Bearcat and twenty-two miles northeast of Saigon, the enormous Long Binh base occupied twenty-five square miles and housed more than 50,000 Army personnel. Doctors, nurses, and medics with the two evacuation hospitals at Long Binh greatly reduced combat fatalities compared to the Korean War, in part due to the speed with which medevac helicopters transported the wounded from battlefield first aid stations to these fully equipped hospitals.

"Rog, it's great to finally have you here full time." Captain Jacob Romo came up to me as I was moving things into my new hooch. Jake would soon complete his year-long tour, and I was his replacement.

"Now that you've arrived, I can kick back and relax for the, let's see," looking at his watch, "for the 26 days, five hours, 37 minutes, 15 seconds, and a wake up until I can say, 'gặp lại sau nhé.'" Jake had mastered a number of Vietnamese phrases, including the translation for "see you later."

A career Army social worker, Jake was a schmoozer. He loved telling anecdotes and seemed to know everyone working in mental health in the Department of Defense. So much work gets done in the military through personal contacts, knowing someone who knows someone who can bypass bureaucratic hassles. Jake's affability, his phenomenal memory, and the contagious enthusiasm he brought to working the system to make things happen all served to bolster his successful career in the Army.

Jake laughed when he saw my personalized version of the short-timer calendar, a daily reminder of exactly how many days remained before I'd get to go home. It was a WWII Bill Mauldin cartoon of Willie and Joe, the two "grunts" the artist created to capture with dark humor what life was like in the trenches. Divided into 365 tiny sections, this one showed them hunkered down in a foxhole in the middle of a snow storm, and Willie asks Joe, "Remember that warm, soft mud last summer?" There was something very satisfying in penciling an X each evening over one more tiny square in the cartoon.

I had attended weekly case consultations with the mental health staff at the 935th over the previous few months and had come to highly respect Jake and Captain Paul d'Oronzio, another career Army social worker officer, for their savvy in very expertly manipulating the Army power structure on behalf of their clients.

Paul usually had a tobacco pipe in his hand and liked wearing a side arm, an image that coalesced fighter and philosopher into one.

A month earlier, the three of us had had a chance to get to know each other a lot better. We took a week-long trip to Japan where we attended a conference in Tokyo of military social workers serving in Korea, Japan, Vietnam, and other locations in the Far East. Attended part of it, that is.

At the earliest possible moment, we went AWOL and took the bullet train to the imperial city of Kyoto for several days of decidedly non-official and unauthorized R&R. Amidst a whirlwind tour of shrines, temples, palaces, and gardens, a highlight was being invited to attend a Kyoto University graduation party held at the Inn Raku-toso, a ryokan where we were staying. Following the party, several students and their professor invited us to go out drinking. Most memorable for me was the price paid for imbibing far too much sake.

The major who organized the Tokyo conference was irritated by our absence but never wrote us up, perhaps thinking that the "delegation from Vietnam" deserved a break. Paul and Jake were certain we could get away with it, and their confidence elevated each of them a few notches in my view. We became a band of miscreants, a bit of defiance that cemented a long-term friendship.

On that first day as we toured the 93rd Evac, Jake and I walked over to Paul's office and the three of us then took a quick tour of the hospital. They pointed out the various medical and surgical departments, most of which were located in four rows of four-winged Quonset huts made of corrugated steel. A large helipad was situated directly outside of the hospital's emergency room, and we watched two choppers land and unload wounded soldiers onto gurneys that were then rushed inside.

As we walked through the hospital grounds, the air was filled with pungent smells of burning excrement, a ubiquitous and noxious aroma that must be experienced to fully appreciate, and fuel, both from aircraft and the constantly running generators that powered the hospital. Just outside the base, traffic made up of both civilian and military vehicles was heavy on Route 1. The noise from the choppers, generators, and highway traffic made it difficult to hear one another.

At Paul's suggestion, we checked a jeep out of the motor pool and drove over to the stockade, the Army's term for a jail. I'd work part-time staffing the mental health clinic there and Paul wanted to let me know what I'd be experiencing. Driving outside the perimeter of the compound, I saw that it was enclosed by cyclone fences topped with concertina wire. Seven elevated guard towers stood at fixed intervals around the stockade and flood lights were mounted on tall poles to illuminate the area at night. One of the internal yards had twenty large dormitory tents erected on wooden frames. Another yard, sectioned off by high fences, included a chapel, administration buildings, the mess hall, a medical clinic, and the mental health office. Its official name was the US Army Vietnam Installation Stockade, but everyone called it the Long Binh Jail or sometimes "the LBJ," not quite in honor of the president.

The LBJ would have been where Specialist Gordon served his four month sentence for possessing pot. PFC Wilson, on the other hand, presumably with a much longer sentence for what was essentially desertion, would have been incarcerated at the U.S. Military Barracks at Ft. Leavenworth, Kansas.

Civilians are more likely to be aware of confinement camps for prisoners of war than jails to imprison members of our own military. Yet punishments such as demotions, loss of pay, dishonorable discharges, and confinement long have been part and parcel of military history. During the Vietnam War, more than two million young men were drafted, more than half a million of them receiving less-than-honorable discharges. Thirty-four thousand were imprisoned following courts-martial.

Cecil Barr Currey, in an oral history of the LBJ, described how the stockade was viewed by the troops: "Every soldier assigned to Vietnam detested the name LBJ. It was the most hated place in the combat zone, always a brooding presence in the lives and consciousness of young soldiers. Fear of being sucked into its coils kept many an unwilling, and sometimes unruly, American soldier on the path that is called narrow and straight."

Paul said, "Roger, you'll meet some pretty tragic people here. Many are in for going AWOL, and some for drugs, but there are also guys here who've committed theft, rape, assault, and even murder. Unfortunately, this place keeps growing to handle the steady increase in the number of prisoners, and things could get out of hand if the stockade isn't staffed adequately."

That, indeed, did happen fifteen months later when, in August of 1968, the stockade was largely destroyed by a group of about 200 of the 719 prisoners who rioted and held control of the compound for nearly a week. Those who were there attributed the destruction to gross overcrowding, insufficiently trained guards, racial violence among prisoners and between prisoners and guards, and many prisoners being high on smuggled marijuana and a French barbiturate named Binoctal, cheap and widely available in the civilian economy.

In the spring of 1967, however, with a much smaller prisoner population, the stockade was a safer place for prisoners and guards alike. I became the stockade social worker, spending two days each week conducting mental health assessments and offering individual and group counseling. Confinement in this bleak environment, particularly for those younger men who had tried and failed to escape from their units and from the war by going AWOL, commonly contributed to depression and sometimes suicide.

It was a sad place.

8

ANSWERS FOR GENERAL WESTMORELAND

U.S. ARMY VIETNAM INSTALLATION STOCKADE ("LONG BINH JAIL")
LONG BINH, JUNE 1967

"Lieutenant, what do you know about marijuana?"

It was two months later, and a major I hadn't met poked his head into my office at the LBJ to ask if I had a minute. I wondered if he noticed how flustered I quickly became when I immediately concluded he knew about my personal "experiment" back at Bearcat and was there to interrogate me.

Fortunately, he had something else in mind. "I'm Ron Berry, assigned to the USARV Provost Marshal's Office. Marijuana has suddenly become a hot topic in General Westmoreland's Office, and I've been asked to pull together a brief report. I figured a social worker would know a hell of a lot more about it than I do."

Unlike many MP officers who were built like linebackers, Major Berry was about 5'6", a bit overweight, and balding, and his drawl gave him away immediately as a west Texan. He opened his briefcase and pulled out a file and some newspaper clippings.

"Earlier this month, General Westmoreland was back in D.C. for meetings in the Pentagon. Someone told him to be prepared to receive a formal request, probably within a few weeks, to estimate the percentage of U.S. military personnel in Vietnam who smoke marijuana. Apparently a Congressional committee has held hearings and one of the witnesses said he was certain there were approximately 100,000 servicemen involved with pot. Let me see, I've got some clippings about this somewhere. Yeah, here they are.

"Okay, let me read this first one to you. It's from the New York Times and dated June 15, 1966. The headline reads ADDICT SAYS HE SHOT 2 SOUTH VIETNAMESE WHILE HIGH.

A former Marine helicopter crew chief told a Senate subcommittee today that he had taken four "goof balls," had drunk a glass of beer, had gotten "high," and then shot and wounded two South Vietnamese soldiers while on a mission.

Major Berry paused and looked at me, rolling his eyes and muttering, "The son of a bitch fired on our fucking allies!" He went on:

The 23-year-old former sergeant, identified only as "Frank," said he had flown more than 100 missions in Vietnam and had been under the influence of drugs "a good portion of the time." Pep pills and barbiturates, he said, were easily available to servicemen either by purchase or by "conning" medical corpsmen. No disciplinary action was taken against him, the Senate group was told, because no one was aware that he was under the influence of drugs at the time.

"Okay, enough about this poor bastard. Let me find the quote about the doctor. Yeah, here it is."

Frank, accompanied by his wife, was introduced to the Senate Juvenile Delinquency subcommittee by Dr. Robert W. Baird, director of the Haven Clinic, a narcotics treatment center in Harlem. Dr. Baird testified that he was concerned about the "increased amount of addiction of boys in the armed services."

"Then, get this, he pulls these unbelievable numbers out of the air."

"Based on the statistics that I have seen, plus talking to various addicts and other servicemen in New York, Miami, California, Boston, and New Jersey, I would predict that there are a minimum of 10 to 15,000 heroin and barbiturate addicts in the service and easily 100,000 marijuana smokers."

"Can you believe this? A civilian doc who thinks he's an expert makes some wild guesses and, just because he's a doctor, his numbers are taken seriously." Major Berry was clearly bewildered by how such unfounded estimates could shake up the Pentagon.

The kernels of myth and half-truths surrounding marijuana use by GIs were already taking root, soon to grow into a formidable bean stock of lore and hyperbole. Experts in mental health, addiction, and criminology, Dr. Baird among them, would, in the coming months, be widely quoted in the media, offering their perspectives of what the scant data and early anecdotes about pot use by soldiers might portend. I sometimes wondered the extent to which self-aggrandizement contributed to the motivations of some who were issuing the direst projections.

"Okay, so here's another clipping from a couple of days later. Really not any better than the first one if you're at all interested in getting at the truth."

The next article, also from the *New York Times*, was headlined WIDE NARCOTICS USE BY MILITARY FORCES DENIED BY PENTAGON.

He scanned the article, found what he was looking for, and then read it aloud.

In a formal statement, the Defense Department said: "Widespread use of marijuana or narcotics by members of the armed forces could not go undetected, either in the United States or overseas, because of the very nature of military service, which involves a close degree of supervision."

"Okay, enough of that. Obviously there's some big time 'CYA' going on. Let me read you something else. While they were back in D.C., one of General Westmoreland's aides got a copy of testimony Henry Giordano gave at these hearings. Do you know who he is?"

I didn't.

"He's the Commissioner of the Federal Bureau of Narcotics, and listen to what he had to say." He removed a mimeographed document from his briefcase.

"From my studies and experience, one theme emerges—that marihuana is capable of inducing acts of violence, even murder. The drug frees the unconscious tendencies of the individual user, the result being reflected in frequent quarrels, fights, and assaults. In Colorado, a man under the influence of marihuana attempted to kill his wife, but killed her grandmother instead, and then committed suicide. In Baltimore, Maryland, a 25-year-old Puerto Rican charged with criminally assaulting a ten-year-old girl entered a plea of not guilty

on grounds of temporary insanity caused by smoking marihuana. He was subsequently found guilty and sentenced to death by hanging."

"It goes on and on, but I think you get the point."

He dropped the documents into his briefcase, sat back in his chair, wiped his brow with a handkerchief, and shook his head slowly. He was quiet for a few moments, and then said, "So you see, Lieutenant, I'm the smallest fish in the food chain right now and somehow have got to quickly come up with some answers for the CG that are a hell of a lot better than this bullshit. Can you help?"

I hesitated, but decided to take a risk. "Sounds like you're not interested in just spouting the party line."

"Damn straight, Roger. If I'm going to submit a report over my signature, I want it to be credible, not a bunch of fantasies patched together just to make the top brass happy."

As Major Berry was talking, I thought about Majors Evans and Henley from Specialist Gordon's court martial and how adamant they had been about imposing a jail sentence on him for possession. They had a black or white outlook, and for them marijuana was entirely black. It seemed as if Major Berry was far more willing to look for the truth, not needing to either demonize the drug or cover up the use of pot by soldiers. He wanted hard data, and then he'd draw his conclusions.

"Sir, I've got an idea. We could conduct a survey of GIs here at the stockade and make sure that they know that their answers couldn't be traced back to them. It'd have to be truly anonymous. Obviously, you couldn't use data from inmates to estimate how prevalent marijuana use is among all Army personnel in Vietnam, but the findings would give you part of the picture. Maybe you could even argue that they give you an upper range of the estimates for what's going on among troops not in jail. A survey here could be done pretty quickly."

"How quickly?" he asked.

"I think it'd take a few weeks to design the questionnaire, collect the data, and write it up. But I'd need clearance from the Stockade Commander and Major Blechschmidt, my CO at the 935th."

He smiled, stood up, and reached over to shake my hand. "Lieutenant, I believe I've found the right man. Look, there are two questions I'd like you to start asking. First, tell me how many have used it, and second, tell me how frequently they smoke it. Give me a report that can answer those questions in a month and I'll be a happy man."

That evening I began to sketch out the form that the questionnaire might take, and what I'd need to do to get prisoners to cooperate and safeguard their identities. I was excited about getting a chance to make use of my research skills, all the more so because of the controversial nature of the topic.

Since Specialist Gordon's court martial four months earlier and my own attempt at getting high a few weeks after that, I'd been curious about pot and how it was actually affecting soldiers' lives. Over time it was more and more evident that GIs, lots of them, were getting high. I'd heard quite a few were being tried by court martial. I wanted to know just how common pot smoking was by service personnel in Vietnam. It seemed as if a new chapter was being written. Marijuana's popularity in our country had begun in the early 1900s when the drug was introduced by Mexican immigrants in the southwest. Later chapters included the jazz scene of the 1920s and the beat generation of the 1950s and 1960s, and now there was a resurgence in its popularity on a wider scale than ever before with the hippie and counter-culture movement in America, and then abroad in Southeast Asia. How would the Vietnam War era rewrite the textbooks about this drug?

After receiving the go-ahead, I began the study. I selected a random sample of the 425 inmates confined as of July 1, 1967. Between mealtimes I used the mess hall to meet with groups of ten, explaining the purpose of the study and assuring them that their answers could not and would not be traced back to them. To avoid coercion, I said anyone who didn't want to answer the questions could simply hand in a blank questionnaire.

Among the key findings were that while only 5% had been charged with a marijuana offense, 63% of those confined for some other offense declared that they had smoked pot since coming to Vietnam. Almost half of these men had never used marijuana before this deployment. Nearly 60% said they had used it more than 20 times in country, the arbitrary benchmark I used to indicate more than experimentation.

My report went up the command channels. Eventually I was told by Major Berry that his boss, Brigadier General Harley Moore, the Army's Provost Marshal for Vietnam, said it was "a damn fine job."

I soon had another visitor, Lieutenant Colonel Arnold Johnson, the Consultant in Psychiatry and Neurology to the USARV Surgeon. He had read the stockade survey report and asked if I'd replicate the study with GIs who weren't incarcerated. Knowing how popular marijuana smoking was becoming back home, he had been advocating such a study for months.

Only later did I wish that LTC Johnson had put his request in writing.

9

SACRIFICED TRUTH

T he second marijuana survey began well enough.

I asked Captain Ely Sapol, a psychologist on the psych clinic staff, if he'd work with me on the next study. He quickly agreed.

A son of Brooklyn through and through, Ely had attended Brooklyn Technical High School where he was elected president of the student body, and then enrolled in ROTC while studying at the City College of New York. Headed for a career in engineering, he got sidetracked by psychology, eager to understand human adaptability. Determined that he'd be prepared to protect himself if he had to go to Vietnam, he'd purchased and brought along his own personal Smith and Wesson pistol, ammunition, and shoulder holster, all of which were promptly confiscated the day he arrived. He was taken aback by the irony of having to surrender his weapon as he entered a combat zone, but that wasn't the only memorable event of his first day in country, Christmas Eve of 1966.

That first evening, he'd found his way to the Officers' Club where he spotted someone who was quite drunk and bawling. Ely asked if he needed any help and learned that the fellow was disconsolate about being apart from his wife. The next morning, as Ely boarded a helicopter that would take him to the 93rd Evac, he was shaken to see that the pilot was none other than the fellow he had tried, quite unsuccessfully, to help the night before. Ely wryly commented, "It gave me pause about getting into that chopper."

Neither of us anticipated that a project LTC Johnson asked us to take on would eventually be turned on its head, with our research later being labeled as almost subversive. In the coming months, learning to appreciate the irony in how our study of marijuana use would be perceived by Army brass became an important adaptive skill for the two of us. Ely was the perfect partner.

We arranged to conduct the new study at the 90th Replacement Battalion. Hundreds and sometimes thousands of Army personnel passed through the 90th each week, either just after arriving and awaiting transportation to their assigned units or on their way home. We'd survey those about to return to the States after a year's tour in-country.

The 90th was a camp within the larger Long Binh post, with its own quarters, mess halls, PXs, laundry facilities, barber shops, medical dispensary, and clubs. Here the new arrival in Vietnam would see row after row of two-story unpainted wooden barracks buildings, olive drab tents, and sand-bagged bunkers. First impressions would result from a conglomeration of the familiar (being issued field equipment, standing in formations, moving into assigned spaces in barracks) and the unfamiliar (the sounds of nearby mortar and artillery fire, oppressive heat, and the presence on base of Vietnamese civilian employees).

Upon arrival, all were required to exchange their American currency for Military Payment Certificates, the scrip used in Vietnam. The orientation handbook noted where the mailroom was located, the hours when the mess halls were open, and—just in case it might not be evident—that "notification of a red alert will be incoming artillery, mortar rounds, or one long blast on the post siren." The recommended response was "(a) hit the dirt; (b) if a drainage ditch is nearby, move quickly into it; and (c) if you are in the billets, crawl under a bed and cover yourself with a mattress." The introduction to the handbook, written undoubtedly with a substantial dose of irony, said that these guidelines were intended "to make your stay here more pleasant."

Beginning on August 2nd, we started visiting the unit two or three days each week. Our plan, over a three month period, was to ask 600 GIs who had completed their year's tour to fill out a questionnaire. We worked to design the study's methodology to meet the standards for competent survey research.

At that time, marijuana's popularity in the U.S. was rapidly escalating, above all on college campuses, and its prevalence, as well as debates about its effects and whether it should continue to be illegal, were receiving increasing coverage in American news media. Editorials calling for legalizing pot began to appear, particularly in student newspapers at the University of Michigan, Yale, and the University of Wisconsin.

The controversy heated up even more when two senior health officials squared off on the issue. When the Director of the Food and Drug Administration, Dr. James Goddard, described pot as less harmful than alcohol and called for the elimination of criminal penalties for its possession, critics called for his resignation. Not

surprisingly, Dr. Henry Giordano, the Commissioner of the Federal
Bureau of Narcotics whose quotes Major Berry had read to me,
was one of those critics.

News coverage of marijuana use by GIs in Vietnam was also
increasing. One reporter wrote it was as easy to buy as candy, often
from old women at street-side stands and pedicab drivers. The article
quoted Harley Moore, the Provost Marshal who had praised my
stockade survey report. He said young people in the military reflected
what was happening in their age cohort at home. He added that pot
was not much of a problem in his view. When I later met Brigadier
General Moore, he told me confidentially that he had been criticized
by General Westmoreland for having made those comments.

Eventually, one of those reporters found us. "Gentlemen, can
I have a few minutes?" Twelve soldiers who had taken the survey
in one of the mess halls at the 90th that morning had just left and
Ely and I were packing up the filled-out questionnaires.

The fellow who approached us wore Army fatigues, but because
there were no insignia to indicate rank or unit, it was evident he
was a civilian. "My name is Tom Corpora and I'm with United
Press International. When I interviewed the CO here this morning,
he told me about your work." Corpora was about thirty, tall and
with a weathered look, his hair graying prematurely. He had been
writing first-hand accounts about the war from the field for some
months. Corpora had been with units while they were under fire,
knew well both the Army bureaucracy and culture, and seemed
well suited for a battlefield beat.

The three of us walked outside to talk. He glanced at the tags
on our uniforms, jotted our names in his notebook, and said, "I
understand you did a study of pot use by stockade prisoners, and
now you're doing another survey here. I'd like to know what you're
hoping to learn. There'll be a lot of interest in this back home."

The reporter had his pencil at the ready, but this seemed risky, I thought. Ely apparently agreed. He said, "Tom, USARV Headquarters has a Public Information Office. Will you talk with them about this first? We'll be in deep shit if we give an interview without clearance."

The reporter readily agreed, and the next day we received a call from a Major Summers, the Assistant USARV Public Information Officer. General Moore had approved releasing the stockade study report to the UPI reporter.

But before Corpora could get back to us that decision was countermanded just a day later. The USARV Surgeon decided that not only would the press *not* be given the report, but also that all extra copies of it would be destroyed, copies presently held by officials would be classified "For Official Use Only," and Ely and I were ordered to refuse any requests for interviews. Once again we got a call from the USARV Public Information Office. This time it was a colonel who warned us about reporters who, under the guise of friendly interest, would do their best to pry information. My colleagues at the hospital had a field day riding me about the notorious "Roffman Report."

About a week later, Tom Corpora showed up again while we were administering the survey at the 90th Replacement Battalion. "Fellows, I think I may have upset a beehive with this one." Shaking his head and with a sardonic grin, he said, "After I left you, I got the okay from General Moore to see your stockade report. I got a short glance at it and took some notes, but when I returned to ask a few more questions, suddenly no one was available to talk with me. I'd sure like to know more about the findings and what you make of them."

Ely and I both felt stymied. A green light had been given by the USARV Provost Marshal, and that had been quickly countermanded by the USARV Surgeon. Neither of us was willing to take the chance and hoped Corpora would appreciate the bind we were in. In a sense, I thought, the story of the dueling generals was far more interesting than the stats about pot use.

About a week later, it became evident that the truth about marijuana use by GIs was going to be sacrificed in the service of propaganda. At Corpora's urging, a meeting was convened by the new USARV Psychiatry Consultant, Colonel Matthew Parrish. COL Parrish had replaced LTC Arnold Johnson, the former Consultant who had proposed the new survey we were now conducting. Also attending were Major Summers from the Public Information Office, our new CO at the 935th, Ely, and me.

During this meeting, Corpora attempted to ask further questions about both the stockade survey and the study that was currently underway. COL Parrish immediately dampened any discussion of the surveys by saying that in essence no actual studies had been completed, but rather very preliminary pilot work had been done from which no valid conclusions could be drawn. It wasn't certain, COL Parrish continued, that any further efforts would be made to collect information on this topic.

What an incredibly frustrating experience this was turning out to be. It was as if our work had been judged as worthless.

The reporter recognized what was happening and rose to leave, saying, "Gentlemen, I think we are wasting our time." I wanted to defend our studies, believing that our data were certainly more useful than they had been made out to be. With just a glance at COL Parrish's face I knew I'd have been rebuked had I done so.

Approximately two weeks later, a wire service article about our two studies was published across the U.S. with Tom's byline. He added a personal anecdote in his article about having gone into combat with a platoon. As the men readied to leave base, their sergeant ran through an equipment checklist and ended with "and if you've got any pot or pills, share 'em." Tom wasn't sure whether the sergeant was serious or perhaps had been joking for his benefit.

But for Ely and me, it only got worse.

COL Parrish called us into his office. He noted that his predecessor had not authorized the current survey in writing and he told us he had a plan to rectify that problem.

"Gentlemen, the survey you're conducting is unauthorized. To change that, I want you to submit a request through channels for authorization to do the research. In that request, do not mention that you've already collected data. Instead write the request as if the study has not been started."

I asked if he could simply issue a retroactive order, but he cut me off, standing up to signal that our meeting was over. "By the way," he said, almost as an afterthought, "you have my oral permission to continue collecting data. And no, Lieutenant, I do not intend to put that in writing."

Decades later I learned that all was not how it appeared. In actuality, COL Parrish was unhappily carrying out instructions from the USARV Surgeon, the general who had cut off Tom Corpora's access to us and our findings. At the time, however, COL Parrish gave us no indication that he sympathized with our plight. What does seem evident, however, is that by refusing to issue orders for us to continue with the survey, he was protecting his deniability.

During our final week of administering the questionnaires, one bright spot appeared on an otherwise increasingly gloomy horizon. I was promoted to the rank of captain. Yet even that cause for celebration had its own ironic twist. At the promotion party, the hospital Executive Officer got drunk, tripped, got a nasty gash on his forehead, and required six stitches.

The stage was now set for the penultimate chapter in our demise as marijuana researchers in the Army. We'd finished administering questionnaires, but our request for written authorization to even begin the study continued to go unanswered. The dates when each of us would return to the States rapidly approached. Now the issue was whether we'd be permitted to take the completed but unanalyzed data with us. Once again, we were told to submit a written request. This time there was no delay in the Army's response. Permission was denied. Every bit of this study's data set was to remain in Vietnam.

We quietly seethed. Just in eyeballing the completed questionnaires, it seemed highly likely that they'd tell an important story, one that might contribute to a better understanding of how pervasive pot use actually was. But now it appeared that our work was being deep-sixed.

Back home, John Steinbeck IV, the famous author's son, had recently returned from a year's tour in Vietnam. He was widely quoted as saying that 75% of soldiers in Vietnam smoked pot and did so most of the time. Our survey could support or refute his claims. But we now were convinced the findings would never see the light of day.

It seemed as if there were no options.

Then, an inspiration. Believing that we'd certainly be free to publish the results after leaving the Army, Ely and I left a stack of randomly filled-in fake questionnaires with our CO and I mailed the real ones to my home address in the States.

Having taken this now irrevocable step, the days remaining before my departure were anxiety-laden. I worried that I'd somehow be found out. Then, transfer orders arrived requiring that I spend the final three days at the 90th Replacement Battalion for out-processing. Even after moving there I feared the worst in the knowledge that disobeying a direct order was an offense not taken lightly. Succeeding in rescuing the data would be a victory for science, I thought, but knew that my Robin Hood fantasy was just that.

The MPs never showed up, and on December 11, 1967, a little more than eleven months since arriving, I boarded a chartered TWA flight at Tan Son Nhut airfield for my return to the States. Ely's departure was about a week later.

Cheers erupted as the plane lifted off the runway, and then the cabin went silent as, I suspect, each of us became absorbed in thoughts about what we were leaving behind and our collective relief in getting out of that country alive. As the plane gained altitude, the bomb craters and military bases grew smaller and smaller, eventually giving way to a vista of the lush tropical forest canopy and the sparkling azure waters of the South China Sea. Then we were in the clouds and Vietnam disappeared.

10

YOU COULD BE TRIED

BOSTON, MASSACHUSETTS

12 DECEMBER 1967

Following a refueling stop in Alaska, continuing on to McGuire Air Force Base in New Jersey, a bus ride to a civilian airport, and then the final leg of the journey to Boston, I was home. It had taken a month to get to Vietnam by ship, and the 24-hour return trip seemed almost too quick. Transitioning from the all-military environment to the civilian world was surprisingly uncomfortable. On the commercial flight to Boston, there were just a few of us in uniform, most still grubby with Southeast Asia grime. Occasionally, someone would smile or nod, but I wondered what they were really thinking.

Once the plane had taxied to the gate and the passenger stairs were being rolled up, I scanned the waiting crowd on the tarmac and quickly spotted my parents. People were all bundled up in hats, scarves, and gloves, but I'd have recognized Dad's gray fedora hat anywhere. Mom and Dad looked anxious and were holding hands, something I rarely saw them do.

It was hard to remain patient as the passengers ahead of me gathered their belongings and deplaned, but then my turn came to walk down the steps and I was soon in my parents' arms. Had they quickly checked me over as I walked up, just to be sure I hadn't kept some injury from them in my letters? We held one another, each in tears, and over Dad's shoulder I glimpsed compassionate glances from several others who were entering the terminal. They understood what they were seeing.

I'd have thirty days of leave before reporting to my next duty assignment for my final 18 months in the service. While living in my parents' home in Marblehead, I experienced that month as surreal, struggling with disbelief that day-to-day life in the U.S. could be seemingly entirely unaffected by the tragedies in this continuing war. Were people that unaware?

The incongruity troubled me deeply, a kind of flashback to my rant to Bill Baker just after he arrived at Bearcat. Back then, I railed about how some of us got to dine in fine restaurants and spend hours at a swimming pool while kids were getting maimed or killed. Something was terribly wrong with both pictures.

After several days, I realized that I wasn't feeling the happiness I had expected. No exhilaration, no joy, and—for that matter—no sadness or unhappiness. It seemed I was having no feelings whatsoever. My parents let me know they understood it might take some time before I'd be ready to talk about the past year, but they were as unprepared as I was for the chasm into which I had slipped.

Much later I managed to sort out what that was probably all about. It wasn't as if I couldn't have found words to tell them about the traumatic experiences of soldiers I had counseled and what it had been like for me to talk with them. I could have told them what it was like when medevac choppers carrying the wounded and the dead suddenly arrived. I could have described the scenes of hospital triage. I could have read to them from my journal about the intense emotions I had when sending soldiers back to their units just days after having survived combat and witnessing their buddies' deaths or severe injuries.

But they wouldn't have understood, at least not in the way I needed them to understand. They'd have listened and asked questions, I was certain of that. But I was just as certain that they'd do what people who love you do. They'd try to comfort and reassure me. They'd offer sympathy and encouragement that with time the intensity of painful memories would ease. Perhaps seeing a therapist might help. Just a few sessions. And then the subject would change. It would be time to get dinner prepared, or a favorite television program would soon begin, or a suggestion that we visit Aunt Eleanor and Uncle Jack on Saturday.

And I wouldn't have been able to bear it. That's the reality that occurred to me when I tried to understand the chasm. Were we to have the conversation, I would take my parents through the looking glass into the Vietnam experience, my memories of the past year, emotions barely unpacked and hardly stowed away, and they'd leave before I could. Not because they didn't care, but because they'd have no way of staying with me.

So I kept much of it in.

Decades later, a conversation with a friend brought me back to that period, the initial weeks of being home from Vietnam. Knowing what I had experienced, she offered a thought that moved me deeply. Pauline, following the death of her mother in Jerusalem, had flown back to Israel and sat Shiva, traditionally a multi-day bereavement ritual practiced in Judaism. The mourners receive relatives, friends, neighbors, and well-wishers. As Pauline described it, "We talked and talked and talked, and cried, and talked, and laughed, and cried. People shared anecdotes, stories were told and memories recalled, and I even learned some aspects of my mother's past that I hadn't known. Sitting Shiva gave us the time to begin the grieving, time devoted completely to just that, nothing else." She paused, and with a loving look of compassion on her face, said, "Roger, you never sat Shiva when you came home from Vietnam."

I realized the truth of her comment, and wondered whether I'd have found my way more quickly had I sat Shiva on returning. Would fewer in the military have experienced PTSD had they done the same, sat Shiva for their buddies and for themselves? Sat Shiva for who they had once known themselves to be and would never be again?

I was fortunate. The period of numbness in which I found myself upon returning from Vietnam lasted for only a few months. For so many others, the psychological re-entry process was far more traumatic and long-lasting. For some, it has never ended.

In mid-January of 1968, I reported to Walter Reed General Hospital in Washington, D.C., where I was to serve on the staff of the Medical Social Work Department. As I settled into my new responsibilities, my capacity to feel gradually returned. There wasn't a specific incident or an identifiable day when my emotions switched back on, but eventually I became aware a change had occurred. Even today, I can easily access the keen memories of pleasure from music while attending an outdoor concert with my friends, Larry and Edna, and the joy of driving in the Virginia countryside, the top down on my new Pontiac convertible. The fog had lifted.

I wondered if I had experienced a short-lived episode of a delayed stress reaction. In preparing an in-service training for social work colleagues on the mental health consequences of trauma, I read of people being capable of delaying reactions until it was safe to experience those feelings. Is that what happened to me?

—⁂—

This period of numbness and subsequent calm and seeming transition into a new, post-war and post-pot routine was not to last. Several months after I had returned to the US and begun my work at Walter Reed, Ely and I learned we had been wrong about the possibility of publishing our survey results. We'd thought that once we were discharged there'd be no issue, but a civilian lawyer advised us that the questionnaires belonged to the Army. If we published the findings without authorization, we could be prosecuted.

And then I met a guy at a bar and our fortunes changed.

At a psychiatric conference at Walter Reed Hospital, Lieutenant Colonel J.D. Lloyd, the Assistant Psychiatry and Neurology Consultant to the Army Surgeon General, had presented a talk on substance abuse in the military. A soft-spoken man who nonetheless was clearly intensely interested in his topic, he told the audience that he recently had been appointed to serve on the newly formed Department of Defense Task Force on Narcotics and Drug Abuse.

Later, at the Officers' Club, I spotted him sitting alone at the bar reading a newspaper. As I walked up, I thought about what he had said in his talk that afternoon and the attitude he'd revealed in his characterization of drug use by military personnel. Quite unlike some hardliners who favored severe penalties and perceived any drug use as a threat to military discipline, LTC Lloyd had spoken of the need to better understand the motivation to use drugs, particularly by young people who were living in extraordinarily stressful circumstances. From his perspective, appreciating the reasons why soldiers got high could contribute to a more effective response than simply relying on punishment. I wanted to meet him.

I asked if he had a moment and introduced myself. "Sir, in your talk you said that there hadn't been any surveys of drug use by military personnel in Vietnam. I thought you'd be interested in knowing about two surveys of marijuana use by GIs that I conducted there."

"You've done what?" LTC Lloyd had a shocked expression. "I'm sorry, but I'm really surprised. We asked USARV about whether any data existed about drug use in Vietnam, and they said no studies had been done."

"Well, Colonel, I guess you got a technically correct answer, but not an entirely truthful one. Both studies have been suppressed."

I waited to see how he'd respond, knowing that my accusation might have raised his hackles, but he simply nodded as I spoke. I told him about the stockade survey and the fact that the USARV Surgeon had ordered that the report of the findings be classified and extra copies destroyed. I also talked about the still uncompleted second survey, omitting the fact that I had mailed home the actual questionnaires after having been ordered to leave the data in Vietnam.

He had questions. What populations had been sampled? What were the response rates? When had each study begun and ended? And more.

As I replied, he removed a business card from his wallet, handed it to me, and said, "Captain, I think I can help you get those questionnaires out of General Westmoreland's headquarters, but I'd like you to put what you've told me in writing. Give me the details about both studies and I'll see if we can't get those questionnaires sent back so you and Captain Sapol can analyze the data."

He slowly shook his head and smiled in apparent disbelief, raised his bottle of Budweiser in my direction, and said, "Thanks for introducing yourself. This is really astonishing to me, although maybe it shouldn't be given how political drug use in Vietnam has become. I guess one of the ways some people deal with the heat is to stick their heads in the sand. Get that memo to me this week, will you?"

He turned back to his newspaper and as I was about to leave, I quickly made a decision. "Uh, Colonel, there's one more piece of information you ought to know. Can I tell it to you off the record?"

With a questioning look, he paused to think, and then said, "You know, nothing's really off the record in the Army. But if you think it's important, you'd better tell me."

I spilled the beans. I told him Ely and I had mailed the questionnaires back to the States and why, that we had left a stack of bogus questionnaires there, what we had learned from the lawyer, and the corner into which we had painted ourselves. Even though the questionnaires left in Vietnam were phony, we had to get them back.

Before I finished, he had started to laugh and then, perhaps in an attempt to make me feel better, asked if he could buy me a beer. "Captain, you may end up in more trouble than you can imagine for this, so let's have a drink while you're still a free man. By the way, for God's sake don't mention *this* part of your story in the memo you're going to send me."

I quickly did as he asked and two weeks later he phoned and requested that I come down to the Office of the Surgeon General for a meeting. A reply to his request for the questionnaires to be returned had been received from General Westmoreland's headquarters. It wasn't good news.

Entering the Main Navy Building, an enormous three-story office building on Constitution Avenue west of the Washington Monument, I had a sense of foreboding. Walking down the battleship gray main corridor that stretched for nearly a third of a mile, I wondered just how bad the news might be, not only about the questionnaires but also about the possibility that I'd be charged with deception for swapping out the surveys and smuggling.

Attending the meeting were the Psychiatry, Psychology, and Social Work Consultants to the Surgeon General, all high ranking officers. LTC Lloyd made the introductions and then read a telex from USARV. It said that our data couldn't possibly be valid and that a special research team from the Walter Reed Army Institute of Research ought to be sent to Vietnam if such a study needed to be done. In hearing our research described as faulty, I wondered if the telex had been written by COL Parrish himself.

Finally, LTC Lloyd read from the telex, there was no need to send the questionnaires since "Captain Roffman had the data" anyway. He stopped reading and glanced in my direction. Damn, I thought, he must have told Westmoreland's headquarters that I mailed the real questionnaires home.

I felt my face becoming red. The silence in the room and my awareness that each of these senior officers was looking at me had a sobering effect.

"You know, Captain, for what you've done you could be brought up on charges and tried by court-martial." The speaker was LTC Sid Couch, the Assistant Social Work Consultant. From the look on his face and his stern tone, it was apparent that a trial was not out of the question.

He went on: "General Westmoreland's staff has every right to charge you for disobeying an order to leave the data." He paused for what seemed like several minutes, clearly steamed that one of his junior officers could have caused this mess. "We also have a memo from a Colonel Hyde with the USARV Provost Marshal's Office. This memo says you conducted the second survey after being refused permission to do it." The memory of not getting LTC Johnson to put his request in writing flitted across my mind for the umpteenth time.

I thought that I was about to be arrested, that MPs were going to be called into the meeting room and place me in handcuffs. I began to feel panicked. Remembering how powerless I had felt when COL Parrish, in that last meeting with the UPI reporter Tom Corpora, denied that any actual studies had been done, I was determined to not miss the chance to defend myself and began to hastily prepare for a last oratorical stance.

"Sir, that's a flat out lie." I was flustered by this gross misrepresentation and was about to continue with my protest, but LTC Lloyd raised his hand and interrupted.

"Calm down, Roger. It's obvious that this fellow from the Provost Marshal's Office was trying to protect the Army by writing that memo. None of us believe it for a minute."

For the first time in that meeting, it seemed as if I might have allies. He looked to the others, each of whom nodded in agreement.

"Let's just ignore it."

LTC Lloyd changed the focus by suggesting that a new telex be sent to Westmoreland's headquarters saying that while we indeed had part of the data, the questionnaires that had been left in Vietnam were necessary in order to complete the study. The men in the room knew those questionnaires were fake, but they agreed with his plan and the meeting mercifully came to an end.

It took about six months, but to my enormous relief the counterfeit questionnaires eventually were returned. Ely and I replaced them with the real ones and, with approval to proceed with the study now granted by the Office of the Surgeon General, we began the data analysis, and there was no more discussion of pressing charges. The upsurge of drug use in the military, both at home and abroad, merited such immediate attention that what Ely and I had done and the politics that had lead us to do it did not merit serious attention any longer.

11

*

32%

Beginning in late autumn of 1968, Ely made several trips to Washington, D.C. from his duty assignment at Valley Forge General Hospital in Pennsylvania so we could work on the project. It quickly became evident that if the effort to suppress the study had been out of fear that it would put the Army in an unfavorable light, the opposite appeared to be the case.

The findings supported the conclusion that BG Moore had asserted when he said that pot use among troops largely mirrored what was happening in that age group back in the U.S. In our sample, 32% had "ever used" marijuana, and that was within the range of prevalence estimates of 18% to 49% from student surveys in U.S. colleges. Two other surveys of GIs in Vietnam conducted within a year after our study came up with "ever used" estimates of 31% and 35%, so we seemed to be in the ballpark.

Similarly, we estimated that 75% of GI pot smokers in Vietnam were using the drug casually or experimentally, and we defined this as less than 20 times ever. The range of casual users in the college surveys was 60% to 80%, once again suggesting that GIs in Vietnam were similar to their age cohort at home.

All well and good, but what about what John Steinbeck IV had to say? He published an article titled "The Importance of Being Stoned in Vietnam" in *The Washingtonian* in January of 1968. From his perspective, our numbers greatly underestimated what was really happening. Over dinner at the Officers' Club, we tried to make sense of the discrepancy.

"You know, Ely, for all we know Steinbeck could be right when he said 75% got high. Maybe all of our assurances about anonymity when we administered the survey weren't all that convincing."

"Some probably lied," Ely replied. "But look, isn't it also possible that Steinbeck overestimated based on a biased view he got by only talking to people he knew? After all, he didn't conduct a survey." Additionally, inflating the numbers made his article more striking and headline grabbing.

Ely thought for a moment and then continued. "Take a look at the difference between pot smokers and non-smokers in our study. The guys who smoked pot said 83% of their close friends got high. But the non-smokers told us that just 42% of their close friends got high. Steinbeck clearly smoked a lot of pot while in Vietnam and it's likely he hung out with other guys who used a lot. Wouldn't he have based his estimate on them?"

"I think the best bet is that our data underestimates and his figure is an overestimate," Ely said. "The truth is probably somewhere in between."

He had a good point. Steinbeck clearly wanted readers of his article to see marijuana in a positive light. One of his passages was almost lyrical in the effect it created. He reprinted it in his memoir, *In Touch*, published in 1969.

Because of what marijuana does to the brain's interpretation of light, and what we call beauty, a wonderful change in war can occur. . . . After smoking marijuana, explosions modulate musically instead of being heard in grim terror. Death takes on a new, approachable symbolism that is not so horrible. All the senses, including the emotions, may seem muted by being hypercharged with their own capacity. There is not enough time to delve into the unusual manifestations of fear with this entirely new lexicon of sights and thoughts to deal with.

And the changes keep occurring. I well remember sitting on top of a bunker with about twenty friends during what we thought to be a surprise attack on our mountain. It was about midnight. The South China Sea was behind us, with an opaque moon spreading its glory out over the mixture of Navy ships and sampans in the harbor a mile below us in Qui Nhon. Their lights seemed to twinkle back recognition of our appreciation. Many an Oriental artist has tried to capture just such a scene. In front of us, in the direction of the supposed attack, lay the beautiful mountains and valleys of the central highlands. The blue-green rolling hills were studded here and there with volcanic boulders that shouted their blackness back at the stoned eyes that beheld them in the delicate moonlight. When the flares and fifty-caliber machine guns started up for cover, you could barely hear the noise of the ordnance over the ohs and ahs coming from our little group of defenders, smoking Papa-san's marijuana.

The beauty of all that gunpowder (an Oriental invention, you remember) was almost too much to bear. Up would shoot a white star flare on a parachute, and all eyes would be transfixed by the glow. Of course it was intended to show whether the enemy was coming up our side of the crest, but a sigh of "did you dig that?" whispered past the shuffling of grenades and ammunition. The mutual feeling was "If this is it, what a nice way to go." The clatter of the machine guns was like a Stravinsky percussion interlude from "Le Sacre du Printemps." Later we found out what we had expected, that there was no attack, but it was a "good show." There isn't a psychedelic discothèque that can match the beauty of flares and bombs at night.

I laughed. "You know, this guy takes you into this scene much as his dad did in describing the devastation of the Dust Bowl in *Grapes of Wrath*."

I read a bit further, and then said, "He also writes about the release from war that being high provides at the last moment. Listen to this: 'Sometimes you would hear friends of a dead soldier say 'Thank God he was stoned.'"

"You know, Ely, I'm glad he wrote this. It at least sheds some light on what people who got high were thinking about."

I thought about LTC Lloyd's interest in better understanding what motivated GIs to smoke pot and wondered if he had read Steinbeck's article. I was a novice pot researcher, but it quickly had become all too evident that only the drug's dangers were of interest to most of military officialdom.

Our completed report was titled "Marijuana in Vietnam: A Survey of Use Among Army Enlisted Men in the Two Southern Corps." It went up the chain of command and eventually was evaluated by a major general who served as Special Assistant to the Army Surgeon General for Research and Development.

Having our work derided as invalid a few years earlier, it was particularly satisfying to read the general's conclusion. He wrote:

"The survey was conducted in accord with sound scientific principles, and great care was exercised to insure reliable and valid responses from the soldiers being processed for return to CONUS." He recommended "that the authors be commended for an outstanding job within a difficult, highly sensitive and timely subject area." While a part of me knew that the survey and the continuing dialog on marijuana meant bigger things would be at stake for a while to come, vindication still felt sweet.

12

GRIEF AND SHAME

U.S. SENATE, WASHINGTON, D.C.
3 DECEMBER 1969

"**M**r. President, a pall of grief and shame and sadness has descended on our land and our people in the wake of the reported massacre at Mylai [sic], South Vietnam." Thomas J. Dodd from Connecticut was speaking on the floor of the Senate on December 3, 1969.

"For most of us, I believe, our first reaction to the initial reports of the alleged massacre was one of shocked disbelief. Never before in our history have American troops been accused of mass murder in cold blood. Our Armed Forces have strict rules of combat prohibiting the maltreatment of civilians. Moreover, the American GI is universally known for his compassion and kindness to young and old; friend and foe. The pictures and stories of American troops feeding candy bars and chewing gum to children are legion.

Literally thousands of women and children throughout the world are alive today thanks to the generosity of our troops. . . . If the massacre at Mylai [sic] took place as alleged, then it represents a total and almost incomprehensible aberration from the normal conduct of American GIs, in previous wars and in the Vietnam war as well."

As he continued, the senator was prepared to offer an explanation for how this atrocity might have happened.

"Mr. President, the grisly incidents alleged to have occurred on March 16, 1968, in Mylai [sic], South Vietnam, present us with a major confrontation in character. Have American soldiers suddenly been transformed into brutish monsters overnight? Or is there some other cause, another factor that has induced this terrible aberration? There is reason to believe that this new image of the GI as a stormtrooper could well be the direct result of the toxic effects of certain drugs which are abundant in Vietnam!"

And there it was. *Reefer Madness* revisited.

The 1938 film, also known as *Tell Your Children*, had portrayed numerous tragedies, including suicide, manslaughter, rape, and psychosis, which befell a group of high school students lured by pushers to try marijuana. Promoted as a fictionalized story of a real menace facing youth, *Reefer Madness* was not widely seen until the 1970s when it became a cult favorite among pot smokers. For this new generation, it was a satire of the hyperbole about the drug's risks.

Senator Dodd was speaking of the mass murder by U.S. Army forces of 347 to 504 unarmed people. The final figure was in dispute between the U.S. and Vietnamese governments. The victims were mostly civilian women and children, living in the hamlets of My Lai and My Khe in Sơn Mỹ village. Rape, torture, and the mutilation of dead bodies were among the additional horrific acts committed by members of Charlie Company, a unit of the 23 Infantry Division's 1st Battalion, 20th Infantry Regiment, 11th Brigade.

Nearly 18 months went by before, in an exposé written by Seymour Hersh and published in *Harper's Magazine*, the facts became known to the American public. As the truth gradually emerged, a very different set of factors than drug use appeared to have contributed to the brutality. One was that, after recently suffering five deaths and numerous non-lethal casualties in firefights with the Viet Cong in that region, the members of Charlie Company were told at the beginning of their mission that "this is what you've been waiting for—search and destroy—and you've got it." It was believed, inaccurately as it was later learned, that the enemy was deeply entrenched in Sơn Mỹ village. The commanders described that day as an opportunity to get revenge.

Other factors were the military's emphasis on body counts and kill ratios, and widespread failures of leadership, discipline, and morale. Twenty years after the war had ended, Jonathan Shay, a Boston-area psychiatrist, wrote a book titled *Achilles in Vietnam: Combat Trauma and the Undoing of Character*. Based on his work with combat veterans with PTSD, he describes a state of being berserk characterized by being enraged, cruel without restraint, devoid of fear, indiscriminate, coldly indifferent, and beastlike. Shay wrote that events that drive soldiers berserk include feeling betrayed (for example, being issued malfunctioning weaponry or being led by inexperienced officers who made costly mistakes), grieving the death of a friend, and seeing dead comrades whose bodies have been mutilated. Each of these described the circumstances of the men of Charlie Company.

Shay offered one soldier's description of his descent into a berserk state.

I was eighteen years old. And I was like your typical young American boy. A virgin. I had strong religious beliefs. For the longest time I wanted to be a priest when I was growing up. You know, I didn't just go to church Sundays, it was every day of the week. I'd come home from school and go right down to the church, and spend an hour in the church. And I was into athletics, sports. I was nothing unique. I was just a typical American boy,—High School, Class of 1965. . . . It was the way you were taught, like, "Whenever you're alone, make believe God's there with you. Would he approve of what you are doing?" That's basically—sure, I wasn't no angel, either. I mean, I had my little fistfights and stuff. It was, you're only human. But evil didn't enter it 'till Vietnam.

I mean real evil. I wasn't prepared for it at all.

Why I became like that? It was all evil. All evil. Where before, I wasn't. I look back, I look back today, and I'm horrified at what I turned into. What I was. What I did. I just look at it like it was somebody else. I really do. It was somebody else. Somebody had control of me.

War changes you, changes you. Strips you, strips you of all your beliefs, your religion, takes your dignity away, you become an animal. I know the animals don't—the animal in the sense of being evil. You know, it's unbelievable what humans can do to each other.

I never in a million years thought I would be capable of doing that. Never, never, never.

Shay noted that for this soldier, all of his earlier relationships lost meaning, even his caring about the other men on his tank. He no longer wrote to his family. His one focus was revenge.

So had marijuana smoking transformed beneficent young soldiers into brutish monsters? My first thought was to simply dismiss Senator Dodd's notions as a vestige of *Reefer Madness* propaganda.

There were some case examples, however, of soldiers experiencing a psychotic episode while high. Two psychiatrists at the 935th had documented cases of a marijuana toxic psychosis.

One case involved a GI on guard duty who smoked pot with a buddy who had never before been high. The first man began to pick on some nearby Vietnamese children telling them he was Ho Chi Minh, and then fired his weapon in their direction. The novice pot smoker became terrified, saw the words Ho Chi Minh on his partner's t-shirt, shot him and returned to the base camp saying he had killed Ho Chi Minh. Other soldiers quickly returned to the guard post and found the dead soldier. A psychiatrist diagnosed the shooter's condition as delusional and manifesting a toxic psychosis.

Other instances of marijuana toxic psychosis in the combat zone became known, including episodes that also involved acts of murder. Typical symptoms included hallucinations, perceptual distortions, and paranoid delusions. But the toxic delirium in these case studies involved individuals who experienced temporary psychotic states, not entire units of men simultaneously becoming psychotic and engaging in mass killing of civilians.

In my opinion, Senator Dodd's claim that marijuana psychoses were to blame for what happened at My Lai was unfounded. Reading Shay's book many years later reinforced the sense I had at the time that a much more parsimonious explanation for their behavior existed: the experience of feeling betrayed by incompetent leaders, the horror of seeing the mutilated bodies of buddies, grieving, and being encouraged to take revenge.

Sen. Dodd's speech on the Senate floor troubled me for another reason. His portrayal of the American soldier's generosity and kindness, resounding with patriotism, told only part of the story of what war does to its combatants, leaving out the much darker truths of how combat affected many GIs.

Later I learned that Senator Dodd had served as one of the lead prosecutors in the Nuremburg Trials, which he described as "an autopsy on history's most horrible catalogue of human crime." I wondered, wouldn't he have known that atrocities are realities of war, perhaps even of all wars and of all armies? Or was it possible he couldn't bear to think Americans could engage in such similar acts?

Just two years prior to his My Lai speech in the Senate, his distinguished political career was tarnished when he was formally censured by his colleagues for having used campaign funds for personal purposes. Was he trying to resurrect his standing with the public by sounding the alarm about marijuana's dangers to youth? He would neither be the first nor the last to promote fear about marijuana for political gain.

In a letter to the editor of *Harper's Magazine*, commenting on Seymour Hersh's exposé, I raised the possibility that sustaining myths about American soldiers seemed to take precedence over finding the truth:

> *Is it possible to objectively and rationally inquire about man's nature in terms of behavior in combat, or the use of drugs? Or is the preoccupation with preserving notions of man's nature as it ought to be so entrenched that rational inquiry can not occur?*

I wanted my voice to be heard on both of these matters, and wrote to Senator Dodd to express my concerns. Inadvertently, by virtue of my being one of only a handful of people to have conducted such studies, and probably because of an article about our work that Ely and I had published in the *Journal of the American Pharmaceutical Association*, I had become something of an expert on pot use by GIs in Vietnam and felt compelled to challenge what I perceived as myths.

13

CONTRASTING AGENDAS

SENATE SUBCOMMITTEE TO INVESTIGATE JUVENILE DELINQUENCY
WASHINGTON, D.C.
19 AUGUST 1970

I had been invited to testify before Senator Dodd's subcommittee in a public hearing and flew to Washington, D.C. from Berkeley, where I was living while studying in the social work doctoral program at the University of California. It had been a year since my Army discharge.

On August 19, 1970, I walked up the grand marble staircase in the Russell Senate Office Building and momentarily stood at the door to the large Caucus Room, taking in the scene. The walls of this palatial space, reminiscent of a Greek temple, were lined with paired Corinthian columns. An ornate frieze with intricate molding and guilded rosettes capped the columns, joining the walls to a richly textured ceiling from which four three-tiered crystal chandeliers were suspended.

Frequently seen on television newscasts, the Caucus Room was the venue where in 1954 the attorney Joseph Welch confronted Senator Joseph McCarthy, at the apex of the latter's relentless and unfounded campaign to uncover communists in the Army, with the famous plea, "Have you no sense of decency, sir, at long last? Have you left no sense of decency?" Hearings held in this room in coming decades would focus on the Watergate break-in and cover-up and the Iran-Contra affair, and it was here that Anita Hill would charge sexual harassment in the Supreme Court confirmation hearings for Clarence Thomas. And here today, as part of hearings of the Senate Subcommittee to Investigate Juvenile Delinquency, I would be testifying about our marijuana research in Vietnam.

A bank of television cameras lined the back of the room, and as I walked through the door I saw that Senate staff members were placing materials on the felt-draped table set on the dais at the front. I spotted Ely and sat beside him.

Paraphrasing Andy Warhol, Ely said, "Rog, I think you're about to get your fifteen minutes of fame." He glanced back at the television cameras and then forward to the news photographers setting up near the witness table, adding, "When you get to the part about the Army's attempted cover-up, I'll bet the flashbulbs will be popping and every one of those cameras will be homing in on you."

Just before I could reply, Carl Perian, the Subcommittee's Staff Director, came over to introduce himself. He and I had been corresponding since my original letter to Senator Dodd was received, and he offered some advice intended to help me feel less nervous. "So if you start to feel intimidated, just imagine that the senators are sitting there without any pants on. That always helps me when I start thinking that they're gods." He paused, and then added, "But don't start chuckling or millions of people will think you're nuts when they see you on the news tonight." Carl winked and walked back to the front table. Ely and I laughed, and then glanced at each other and groaned once Carl was out of hearing range.

Pants or no pants, the grandeur of this historical setting was getting to me. Ely patted me on the shoulder and said, "You'll be fine once you get started. Just remember to breathe." I replied, "You know, I think I'll be able to handle the nervousness, but I'm worried more that what I really want them to hear will get lost."

In our correspondence about my testimony, Carl Perian had specifically asked me to speak about the efforts to suppress the two surveys, reminding me that Senator Dodd himself had felt stymied by the Department of Defense, which he thought had ignored his warnings about an increasing drug problem in the military. My testimony about obstructions I had experienced in the Army to conducting research on marijuana use would help make his case.

In preparing my testimony, I included mention of these barriers but I did not belabor them, as the points I really wanted to make had more to do with misattributing the cause of the My Lai massacre to drug use. I found problematic the starting assumption that pot use by soldiers in Vietnam was inevitably a problem and never beneficial. I wrote:

> Adequate research has not yet been done that will answer many of the most critical questions. We really have little idea what the impact of marihuana use has been in Vietnam. From several case studies of psychotic episodes and violent behavior associated with its use, it is a fairly simple step—although not an objective one— to infer that this reaction will be likely to occur in great numbers of people using the drug. Events such as the alleged massacres in Vietnam cause all of us to cry out for an answer to the question "Why did this happen?" And yet it is too easy, too tempting, and far too dangerous to make the giant and indefensible step to

explain the tragedy by pointing to case histories which may bear little or no relevance to what happened at My Lai. It is within the realm of possibility, for example, that moderate marihuana use for some soldiers—perhaps for most soldiers—reduces the likelihood of mental illness, personality disorganization, and aggressive or violent outbursts. I, for one, am willing to remain open to that possibility.

I do not want to be construed as in any way advocating the use of marihuana. However, we know that for most people the typical pattern of use of this drug produces a mild tranquilizing effect. We also know that there are acute and prolonged stresses faced by men in a combat setting. The objective investigator therefore must consider the possibility that marihuana smoking may for some users assist with healthy efforts at coping with a hostile environment.

Ely was right. The flashbulbs did pop at the point when I spoke about our research being obstructed, and most of Senator Dodd's questions to me pertained to just this one issue. That evening, I did indeed have my 15 minutes of fame on all three television networks' newscasts, and the portion of my testimony that each turned into a sound-bite was about the suppression of the studies. Newspaper stories published the next day about the hearings had headlines such as ARMY HUSHED 'POT' STUDIES, SENATORS TOLD, POT HUSHUP IS CHARGED, DODD CHARGES COVERUP BY PENTAGON ON DRUGS, and ARMY CLOAKS GI DRUG ABUSE IN VIETNAM, PROBER SAYS. My comments about the possibility that marijuana smoking could be beneficial or that attributing the My Lai massacre to marijuana was unsupported were ignored by both the senators and the media.

As I thought about the hearings while flying back to Berkeley the next day, it occurred to me that I had an answer to the question I had raised in my *Harper's Magazine* letter in response to their exposé on My Lai. I had asked if we were able to rationally examine what actually happened to people when we made them into combatants, and whether we could objectively seek an understanding—and acceptance—of both the negative and positive effects of drugs such as marijuana on human beings. At that moment, it seemed as if the answer was "No, not if that isn't your agenda."

Parsing what motivated the various "actors" I'd met during my military experience revealed multi-faceted and telling slices of American society's reactions to marijuana. COL Parrish had denied that our survey findings were valid. He seemed most comfortable with his head in the sand. BG Moore, more willing to acknowledge what was true, had noted that young people in the military simply mirrored the behaviors of civilians of their age. The UPI reporter had written of the sergeant who encouraged his men to share pot or pills if they had any, not seeing any particular evil in it, while Dr. Baird had warned of a massive drug problem among troops. Senator Dodd had wanted to attribute a horrific atrocity to drug use, and the Senate hearing had been designed to expose the Army as having deliberately neglected a festering problem. Perhaps there was a festering problem, but these people had very different ideas about how it should be defined. There seemed to be many lenses through which soldiers' behaviors were being perceived, yet science was given short shrift. Was the prevailing agenda something as mundane as image management?

14

TOXINS

MARBLEHEAD, MASSACHUSETTS
SUMMER 1969

Months prior to the disclosure of the My Lai massacre and my subsequent testimony before the Senate Juvenile Delinquency Subcommittee, I formally completed my term of active duty and was discharged from the Army. In late June of 1969, I returned as a civilian to my parents' home in Marblehead, Massachusetts to spend the summer before heading to California to begin doctoral studies at Berkeley, something I was in the thick of when I went to Washington DC.

Soon after I got there, a friend told me about an International 110 sailboat that was available for rental. In my teens I had learned how to sail in just such a boat. I contacted the owner and arranged for a summer-long charter. The white 24-foot sleek double-ended racing boat was one of a few thousand crafts of various types and sizes in this popular north shore historic town's harbor.

Long sails each day, usually alone, became an effective therapy. The searing sun and the offshore winds helped leach out much of the lingering detritus after my year in Vietnam and from the political skirmishes in which I had become involved.

So much of the emotional heaviness I felt during those days on the water concerned myths that had troubled me deeply: myths about how young men ought to experience the role of warrior and myths about how they were expected to simply set aside that role when it was time to again be civilians. My experience as an Army social worker had immersed me in a culture that required myths to sustain itself, and I'd had the choice of either learning to subscribe to those ideas or be made into the other, an outsider. And then when I returned to civilian life, being an "other" was yet another element of Vietnam's effect that I had not foreseen.

Out on the water that summer I scrolled through a collection of memories. I thought of Specialist Gordon, the mechanic with a clean record whom we sent to prison for possessing a tiny amount of pot. And Calvin Phelps, the 19-year-old PFC who got loaded aboard the *Upshur* on his way to Vietnam and the adamant demands from some of my colleagues that he be court-martialed because his injury caused us to miss the cut off for a combat zone tax credit. I remembered the tragedy of his death from a hematoma.

I was haunted by what had happened to PFC Edward Wilson, the guy who quit the war after his unit was decimated, and what it had felt like conducting a mental health assessment of him, knowing he was going to spend years in prison. I re-ran the memory tapes of guys who came to the clinic acutely traumatized because of what they had experienced in the heat of combat, and what it had been like to send them back to their units just a few days later.

I remembered the apparent inconvenience to the Army's upper echelons of the studies I had conducted. Because some of the brass were eager to bury the truth about pot use by GIs, the work I had done was suppressed.

My gut hurt as I relived the powerlessness I had felt so much of the time in the Army. I needed to be a student again.

The wind and the waves that summer, and the work of maneuvering the boat up and down the coast off Marblehead, cleansed the pores of the identity I had chosen to retain while discarding the toxins of myths that I could increasingly recognize as aberrant. I had gained my sea legs at the beginning of the summer and had begun to find my footing by the end.

I thought I was leaving the marijuana issue behind along with my Class A Army uniform, pressed and hung in a garment bag in the back of a closet in my parents' home. How wrong I was. I had no idea that it would be the focus of much of my professional life as an academic. I didn't foresee how embroiled I'd be in challenging misinformation and half-truths about marijuana during much of my later career, nor did I expect that I'd become an activist, advocating for an end to sending pot smokers to jail. At that point in my life, I had never even been high.

The summer months passed quickly. On the last day of August, I returned from a final sail as evening approached, skirting Marblehead Rock and rounding the tip of the Neck to enter the harbor. Most of the benches at Ft. Sewell were occupied, this park being an ideal spot for witnessing the grandeur of a New England sunset. The beam from Marblehead Light was already sweeping its warning to navigators still at sea.

A new chapter of my life was about to start. The past few months had given me what I needed, a retreat from roles and their responsibilities, a time to air out. By the summer's end, the residual sting from the past several years had quieted. In its place was a hunger I'd bring with me to Berkeley, a hunger for understanding and for deciding where and how I would find my niche as a social worker.

At day's end I headed into the wind, quickly lowered the mainsail, and for the last time dropped anchor in Marblehead Harbor.

PART 2

BERKELEY

I let it fly in the breeze and get caught in the trees, Give a home to the fleas in my hair. A home for fleas, a hive for bees A nest for birds, there ain't no words For the beauty, the splendor, the wonder of my Hair. . . .
—Hair: The American Tribal Love-Rock Musical
Lyrics by James Rado and Gerome Ragni
and music by Galt MacDermot

15

THE FIRST TIME

UNIVERSITY OF CALIFORNIA, BERKELEY
AUTUMN 1969

P rofessor Scott Briar had lectured that morning on how people arrive at beliefs. He exhorted his first year PhD students to think critically. "When you find yourself believing X explains Y because 'everyone knows that's true,'" he said, "remember that commonly accepted truths can be wrong."

He looked around the room, perhaps to reassure himself that all ten of us were listening. It was going to be important.

"Let me give you an example. Owning slaves was once legal in the United States, but this country was created as a bastion against the infringement of human rights," he said. "On the face of it, slavery was inconsistent with one of the country's founding principles. How could slavery have been possible here?"

A classmate named Peter chimed in right away. "There wasn't really any inconsistency," he said. "As long as people believed that Africans were less than human, abducting and selling them were acceptable. And the same 'slam dunk' kind of thinking must have justified the theft of Native American land. Andrew Jackson could throw out treaties based on the premise that Native Americans were less than human."

"Good points," Scott said. "The idea that certain groups were less than human was used to justify actions, and then the economic benefits from those actions enjoyed by the powerful reinforced the initial idea. But surely we'd not find that kind of reasoning acceptable today. Would we?"

He looked around with a questioning smile, his squinting eyes signaling that he was enjoying the moment. "Okay, it's 1970, not the mid-1800's. But wait a minute."

He was on stage, acting as if he were truly confused. "How do we explain homelessness and hunger today, right now, in a country with all of America's wealth? Surely there's enough money to feed and house everyone. Why don't we? We're a compassionate people, aren't we?"

It took a moment, but soon a number of hands shot up. Scott called on Riley. "We blame the poor," Riley said. "We say they've made bad choices and basically failed to work hard enough. We convince ourselves that the poor deserve what they get."

Several other hands were raised, but Scott interrupted us, saying, "Okay folks, we could spend all day on this, but we need to move on. There's a message here. We've been talking about some beliefs, beliefs that 'everyone knew to be true' that have been egregiously detrimental to the rights of fellow human beings. Yet they've been endorsed and reinforced, with economic incentives playing a major role in how they came into being and were sustained.

"Remember this conversation," Scott said. "Remember to wonder who benefits from oppression. I want to challenge you to question what you believe you know. Be willing to acknowledge when your assumptions are flimsy."

Upon hearing this phrase, my thoughts drifted back to my Senate testimony a few months earlier as a supposed marijuana expert. If the truth were told, despite having smoked pot twice, not at all certain either time that I was actually high, I had been totally in the dark. What I thought I knew about being stoned was all from descriptions given by others.

Listening to Professor Briar, I began to understand and regret the unquestioned assumptions I had made when deciding what to ask in those Army surveys. I'd only been interested in how many used pot, how often they used it, and the problems they might have experienced. I had entirely missed the chance to learn *why* soldiers got high, to try to understand the benefits that they perceived.

Unwittingly, I had worn blinders while designing those surveys. I wondered who gained by maintaining a view about pot smokers that only considered negative consequences, and felt my face reddening as I realized the part I had played in maintaining that view. My thoughts shifting to what had happened with two friends the previous evening, I entirely tuned out the remaining class discussion.

—⚓—

Seth and Emily had moved to Berkeley with their two kids from the east coast where Emily had been a child care worker in a state school for developmentally challenged youth. Seth had been a social worker in a mental health diagnostic facility serving children and adolescents.

Sharing a love of working with children, each seemed cut out for this line of work. Seth wore his hair long and drooping over his left eye, sported a moustache, looked a bit like Ricky Nelson, and spent hours jamming with that era's version of a garage band. With her youthful appearance, long straight hair parted in the middle, and hip clothing, Emily could easily have been mistaken for a high school student.

It was Seth's turn to go back to school, and Emily agreed to be a stay-at-home mom for the next several years. While I keenly felt the disdain of many at Berkeley for the role people like me had played in the Vietnam War, Seth and Emily made it clear that issue wasn't on their radar in our relationship.

I had joined them the night before for dinner in their rented mission-style stucco house. When we finished eating, I read a book to their son and daughter while the dinner table was cleared. After a while, the kids went up to bed, and Emily put a Miles Davis record on the turntable.

After we had listened for a few minutes, Emily asked, "Roger, ever heard Roberta Flack?" As she pulled another album out of a stack of records, Seth unlocked a filing cabinet, removed a cigar box, and took out a package of rolling papers, a baggie of pot, and a rolling machine. After looking my way with a questioning glance, to which I responded with a smile and a nod, he began the preparations.

"No, what kind of music is it?"

"Think of what you're about to hear as dessert," Emily replied, laughing.

Seth lit the joint, inhaled, and a pungent odor of a brush fire, maybe with a hint of skunk, began to fill the room. He held the smoke in his lungs and exhaled slowly. I doubt he was aware of how closely I watched in order to see how this was done.

Seth passed the joint to me and, remembering how easily a deep inhalation could set off a bout of coughing, I took in a small amount, waited, exhaled, and then inhaled again, holding it this time. It felt hotter and more raspy than cigarette smoke. The joint went back and forth two more times, and I sensed—initially from light-headedness and a rush of warm feeling in my body—that this time would be different.

A minute or two later, Emily switched the records, plugged in and handed me a headset, and invited me to lie on the plush blue carpeted floor with my head on a throw pillow from the couch.

"Prepare yourself for some magic." She moved the tone arm to the specific cut she wanted me to hear. I closed my eyes and noticed how good it felt to be cushioned by the thick carpet and the soft weave of the pillow on which my head rested.

The music began with three strummed notes on a lone bass, repeated and then repeated again, a rhythmic percussion that would even have been enough to elevate had nothing else followed. It transported me into a hypnotic groove, a groove with a hint of infinity. I experienced these tones both as deep mellifluous sound and as a tingling reverberation in the back of my skull.

A guitar added just a few simple notes of reply to the bass foundation and then a piano, its tones higher, expanded and brought lightness into what had been a darker musical patina. The resonance of each note from each instrument seemed to hang in my hearing, and I found myself enveloped in this music, a part of it rather than a listener, aware of each tone, feeling a sense of awe at the music's structure, even at the beauty of the moments of silence. I hadn't dreamed music could be experienced this way.

As the music flowered, a fourth instrument joined in: Roberta Flack's voice.

The first time ever I saw your face
I thought the sun rose in your eyes

As her smoky voice filled my head, all my senses magnified and I felt as if I might implode. The lyrics of this sumptuous love ballad captured the earliest breath-taking moments of romantic spark, her voice, the bass, the piano, and the guitar seemingly flirting with one another phrase after phrase. And then, from a near-whispered beginning, her voice rose and then soared with a full-throated and pure crescendo and my pulse quickened. I felt carried deeply into her story.

The music ended and I lay there with my eyes closed. Time passed and my friends waited while I resisted letting go of this reverie, resisted the necessity of departing from a space I hadn't known existed. The high had been immaculate, and I had flowed—physically and emotionally—with the music and story, feeling enraptured and spellbound.

"I can't. . . . I can't find the words." I had removed the headset and sat up, wanting to talk about what had happened, but was incoherent. Seth and Emily laughed, sensing my consternation, and I laughed with them. There'd be another time for a conversation. For now, however, we just listened to the rest of the album.

I later learned and came to appreciate the diversity of marijuana highs, the various circumstances in which being stoned could enhance experience, and the differing levels of intensity that were possible. What had happened that night, however, was quite extraordinary.

It was my first time.

I wished I had understood this before Vietnam. I'd have wanted to ask so much more about the pot smoker's experience in being high. I hadn't been ready to do those studies. Perhaps if I'd been sufficiently aware, I would have been able to probe deeper into the pervasive question of why they were drawn to pot, whether it helped them cope, maybe fulfilling a desire to share something with people they liked, and whether those benefits came free and clear or possibly with a cost.

I remembered this experience some years later when reading a passage from the astronomer Carl Sagan's novel, *Contact*. He wrote of two women who, while strolling on the Champs-Élysées, noticed a line of patrons outside a tobacconist's shop. As they came closer, they saw a sign in the window advertising that a shipment of American cannabis had just arrived. A mock-up of a cannabis package had a motto, a much earlier example of which had been "I'd walk a mile for a Camel." On this package, however, the motto read: "This shall be deducted from your share in paradise."

16

PREFERRED BY REVILED GROUPS

UNIVERSITY OF CALIFORNIA, BERKELEY
WINTER 1971

J ust as we were winding down our seminar session, this week
devoted to marijuana, Phil surprised us with a question that
seemed to come entirely out of the blue. "Either of you know
anything about absinthe?" Seth and I glanced questioningly at one
another and it quickly became evident we were both stumped.

"Well, now," Phil exclaimed, stroking his beard and clearly
relishing the opportunity to guide our conversation in a new direction. "You know, I have a hunch we'll learn something useful in
understanding marijuana's history if we take a short detour. The
history of absinthe is fascinating. Why don't the two of you see what
you can come up with and let's talk about it next week."

Because we knew Professor Phil Hilyard was a keen observer
of youth and adult subcultures, issues we both wanted to study,

we asked him to meet with us in a seminar with this focus. We expected he'd stimulate us to better understand the user's motivations and societal norms, a perspective that received far too little attention. These conversations were inevitably thought-provoking, and each of us was giving the seminar much more time than we were to our required courses.

As we were about to learn, fears and misinformation had led to a 1915 U.S. ban of absinthe. Very similar fears and misinformation had shaped American 20th century policies concerning marijuana.

When we met the following week, we brought along an illustrated book on Impressionism. Seth found the page he wanted us to look at and the three of us examined the colored plate closely.

He glanced at his notes and then began our briefing for Phil. "We thought we'd start by looking at a piece of art. It's called *L'Absinthe*, or *The Absinthe Drinker*. Degas completed it in 1876 and the scene is the interior of a Paris café." Phil smiled, telling us he'd hoped we'd come across this work.

The painting depicted two people, a man and a woman, seated side-by-side: an actress, Ellen Andrée, and a man, Marcellin Desboutins, a painter. In the picture, Ellen wore a hat, and her white blouse had a frilly collar and a yellow bow. She wore a full skirt, kind of reddish orange. Marcellin had a moustache and beard and was smoking a pipe. He wore a white shirt and a jacket, and his bowler-type hat was perched toward the back of his head.

The two were together, but not interacting. Marcellin was gazing away from Ellen, seemingly deep in thought. But Ellen was clearly the focal point of the painting. She looked numb. Her shoulders were slumped and her hands were in her lap, her face was expressionless, and while her eyes were open, her stare looked vacant.

Seth pointed out the glass on the table in front of Ellen containing absinthe, a whitish-green colored beverage. There was also a carafe on a tray within her reach. Marcellin's drink might have been coffee in a glass mug. The viewer doesn't know exactly what's in the cup, but it's clear Marcellin was not drinking the same beverage that she was.

From our readings we'd learned that the carafe would have contained ice water and there initially would have been about an ounce of absinthe, typically a greenish color, in Ellen's glass. When she was served, the ice water would have been slowly poured over a sugar cube placed on a slotted spoon resting on the rim of her glass. The beverage would gradually take on a cloudy color. The intention would have been to dilute and slightly sweeten the absinthe which, at 50 to 70 percent alcohol, would otherwise have been incredibly potent and nearly undrinkable.

Phil pointed his pencil at the actress. "She does look stoned, doesn't she?" He paused while musing about what we were seeing and then, looking at us with a wistful smile, said, "You know, I particularly resonate to her. I think of her as a disillusioned dreamer, someone I'd like to know and learn her story."

Seth and I cast a quick glance at one another, smiling at Phil's revelation. We were drawn to him for just this reason. He was particularly interested in the alienated, people who were disaffiliated either by choice or through oppression. Vagabonds fascinated him and he was eager to understand their perceptions of the world, reaching for insights unclouded by stereotypes and misattributions.

Phil asked, "What do we know about how the public responded to this painting? And is there a part of its story that also tells us something about marijuana?"

"Actually, Degas got trashed by the public," Seth said. "When it was first exhibited, the critics used words like 'immoral' and 'degrading' because it depicted bohemian culture. It's as if they couldn't have cared less about the quality of the artist's work.

They saw the painting as somehow glorifying an unconventional and dissolute lifestyle brought on by drinking absinthe."

We went on to talk about a history of guilt by association as the first commonality absinthe had with marijuana. Both were enjoyed by 19th century writers and artists who were seen as part of a decadent avant-garde culture. Many of their books and paintings eventually became renowned, but when they were alive they were marginalized, and so were marijuana and absinthe, apparently tainted by the reputations of their enthusiasts.

Seth read two quotes that illustrated how sensationalism and hyperbole played into public fears about these substances. The first was about absinthe:

Absinthe makes you crazy and criminal, provokes epilepsy and tuberculosis, and has killed thousands of French people. It makes a ferocious beast of man, a martyr of woman, and a degenerate of the infant, it disorganizes and ruins the family and menaces the future of the country.

"Wow, whoever wrote that had a vivid imagination," Phil said. "Colorful stuff!"

Seth then read a quote from a 1928 book titled *Dope: The Story of the Living Dead*:

And the man under the influence of hasheesh catches up his knife and runs through the streets hacking and killing everyone he meets. No, he has no special grievance against mankind. When he is himself, he is probably a good-humored, harmless, well-meaning creature; but hasheesh is the murder drug, and it is the hasheesh which makes him pick up his knife and start out to kill. Marihuana is American hasheesh. It is made from a little weed that grows in

Texas, Arizona, and Southern California. You can grow enough marihuana in a window-box to drive the whole population of the United States stark, staring, raving mad.

Beliefs that they caused insanity and violence were two common denominators in the lore about absinthe and marijuana. Phil highlighted another common denominator: the public's belief that a behavior perceived as dangerous is associated with a reviled or feared group. Referring to the history of alcohol, he said that in the years leading up to Prohibition, people feared the kinds of alcoholic beverages preferred by immigrant groups that were perceived as threatening the economic livelihoods of those already living in the U.S. Guilt by association worked, he emphasized, and the same thing happened with marijuana and its use in the 1920s and 1930s by Mexicans and blacks. Two more of the common denominators were racism and bigotry.

Our conversation turned to the banning of absinthe. "We've learned a bit more about it," I said, returning to my notes. "At one time, people thought that a chemical in absinthe called thujone was responsible for people having hallucinations. One of the more likely causes was alcohol poisoning due to the high alcohol content. Absinthe was intended to be diluted, but not everyone drank it as was intended. The other cause was poisonous additives. It seems unscrupulous makers of the drink took dangerous shortcuts such as adding copper salts to artificially create a green tint. Absinthe got a bad rap because, just like moonshine that wasn't correctly distilled, drinkers could get messed up if the production process wasn't done correctly."

Popular rituals, somewhat akin to "Miller Time," were one more aspect they held in common. Absinthe usually had a natural green color before being diluted with water and turning gray. In mid-1800s France, absinthe's popularity in bars, bistros, cafés, and cabarets led to the hour of 5:00 P.M. being known as *l'heure verte* ("the green hour"). In this same tradition, in the U.S., thanks to the Grateful Dead and *High Times* magazine, both the time of 4:20 P.M. and the April 20th date came to be known as occasions to get stoned.

"Okay, guys, nice work. Let's wrap it up," Phil said. "So, what's important here?"

Neither of us spoke for a few moments. We'd talked a lot about unfounded beliefs that seemed to be connected to the marginalization of unpopular groups. But what *was* important in all of this, I wondered, besides an academically interesting set of parallels between the cultural perceptions of these two substances?

Seth spoke first. "I guess what strikes me in the materials we've discussed about pot is that I don't see myself or any of my experiences. The focus in these articles is almost always on harm, pathology, and dysfunction. They tell only one side of the story." We waited as he took a moment to think.

"You know, getting high really enhances life for me. I'm often a better musician when I'm stoned, more tuned in to the structure of a piece I'm playing, and more intuitive about where each of the other musicians is headed when we're jamming. Being stoned also gives me access to a kind of thinking that is creative and imaginative, sometimes even with the ideas we discuss in our courses."

"Look, Seth, I get it," Phil said. "You're not inventing the wheel, here. Generations of musicians and writers would say the same thing."

"It seems the public acknowledged one absinthe," I said, "the poison that killed and caused insanity, and ignored the other, the alcohol beverage that enhanced life. Same distinction with marijuana. Seth's experience stays invisible, even to researchers."

Seth wondered why any in-depth examination of cognitive and emotional benefits from smoking pot was missing from the scientific literature. "Are researchers just not interested in those questions? Don't they see them as at all relevant? Are they wearing blinders?"

His questions brought to mind John Steinbeck's vivid depiction of how being in the war changed for soldiers when they were stoned, the beauty they perceived from looking at flares and machine gun tracer bullets, and his writing that the prospect of dying took on a new symbolism and seemed not so horrible. But, of course, Steinbeck wasn't a researcher. Seth was right. There was a big gap in what science had and had not considered worth examining.

"Sure, there are lots of lab studies looking at reaction times, memory, coordination, and cognition," Seth said, "but none that get at what seems to me to be really important. We need to know what draws millions of people to getting high, what pleases them and makes them want to get high again and again."

Our seminar hour was nearly up. Seth and I gathered our notes together. Just before leaving, however, we noticed that Phil was again gazing at the Degas painting. "I'd really have liked to spend some time with Ellen Andrée in that Paris café," he said. "Au revoir, mes amis."

17

CLAUDE LAY DEAD

SAN FRANCISCO
WINTER 1971

The usher handed me back our tickets. "Might be a good idea if she sat here," she told us, pointing to my date, Mandy, and then to the seat on the aisle. That suggestion didn't make any sense, so we ignored it, and sat where we originally intended. Before the end of the first act, however, when a guy in a loincloth sat in my lap and kissed me on the lips, the reason for her advice became embarrassingly clear. Whoever occupied that specific aisle seat was destined to become part of the performance.

It was just our second date and we had driven into San Francisco to see the rock musical *Hair*. The show began with Claude, the leader of the tribe, sitting alone on the floor of a nearly empty stage. The only set was a multi-level metal pipe scaffold. Slowly, from the back of the theater, others in the cast moved through the audience and joined him. They were adorned with long flowing hair, many with enormous Afros, and their clothes a combination of cast-off military jackets and drab work shirts and jeans. As they converged on the stage, they sang of being children of the Age of Aquarius . . . "harmony and understanding, sympathy and trust abounding."

With the sweetness of youthful idealism, the play and its music expressed themes of the '60s counter-culture—rejecting racism and sexism, deploring destruction of the environment, challenging sexual repression, and protesting the U.S.'s involvement in the Vietnam War.

Hair was solidly anti-war, its message all the more compelling as we in the audience felt the war's impact on Claude, Berger, Woof, Hud, and their tribe-mates, all of whom passionately yearned for a more just world. Claude struggled whether to burn his draft card, and after impulsively throwing it into a fire and then quickly grabbing it back, he wanted this crucial decision to just go away and sang of his desire to be invisible.

Theirs was a personal message, not political or ideological, and the lyrics of their songs told of their pained perceptions of our country. Hud captured the outlook of many in his generation when he said, "The draft is white people sending black people to make war on the yellow people to defend the land they stole from the red people."

In one scene, a Buddhist monk doused himself with gasoline before striking a match and perishing. In another, the song "Three Five Zero Zero" was a harsh reminder of the daily body counts announced by General Westmoreland's headquarters.

As the music played, my own memories from Vietnam began to intrude. Boys turned into warriors, some returning home in caskets, many others carrying wounds of the psychological assault they would endure for the rest of their lives.

Hair was unabashedly pro-drug. In a bizarre LSD-induced hallucination, various tribe members became George Washington, General Ulysses S. Grant, Abraham Lincoln, John Wilkes Booth, Calvin Coolidge, Clark Gable, Scarlett O'Hara, Aretha Franklin, African witch doctors, and George Custer. Two songs challenged the idea that getting high with pot or hallucinogenic drugs is bad. In "Walking in Space" a character sang "How dare they try to end this beauty . . . in this dive we rediscover sensation . . . our eyes are open wide, wide, wide." In "Donna," another sang "I'm evolving through the drugs that you put down." After smoking a joint, a tribe member proclaimed that "Anyone who thinks pot is bad is full of shit."

Several trippy scenes took the audience through a phantasmagoria of free association. I had the thought that pot served as an emotional iodine for the skinned knees from an all too dangerous world, somehow nurturing these half child, half adult hippies.

Hair was wildly sexual. Woof, a boy with a gentle soul, wondered about the repression of normal desire as he sang "Sodomy, fellatio, cunnilingus, pederasty—Father, why do these words sound so nasty? Masturbation can be fun. Join the holy orgy Kama Sutra everyone." As the tribe came together in a "be-in" at the end of the first act, clothes were dropped, their nakedness a clear statement about freedom.

Near the end of the play, members of the tribe began the final song while slowly moving to the sides of the stage. There, in the center background, Claude lay dead on a black cloth, his uniform making it evident that he had allowed himself to be drafted. But his wish to become invisible had been granted, and none of his friends could see him. They wondered what had happened to Claude, and only we in the audience knew.

The tribe members sang and Mandy and I were both in tears, each with our own raw spots, but also sharing in grief for the innocence taken from the children of Aquarius. From the sniffing all around us, it was obvious we weren't alone. And then the tribe members motioned for the audience to join them on the stage, some coming down to offer their hands. As many of us that could fill up that space did so, singing and dancing. "Let the sunshine, let the sunshine in, the sunshine in."

It was healing to be welcomed to their community, even in the knowledge that it was indeed very foreign to both of us. As we left the theatre, we were both unhinged by intense feelings. For me the discomfort came from remembering Phil Hilyard's explanation for how users of drugs such as marijuana came to be vilified, just like some of the young men I met in Vietnam: "Find a behavior that's associated with a reviled or feared group, and tell people that the group's members favor that behavior." Marijuana's historical symbolism of violence and insanity just didn't compute with the values of peace, harmony, and understanding deeply held by Claude and his tribe. Their spirit spoke to me, and I cringed at the thought of their being arrested for getting stoned.

Later that evening, we still felt caught up in what had most touched each of us. For me, it was Claude's doing what he thought was right and then getting killed. The jumble of emotions I was still experiencing, now mostly anger, made it evident my internal conflicts left over from Vietnam were nowhere near being resolved.

18

WHAT THE F*** ARE YOU THINKING?

BERKELEY
SPRING 1971

The pungent smell of smoke wafted under the door to the Haviland Hall conference room where three professors had just begun the questioning. My first thought was how cheated I'd feel if, after months of non-stop studying, we'd have to reschedule the exams because the building was on fire.

Scott Briar, the committee chair, poked his head into the corridor to check out what was happening. As it turned out, a fellow doctoral student, knowing that I was undergoing this final step that morning in my two-week-long doctoral qualifying exams, sought to shift the odds of succeeding in my favor. He lit incense sticks just outside the door, propping them up in an empty Coke can.

Fortunately, the fire alarm was not pulled, the building was not evacuated, and the exam quickly resumed. Phil Hilyard, probably to soothe my quite obvious jitters, asked a question he knew I'd do well in answering. "Roger, whatever happened to absinthe?"

The two hours passed quickly and, after being asked to wait in the hallway for several minutes while the professors evaluated my performance, Scott Briar invited me back into the room with a pat on the back. I had passed. That moment held more than a little irony. The night before, I had gone sailing with Scott and his girlfriend aboard his Norwegian cutter *Aquarius*, sharing a joint and enjoying the sunset over San Francisco Bay. The next morning, he was one of my examiners, with alcohol and drugs among the topics about which I was questioned. "What societal changes led to the adoption of the 18th amendment?" he asked, giving me the chance to talk about the role of evangelical Protestant churches, the push-back against the politically powerful German-based brewing industry, and shifting labor economics that threatened jobs. "So, did Prohibition work?" was his next question. My answer began with "Yes, but only for a while."

Over a post-exam beer with my classmate, Tony insisted my ascendance to the status of doctoral candidate never would have happened had he not lit incense and beseeched the gods for divine intervention. No arguments from me.

That oral exam was predictably tough, but I had been prepared. It paled in comparison with the grilling I received a few weeks later from a group of eight recovering heroin addicts.

—⋙—

Jack Goldberg, the director of an addiction treatment program named Bridge Over Troubled Waters, had asked if I'd be interested in having a conversation with his residents. Only later did I understand what he'd had in mind. His intention was to set me straight, a middle class white guy fully submerged in academia, whose ideas about addiction, from Jack's point of view, were hopelessly idealistic and nowhere grounded in the junkies' reality. But at the time, I took his invitation as simply giving me an opportunity for more input concerning an idea I was mulling over.

Jack was in his mid-forties, wore his graying hair in a short ponytail, and sported a prominent paunch. After overcoming his own heroin addiction a decade earlier while living in New York, Jack had become a drug counselor and eventually a program director.

I had heard him speak at several community meetings about the growing street drug scene in Berkeley. He came across as pragmatic, not wedded to any single philosophy or approach. His primary goal was getting addicts the help they needed to kick their addiction, using a wide variety of means to meet that end. At one of those meetings he said that while methadone maintenance, Narcotics Anonymous, residential and out-patient programs, and detoxification all were important, we still were very much in the dark about how to really be effective in treating the specifics of heroin addiction. Too many people died from overdosing or cycled repeatedly through the detox-jail-treatment-relapse revolving door. He seemed open to new ideas and I had one. I approached him after the meeting and asked if he'd meet me for coffee.

We met at a place on Telegraph Avenue near the Berkeley campus. As soon as we'd been served, I launched into my thoughts, expecting he'd completely agree with me. "You know, Jack, it seems to me that the approach to heroin addiction in England has a lot going for it. The Brits see addiction as a health issue, not a crime problem. In their system, doctors can treat addicts, and that's very different from how things work in our country."

I noticed him nodding in agreement. A good sign, I thought, although I wondered if he'd stay with me as I laid out the rest of my thinking.

"In England, their philosophy is not to demand that every addict quits using. That's 180 degrees from U.S. policy." I went on to explain that British doctors could help people who want to quit by detoxifying with methadone. But for those who didn't want to quit, doctors could write a prescription for heroin that the patient could fill at a local pharmacy. That reduced the incentive to steal or rob to afford black market prices for the drug. There were no illnesses due to contaminants and much less risk of over-dosing or infections due to needle sharing. And while there might be stigma in being an addict, the British system doesn't create the heavy deviant subculture that we see in this country as a result of throwing addicts in prison.

As I spoke, I noticed he now was looking at me with a wry grin on his face. I wondered if he was patiently waiting to knock down my argument, so I hurried on to finish expressing my thoughts before he got started.

I told Jack we had a similar system in this country in the 1920s. Addicts could receive morphine at local morphine maintenance clinics. It was pure and available at low cost, and—once again—the approach was attuned to enhancing public health, not punishing criminality. I told him I wondered why we're not talking about this kind of approach now.

"You make it sound reasonable, Roger," Jack said, with a smile on his face and a questioning look. "But there may be a few problems. For example, I wonder if you've considered the politics. I mean, come on now. What are the chances that President Nixon or Governor Reagan would go for letting doctors maintain addicts with heroin prescriptions?"

I laughed and felt stymied by this political reality check. But I didn't intend to give up.

"Okay, Jack, you've nailed me. But what if there were some small pilot projects that showed dramatic cuts in crime and overdose deaths? Wouldn't that pave the way for shifts in politicians' views?"

Jack looked at his watch and said he needed to get to another appointment, but before he left, he asked if I might like to run my ideas by some of the people who were being treated at his program. I eagerly agreed. Surely his clients, victims of a wrong-minded policy, would like my ideas.

That chance came a week later. The setting was the large second floor community room in a colonial-style residence that now housed Jack's residential drug treatment center in north Berkeley. The building was badly in need of a coat of paint and a new roof, but there had obviously been a lot of care given to the landscaping and the windows were all clean.

The African American man who greeted me at the door was wearing a white shirt and tie. He let me know I was expected, and asked me to wait for a few minutes until a group meeting had ended. Soon, Jack walked down from the second floor and told me the residents were ready. He also had some advice as we headed upstairs. "Roger, don't be too surprised if you get some skeptical comments. You're rockin' the boat and these guys probably won't see things as you do. Don't take it personally."

Hearing Jack's comment led me to wonder where the skepticism might come from. I would be laying out a more humane philosophy. What wasn't I getting? There was no time to figure that out, though, as we walked into the room.

Seated on four couches arranged in a circle, the eight men looked as if they ranged in age from their mid-twenties to perhaps sixty. Most were older than I had expected. Five were African

American and three were white. They looked either bored or ready to fall asleep.

"Roger is a Cal student," Jack said. "He's got some ideas about what needs to be fixed in how this country treats addicts. I want you to hear him out and then you're free to ask questions and tell him what you think. Roger, we've got an hour." Jack and I found some empty seats on the couches.

He asked the men to introduce themselves, and each gave his first name followed by how many days he'd been clean. One was just a week into recovery, several had made it for a month, and a few others, two months. An older African American man, Joseph, had made it for ninety-two days. He smiled and nodded at me when he introduced himself, and I wondered if I might have at least one person in this group who'd lend a sympathetic ear to what I had to say.

"Thanks for making some time for me," I began. "I need to start with an admission. Most of what I know about addiction comes from books. So when Jack invited me to talk with you about some ideas, I think he wanted me to have a reality check. I hope that's okay." No one responded, so I forged ahead.

I spoke about what I thought to be true about heroin. If someone obtains pure heroin, doesn't inject more than their tolerance allows, and uses a sterile needle, the only real health problem, even if they got addicted to it, is constipation. But it's an entirely different matter when possessing heroin is a crime. The cost is much higher, the buyer can't ever know for sure how potent a batch is or what contaminants are in it, and lots of people get ripped off by sellers. Sterile needles are hard to get, so people share them and that causes infections and injuries to the skin and blood vessels. And people who don't have several hundred dollars to spend on heroin every day are very likely to steal or rob or turn tricks to afford it.

I told them I read that addicts steal $8 billion in property each year. All of that leads the public to want to put users in prison, and that adds up to a lot of stigma, a lot of hate for addicts, and a lot of barriers to getting a job and living a free life. For poor people and minorities, the chances of being arrested and jailed are much higher than for whites and those in the middle class.

I noticed many of the men now seemed to be listening, although I couldn't tell what they were thinking. Joseph, however, let me know I was on target as far as he was concerned. "Those books you been reading are all right. You got it right so far. But be careful, son. Watch where you goin'."

The rest of the men laughed at that, and it felt as if there was a little less tension in the room. But, knowing where I was headed, I had a passing thought that maybe I ought to stop right there.

"Okay, I'll watch my step. I have to warn you, though, that I may be headed for trouble. I think it's a problem that possessing heroin is a crime. Imagine for a moment what could be possible if it weren't a crime. Suppose that someone who needed heroin, either people who were addicted to it or people who wanted to try it, could get it at low cost at a community clinic—a clinic controlled by people in the neighborhood, not by the government. The heroin would be pure, there'd be clean needles, and there'd be medical supervision to prevent overdosing. No need to rip anyone off, steal stuff, turn tricks, and no need to risk getting arrested. It'd be as if. . . ."

"Shit, Mr. Cal Student, you really think you doin' anyone any favors givin' out free heroin?" Alex, one of the white men, was glaring at me, his arms folded across his chest. "You'd just be fuckin' up ten times more people, maybe a hundred times more, than now. You ever try heroin? I mean, you got any idea? What the fuck are you thinking?" He had a look of disgust on his face as he shook his head back and forth.

Andrew, a younger African American man, obviously agreed with Alex. "Too many brothers are already under the white man's boot, and heroin has a lot to do with that. Maybe that's why heroin is already so easily available in our neighborhoods. A way of keeping black men down, keeping us from protesting, from having power, from breaking out of the ghetto. Alex is right. These community clinics you're talkin' about would be just another kind of jail, even if they didn't have bars."

Most of the men were obviously seeing it this way, and the conversation wasn't turning out to be just an intellectual exercise. I saw that I was being perceived as either hopelessly naïve or as an oppressor, both totally opposite from how I saw myself.

"But wait a minute. What if these clinics were run by local people, by black people in black neighborhoods?" I said. "And what if the clinics had counselors who could help educate, tell the truth about heroin, not just spout propaganda? And offer help to people who wanted to quit, find a job, or get into school? I mean, maybe more people would use heroin, but maybe more people would do it safely, without robbing and stealing and getting arrested, without overdosing, and without being cut off from their rights as citizens."

I looked around to see if someone, anyone in the room might be seeing some merit in my proposal. Joseph, looking as if he were pondering the ideas I had presented, hadn't said anything yet. But now he was ready.

"Don't say I didn't warn you," he said with a smile on his face.

I nodded back, glad that he was going to add his views. He was older than the rest in the room. Maybe he'd help salvage at least some parts of what I proposed.

"I suspect that you'd describe addiction as a victimless crime if the legal element was removed. Am I right?"

"Yes," I replied.

"So there's the root of the differences we're hearing in this room. Every one of us sitting in this circle has victimized our families, our friends, our employers, even one another. When you're strung out and you haven't the cash for that next fix, whatever morals you grew up with, the 10 commandments, the Bible, the things your mamma taught you. . . . they're all thrown out the window. You do what you need to do, and you make a lot of victims. You following me so far?"

He wasn't speaking in an angry tone, although it was very evident he wanted me to hear him. I nodded, wanting to argue that victimizing others would no longer be necessary if these clinics existed and heroin's cost was much lower, but Joseph wasn't finished. I made myself listen.

"Each man in this room is trying to walk down a new path, trying to make amends for the harms we've caused others, and trying to recognize when we're bullshitting ourselves. It's not just heroin that we're trying to leave behind, it's also a lifetime of scamming, lying, cheating, stealing, and watching ourselves turn into something so shameful that none of us thought we could have become."

Joseph paused, and no one made a sound. He had everyone riveted to the lesson he was trying to teach.

"Now, I'm not saying your idea couldn't work," Joseph continued. "Maybe in some middle class neighborhoods where the schools are good, there are plenty of jobs, access to good health care, and people feel safe on the street and in their homes. Maybe in some places like that your community heroin clinics might work. I've gotta tell you, I seriously doubt it, but I'm willing to think it's a possibility.

"But that's not where most of us in this room grew up and got strung out. In our neighborhoods, there's a lot of unemployment and lousy schools and no health care access. If you turn on the heroin faucet the way like you described, it'll suck the lives out of people, a whole lot of people, including people like me and my brothers you're talkin' to. Right now, we're trying to stand up, and most of us are still on our knees. Turn on that tap and we'll be back on the floor. Understand what I'm saying, brother?"

All eyes in the room, Jack's included, were fixed on me. With his words still reverberating in my mind, I felt stunned by the reality Joseph had conveyed. I sat quietly even though I wanted to continue the debate, to try to convince him that the community clinics would be even more powerful in oppressed and economically stressed communities where they'd empower people to escape the enslaving chains of addiction. I still didn't quite understand why my argument didn't work and why addressing the legal and supply aspects wasn't enough.

As we'd all soon learn, a new version of the morphine maintenance clinics of the 1920s was gaining favor in the U.S. Methadone maintenance, an "opiate replacement" intervention for heroin addicts who repeatedly relapse, was based on the pioneering work of Drs. Vincent Dole and Marie Nyswander who, in the 1960s, demonstrated that the turbulent lives of heroin addicts could become stable if they regularly took oral doses of a synthetic opiate called methadone. It staves off withdrawal and blocks the effects of heroin. That's the good news. The not so good news is many addicts choose to instead live the life of a street addict rather than give up the hugely reinforcing high from heroin.

All well and good, I thought, but wouldn't the heroin clinics that I was proposing add an important service to the continuum of care, each service designed to be the best fit for people at varying levels of readiness to change? Wouldn't it help keep people alive, free of the need to commit crimes, and safe from infections until such time that they were ready for a more conventional life?

Soon, however, I'd experience up close what Joseph and the others were trying to make me understand. Their vehement opposition to creating a legal supply of heroin became all too clear when addiction hit home—my family's home.

19

BRYAN

BERKELEY
AUTUMN 1971

My parents called unexpectedly. We usually spoke on Sundays, but it was a Tuesday afternoon. Bryan, my 16-year-old brother, was in an in-patient drug treatment program. He had been bingeing on downers and was out of control. Would I fly to Massachusetts to attend family sessions there?

Bryan insisted he didn't need help, yet in the last several months he had hit my father while in a rage, punched his fist through a wall, and my mother feared he'd burn the house down. I had known my folks were worried about him, but had no idea he had become violent. Bryan initially had been admitted involuntarily after my parents filed a Child in Need of Services petition with the juvenile court. But he'd soon be free to leave. Too soon.

The program's staff encouraged him to remain and complete the 28-day treatment program. Hopefully, meeting together as a family, we'd convince him to stay and get the help he needed.

I feared if we weren't successful, there'd be no end to the terrible anxieties with which my folks had been living. There would likely be even more frightening violence if he returned to their home.

After the plane reached cruising altitude and the fasten seat belt sign was switched off, I turned back to the book I had brought with me. I looked at the words for a while, but realized my mind was somewhere else. I felt my gut churning as I pictured what the family session might be like. Could it possibly turn out well, with Bryan committing to complete the program? Far more likely, I thought, the session would be rife with defensiveness.

"Excuse me," the fellow seated next to me said. "I see you're reading *Marijuana Reconsidered*. Great book!"

Just recently published by Professor Lester Grinspoon, a member of the Harvard psychiatry faculty, this book took on many of the myths about marijuana. Grinspoon was one of the earliest academics to challenge unfounded beliefs by critically examining the evidence and refuting erroneous conclusions with the findings of science.

My seatmate looked to be in his mid-twenties, with a deep tan and his hair in a ponytail. Californian, I thought. Dressed simply in jeans and a t-shirt, the thick gold chain around his neck and the several flashy rings on his fingers hinted at a lot of disposable income.

"Yeah, the book is impressive," I said. "Doesn't hurt that he's a Harvard professor. It gives him a lot of credibility to take on some of the sacred cows."

"Wouldn't happen to be a dope fiend, would you?" He winked at me, maybe guessing the answer from my beard and choice of reading material.

I laughed. "I dabble a bit."

"Right on," he replied. "Look," he said, lowering his voice and leaning over to whisper. "Just between us, I'm in the trade. You know once it's legal, guys like me will become the next mega-tycoon farmers in the U.S. of A. Just a matter of biding our time, buddy, staying under the radar, and burying all that cash in the backyard."

I saw his broad grin, and then, with a shock of clarity, remembered why I was on this plane, where I was going, and what I'd face when I got there.

This conversation had taken an alarming turn for me as I thought of my brother's spiraling self-destruction. Suddenly, I found myself thinking people like the guy next to me were part of the problem my family was facing, and the families of the recovering heroin addicts who found my idea of heroin clinics abhorrent. I became aware that my heart was racing and I was beginning to perspire.

I pictured my brother at a time in his life when he loved family vacations, played sports, and looked up to me and our two sisters. It had been so easy, in the abstract, to conclude that most drug problems were due to the criminalizing of users, not the drug itself. Now, the clarity of my conclusion was shaken, just like that. Continuing this conversation with the fellow next to me became intolerable.

I mumbled something about needing to get some reading done and put in my earplugs. My thoughts kept returning to my family, though, and I began to recognize my surge of emotion wasn't just about the dealers who supplied Bryan. It also had to do with my own unresolved questions. If criminal penalties for drug possession were eliminated, would the number of users increase as the men at Jack Goldberg's treatment center had asserted? And what then? More Bryans, taking those who loved them down a rathole?

Joseph's words reverberated in my thoughts: "If you turn on the heroin faucet the way like you described, it'll suck the lives out of people, a whole lot of people." His warning stayed in my mind for the next several days.

Our family meetings at the treatment center did, as feared, become acrimonious. Within a short time, Bryan left treatment against the staff's advice. Soon he was using again, and the fights at home with my parents continued.

As I struggled with conflicting thoughts, it seemed as if there were two frequencies broadcasting and I was picking up both signals. Each was strong and compelling, but incomprehensible when I tried to listen to them at the same time. Bryan's life was truly coming apart at the seams, and he was tearing at the fabric of our family. I pictured him escalating his drug involvement, slamming shut the conventional doors of occupational and educational attainment, the possibilities of having a family of his own and making it in this world, maybe even perishing as he lived more and more of his life on the edge. And all of that happening while we stood by, helpless to change the course. Don't do anything to turn on that faucet.

And then the competing frequency. If he had to live in a world in which drugs were available, no matter how much law enforcement had tried to prevent access, and he chose to use, wouldn't he be better off not facing being labeled a criminal and going to prison? Wouldn't the harms of the life he was choosing to live be reduced if we all thought of him and others like him as manifesting a public health problem? Wouldn't that mean providing more services, tolerating and supporting small steps of behavior change rather than vilifying any continued drug use? But what if he never made those small steps? His downward spiral and my family's pain would continue.

And what about the many people who smoked pot and never walked down the road Bryan was on, enjoying the high, but staying on course in their lives? Did they deserve the continued threat of criminal prosecution for what they were doing? Marijuana, for most who used it, was a pleasant diversion, hardly the direct cause of a derailed life.

These two frequencies were and are hard to reconcile. There's a parallel for me with regard to the death penalty, to which I am unalterably opposed. The government should not murder violators of our laws, no matter how heinous the offense. Yet I know in my soul I'd want an eye for an eye if a member of my family were murdered. The only way I can hold these two dimensions of my thinking is to recognize that if it were my family member, I could not be objective. I'd have to recuse myself from the debate. But all murder victims are someone's family members, as are addicts. So my internal debate continued when it came to real life.

Within a year, I'd be even more frequently confronted by this conundrum concerning drug policy. I was recruited to join the University of Washington social work faculty where I'd teach courses on substance abuse.

PART 3

ACTIVISM

20

JOINT HEARING

OLYMPIA, WASHINGTON
15 DECEMBER 1973

t was raining heavily and still dark when I parked the motor pool van in front of the School of Social Work and waited for everyone to assemble. The seven graduate students enrolled in my drug policy seminar were enthusiastic when I told them about our field trip to the state capitol. We'd be observing the law-making process first hand by attending a day-long hearing on a marijuana decriminalization bill. The House and Senate Judiciary Committees would be meeting in joint session.

I was excited, too. There was a growing movement in the U.S. to reform marijuana policy and I had been mulling over the possibility of becoming involved. To be honest, the values of my profession were not the only source of motivation. Because I was getting high occasionally, it was also personal. As I saw it, marijuana was far less of a threat to health and safety than narcotics, stimulants, and depressants.

By 7:30 A.M. we were on our way. The heavy traffic on I-5 eventually thinned out south of the city, although the rain didn't let up. Someone had brought a large thermos of coffee and offered to pour.

A student asked if anyone knew how things worked in legislative hearings. One did. Fred Peters, a lean runner, bald, whose nose had obviously been broken, was back in school in his mid-forties, studying for his masters degree in social work. He'd testified the previous year in favor of a bill concerning addiction counseling in state prisons. In our first class session, as students introduced themselves, Fred disclosed that he served three and a half years of a five-year sentence for drug dealing. His decision to become a social worker was stimulated in part by the respect he had for his parole officer, a man Fred described as "a straight shooter who didn't take any shit from me."

"There'll be a sign-up sheet somewhere in the hearing room," Fred said, "and people who want to testify will need to write down their names and whether they're for or against the bill. Oh, and they won't necessarily call people in order from that list."

"Did they grill you, Fred?" a student asked. "Anyone ask if you still get stoned?"

"Actually, I put the personal stuff out there right away," Fred said. "I told them I was an ex-con and a recovering addict. But I made sure they knew I was now a UW grad student. I also said I wanted them to understand the inmate's point of view about drug rehab in the joint. They asked a lot of questions, like how I became an addict, how I got clean, and stuff like that. I think maybe I had some credibility with them."

"Going to testify today, Fred?" Julie asked. In her mid-thirties and the mother of twin 8-year-old boys, Julie had voiced her ambivalence concerning decriminalization during one of our class discussions.

"Hell, no," Fred replied. That surprised me because of the prison time he'd served, but I quickly got why he was going to pass on the chance to offer his opinions.

"Nobody should do time for smoking pot," he said, "but it's more complicated than just jail time. The thing is, if weed becomes a lot easier to get, I think people like me will smoke a whole lot more and get really screwed up. And more, maybe not a large percentage, but more will someday end up junkies. All I can say is that's what happened to me. I doubt I could back that up with research, but I just know it's real, at least for people like me. Anyway, I don't want anyone getting in my face about what I know in my gut is true."

Joseph's warning when I visited Jack Goldberg's treatment center, the danger of opening the faucet, again came to mind. He would have strongly agreed with Fred.

"We're kind of on the same page about this," Julie said, pulling back her blond hair and tying it off with a blue ribbon. "It's personal for me, too, particularly when I think about my kids. If someone could convince me that decriminalizing it wouldn't flood the community with pot, I mean even more than it is now, I think I'd be okay with this bill." Julie added that although she had loved getting high, things looked a lot different through a parent's eyes.

As we drove further, I half-listened to the hum of several conversations behind me. It was evident that a few of the students were much more positive than Fred or Julie about decriminalizing pot. One argued it ought to be outright legalized and sold in state liquor stores.

I appreciated why Fred and Julie questioned the wisdom of this bill. But as we parked the van and made a dash through the rain for the House Office Building, I hoped the arguments in today's hearing for passing Rep. Kelley's measure would overwhelm the opposition. There had to be a better way, I thought, than continuing to lock people up to avoid the fall-out from decriminalization that worried these two students.

The 4th floor hearing room was nearly filled. Apart from the dozen or so legislators who were taking their seats at the front and a smattering of media, I noticed the audience included two groups, distinctive in their contrasting attire and age levels. Tie-dyed and suits. It was a good bet which group was there to support the bill and which would be opposed.

Representative Kelley began the hearing at 10:00 A.M. With his wavy hair and long sideburns, he reminded me of Kookie, a character from 77 *Sunset Strip*, a popular TV program in the 1960s. Kelley opened by welcoming those present and commenting on the day's business.

"To the fellow members of the committee and to our witnesses and to the audience here, I would like to start by saying that marijuana is a very touchy subject. It has been the subject of an awful lot of scare, of fear, of misunderstanding."

He noted that the bill he had introduced would implement the 1972 recommendations of the National Commission on Marihuana and Drug Abuse, popularly known as the Shafer Commission. Following two years of study and public hearings, the Commission had recommended decriminalization. In other words, marijuana use should continue to be discouraged, although not by punishing users. It should be a crime to sell marijuana, but not to possess it in small amounts.

Kelley added, "I would urge upon the members of the committee and all present here that we keep an open mind about this subject because I think we have a lot to learn. I hope that today's hearing will go a long way in producing that learning and that understanding."

Open minds? Unlikely, I thought. This bill would be highly controversial and it was almost certain that sparks would fly.

Scott Blair, a Republican sponsor, said why he supported the bill. "Jailing citizens for an action which is impossible to demonstrate as doing anyone any harm other than themselves is contrary to my feelings on what is wise and just." I imagined, as I listened to this man quietly articulate his views, that he'd be influential with libertarians.

He was quickly challenged by Representative Ken Eikenberry, a former FBI agent and Deputy Prosecuting Attorney. Much in contrast with his fellow Republican who had just spoken, Eikenberry's voice had a piercing tone of attack. "Representative Blair, would this not be the ultimate in hypocrisy, to say that it is not a crime to possess it, but a crime is being committed if you purchase it?"

Kelley and Blair each responded, acknowledging the legislation was not perfect and that retaining criminal penalties for selling was intended to discourage its use. It seemed evident from Eikenberry's expression that he wasn't buying it. When Kelley then tried to refocus the hearing and begin calling the witnesses he'd invited, he was quickly interrupted by Eikenberry who used a canny bit of maneuvering to bypass Kelley's line up.

"Mr. Chairman, I agreed when I was called by Dr. Gale Wilson of Seattle," Eikenberry said, "to present some testimony on his behalf. He injured his back and is not able to be here today. I am going to quickly read to you what he says, and the letter itself will give his qualifications."

Without pausing to give Kelley time to respond, he began to read. "It is my understanding that if HB 1166 is passed, it will decriminalize possession of up to 40 grams of marijuana in the mistaken belief of some persons that marijuana is a recreational drug. After 38 years as Chief Pathologist and Medical Examiner of King County, I will tell you that in my opinion marijuana in any amount is a very dangerous drug, that it rapidly habituates the user and may be addictive, that in my experience we have had a 300% increase of suicides in the age group of 13 to 25 years in King County, and that many of those young people, especially the early teenagers, have been users of marijuana. It appears that the use of marijuana rapidly loses its hit and that the user then goes on to amphetamines and then to the hard narcotics."

Rep. Kelley looked uncomfortable, repeatedly glanced at his watch, and was obviously impatient to get the hearing back on track. Eikenberry continued reading, however, conveying the writer's belief that many more people would be killed in highway accidents if 40 grams of marijuana were no longer a crime to possess.

When Eikenberry finished, a senator wanted to know how many cigarettes could be made from 40 grams of pot. "What are we talking about?" he asked. "One cigarette, ten cigarettes?" Eikenberry replied that it would probably be 40 cigarettes. Some hands then shot up from others on the committee, but Kelley ignored them, wrested the floor from Eikenberry, and barreled ahead.

"I would like to at this time call upon Mr. Stroup, who is head of NORML, the National Organization for the Reform of Marijuana Laws, from Washington, D.C. Mr. Stroup."

Keith Stroup was a public interest lawyer who had apprenticed with Ralph Nader in the 1960s. He founded NORML in 1970. Stroup testified that making the 26 million Americans who had smoked pot criminals caused far more harm than the drug itself and that moderate use was relatively harmless. More than 700,000 had been arrested for marijuana offenses in the past three years, Stroup added, but 93% were for possession only. The stereotype of the reefer fiend, a depraved criminal, was patently false, Stroup said, noting that many national organizations such as the National Council of Churches had called for decriminalization. He closed by saying current law overburdens the criminal justice system while not effectively deterring pot use, and that discouraging use can be accomplished without saddling the user with a criminal record.

One legislator asked if NORML accepted money from pot sellers. When Stroup replied, "I've never had the option," several legislators and members of the audience laughed.

This fellow was impressive. He seemed effective in speaking to the concerns of middle-aged politically middle-of-the-road legislators. He wore jeans and loafers, but also a white shirt, bow tie, and navy blue blazer. I wondered if he saw himself as bridging two contrasting cultures. I wanted to meet him and learn more about NORML. Once he had returned to his seat, I walked forward and handed him my business card along with a note saying I was interested in talking about becoming involved.

For the next several hours, a series of expert witnesses with impressive sets of credentials rolled out one argument after another for removing criminal penalties for marijuana possession. It gradually became evident that the chairman had choreographed this event. We were getting the unabridged version, chapter and verse, of the rationale for why the law should change. Maybe counterarguments would be heard later in the day, but for now only one frequency was playing.

Pot smoking doesn't cause an amotivational syndrome, we were told, and it isn't a stepping stone on a path to hard drug addiction. Criminalizing users is failing, a former narcotics official said, and families, doctors, the clergy, and the schools can be far more effective in discouraging the individual from using pot than the criminal law. Even the prospect of users becoming hooked on pot was questioned. A Harvard psychiatrist, the author of the book I had been reading when I flew home to be with my family during my brother's crisis, challenged the validity of the concept of habituation. He wondered just how relevant it was since, from his perspective, he was habituated to his trousers, his auto, and his wife.

Fred leaned over and whispered in my ear. "Quite a show, Prof. Wish at least one of them would recognize that the addiction I experienced to pot isn't a damn myth." He shook his head with a look of resentment.

I turned around and spotted Julie sitting two rows back. She, too, looked uncomfortable. Unless later witnesses acknowledged the problems that worried these students, I expected we'd be hearing some angry comments on our trip back to Seattle that evening.

The morning session had extended quite a bit beyond the scheduled ending time and Kelley recessed the committee. After the students and I found a large table in a corner of the Capitol Building cafeteria and began eating, I was eager to get their take on what we had seen. "Let me ask you a question. If you were one of those legislators, would the hearing be helpful to you in deciding how to vote on the bill?"

Jean, who had said she completely supported full legalization during our drive from Seattle, answered first. "Look, all of the research findings we heard were interesting, and maybe they'd have some influence on me if I were in the legislature. But I think when an ex-narc says the laws against pot possession have failed, and that it's unreasonable to expect law enforcement to stop people from using, that's the game winning point."

Several others nodded in agreement. Julie was eating quietly and once again untied and retied her hair ribbon, a nervous habit I guessed. She looked as if she were mulling over an answer. When we made eye contact and I glanced at her questioningly, she said, "Some of those legislators, probably most of them, are parents or grandparents and I'd guess they would have been listening to the experts with the same doubts that I have. In other words, how would making possession legal affect their kids?"

She paused and then added, "You know, something really stood out for me as missing from all of the pro-decriminalization testimony. None of them said that if pot became a lot more available once it was legal, they'd find a way to prevent even more people getting into trouble with the drug. I don't know, it's just that most of their arguments were too neatly wrapped up as a panacea or something."

Fred was animated as he replied. "Yeah, it felt as if the witness list was stacked to sell the committee a used car, no questions asked."

Jean, our legalization advocate, saw their point. "I have to say that I'm still for setting up a legal regulation system for marijuana, but I think these experts could have gone a lot further. If more people become heavy smokers, if more kids get access to it, how could communities deal with those problems without going back to putting people in jail? I wish they had talked about that."

As we bussed our trays and began walking back to the hearing room, the reactions Fred and Jean had had were on my mind. Decriminalization might make things better for some, but possibly worse for others.

When the hearing was called back to order, the first witness was Dr. Richard Seymour from California. It quickly became clear that the pendulum had shifted.

His testimony about marijuana was pointedly about harm. He spoke of pot smoking causing impaired driving and sub-par performance at work and in school, bronchitis, nose and throat irritation, pulmonary function decrement, panic reactions, toxic psychosis, decreased motivation, and impaired relationships. When he said that servicemen who smoked pot risked stupor, coma, and even death, Kelley interrupted and asked for his sources.

Seymour cited an article in the 1904 *Indian Medical Gazette*, and that prompted laughter from both people in the audience and several of the legislators. Kelley kept after him, though, asking if that research had pertained to marijuana or hashish, a more potent form of cannabis. Seymour answered that the study had been about hashish smoking, and that set off yet another series of questions from committee members. Were the harms Dr. Seymour had listed related to the type of cannabis commonly used in America, or the much more potent forms? What about the dosage in these studies?

Seymour wasn't about to be detoured, arguing that if greater potency cannabis in larger dosages caused harm, there was every reason to believe that future studies would also indicate harm with lower potency marijuana. And then he pushed on with his list of harms. Pot smoking caused more venereal disease, the initiation of sex at a younger age, more communal living with members of both sexes, tissue damage to the lungs, the growth of breasts in men, chromosome damage, and severe mental instability.

I found myself thinking that this fellow was throwing in everything but the kitchen sink. He seemed to be a zealot with a calling.

When he told the committee that rats injected with marijuana and deprived of food would become aggressive, the murmurs in the rear of the room erupted into laughter, and Kelley admonished the audience to be respectful. He then looked at his watch and asked if Seymour would try to wrap up his comments.

Eikenberry quickly objected. "Mr. Chairman, I think it's quite evident that you have stacked the hearing with proponents. Maybe Dr. Seymour deserves enough time to help balance what we're hearing."

Kelley replied, "I believe, Representative Eikenberry, that Dr. Seymour has in fact used more time than anyone else." Eikenberry quickly retorted that it was because he had been interrupted more often.

A woman from the audience shouted that she had intended to testify, but would yield her time to this witness. We were going to hear more from Dr. Seymour. As it turned out, we'd be given some insights about underlying attitudes that probably shaped the positions some people adopted about decriminalization.

"Dr. Seymour, the present law doesn't seem to be working to prevent people from smoking marijuana," a senator said. "What would?"

Dr. Seymour replied, "In that sense, Senator, the murder laws aren't working since people are still murdered. Yet no one is proposing to abolish the law against murder. I would say the same principle holds with regard to our laws against speeding."

As this witness returned to his seat in the audience, I thought he had undermined his own standing as an expert by not being more discriminating in the conclusions he presented. Some of the harms he described were probably valid, but became all too easy to dismiss when presented by a witness who had lost credibility.

Dr. Sam Irwin, a University of Oregon professor of pharmacology, was next and his testimony was 180 degrees in contrast from what we had just heard. I scribbled as quickly as I could when he summed up his views about the current law.

"Our national approach to drug abuse, prevention and control, I feel has been misconceived. To me there is no clearer instance in which punishment for the infraction of the law is more harmful than the crime, or a law more destructive to society than our present drug abuse control laws. They label otherwise law-abiding citizens as criminals for potentially hurting nobody but themselves; they alienate many from society; they promote widespread disrespect and flaunting of the law; and they create discrimination in the enforcement of the laws and marked variance in penalties as assigned by judges. They are used as an instrument of harassment of unpopular elements of society; they create the possibility of an illicit drug market with high tax-free profits; they nurture and sustain organized crime; they shape the most dangerous forms of drug abuse; they force addicts into larceny or prostitution to get their drugs; they tie up the courts; they slow the process of justice; they distract the police from the problems of most critical concern, crimes of violence and against property; they create a continuing need to increase expenditures to deal with the mounting problems created by the laws themselves; and they create a great deal of personal tragedy and social waste concealed in the word 'processing' of drug offenders."

Dr. Irwin advocated decriminalization of pot and, later, regulation similar to alcohol. I looked over at Jean, the student who shared the same views, and watched as she pumped the air with her right arm. He was speaking her language.

He was speaking mine as well. What a compelling indictment of how we approach drug problems, I thought. I also appreciated that he was choosing to only propose decriminalizing marijuana, even though his long list of serious problems with our drug laws applied to all types of illicit drugs. Marijuana was different from most of the others in several critically important respects, not the least of which was its not risking the user's life. Marijuana does not suppress the cardiovascular and respiratory systems, stopping the heart from beating and the lungs from functioning. Some people experience withdrawal symptoms after quitting use, but they're short-lived and not life-threatening.

As an alternative to jailing users, he called for reinforcing public attitudes and peer pressure to discourage gross intoxication and inebriation. As he took his seat, a frustrated woman in the audience, clearly someone who had come to oppose the bill, shouted, "That's 11 for vs. 1 against. Oh, come on now."

Over the next few hours, the advocacy continued to bounce back and forth. A final witness, Mrs. Howard A. Barner, representing a national women's organization called Pro-America, presented a copy of their resolution opposing legalization of marijuana. "There are influences at work in our land," she said, "which have as their objective the destruction of our families and youth as their special target. A chief spokesman for the communist party has said we will destroy a generation of your youth and you will have no one to defend you."

In just a few minutes the hearing was over. It was again dark outside as we walked to the van. I suspect the silence for the first few miles was a reflection of how intense the day had been. Finally, Julie blurted out, "That woman thinks that decriminalization is part of a communist conspiracy to destroy a generation of America's youth? God, how do you respond to that?"

Someone replied, "You don't. She wouldn't hear you, no matter what you said."

That comment, I realized, "she wouldn't hear you no matter what," suddenly helped me understand what there was about that day's hearing that, in my mind, had failed. The very label "legislative hearing" seemed a misnomer.

If one goal as an advocate is to get people to listen, particularly people who hold strongly to ideas you're hoping they'll reconsider, you must commit to also listen. Today we saw none of that. Indeed, before any of those opposed to Rep. Kelley's bill had their turn at the witness table, nearly all of the proponents were on a flight heading back east.

Maybe it's unreasonable, I thought, for a legislative hearing to be otherwise. Its structure isn't designed to facilitate negotiation, much less an authentic conversation between people on opposing sides of an issue. That's just not how it works.

Yet, how great it might have been if Eikenberry and Kelley had somehow looked for values they held in common and explored the possibility of a forged compromise. How validating it would have been, particularly for Fred and Julie, if their fears of communities flooded with marijuana were to have been acknowledged as important to consider by those supporting decriminalization.

The arguments for stopping criminalizing pot smokers were powerful, I thought. But a legislative hearing seemed to keep both the proponents and the opponents from making it evident they were hearing one another.

21

WE SEE YOU AS A KEY LEADER

HOUSE CHAMBER, OLYMPIA, WASHINGTON
31 MARCH 1977

Four years had passed. I watched the last few votes being registered on the electronic tote board at the front of the House chamber and suddenly realized we were going to lose. It would be by the narrowest of margins. Forty-six had voted "aye," forty-seven "nay." We needed 50 for passage, a constitutional majority.

When the Speaker announced the result, there was an audible groan from a number of our supporters in the public gallery. We had come so close. The thousands of hours we had devoted to changing the law had all been for naught.

My disappointment was compounded by an inexplicable incident just before the Speaker ordered the vote board locked. The light beside Representative Alan Thompson's name had switched from "aye" to "nay." He had been the prime sponsor of the decriminalization bill. My heart sank in confusion.

As the Speaker moved on to the next item of business, Rep. Thompson walked over to the cloakroom where I had been watching the vote. I expected he'd have some words of consolation, perhaps encouraging me to start planning for the next legislative session, or at least an explanation as to why he had suddenly changed his mind.

But he was smiling. Smiling! What could he possibly be thinking? This was unquestionably the end of the line for our bill.

But as he took me aside to talk, I began to wonder. Did he have another card up his sleeve?

This particular odyssey had begun one year earlier. The phone had rung in my University of Washington office.

"Professor Roffman, this is Keith Stroup from the national NORML office. We met in Olympia back in December, 1973. Maybe you remember."

He paused, and I felt flustered. Why was this guy calling me? I stood up, holding the phone while pacing around the office. Could he be looking for a donation?

"Yes, of course I remember."

"You know, Professor, I was impressed back then that you recognized the importance of Representative Kelley's bill and brought your students to observe the hearing."

"We were studying drug policy, so it was a unique opportunity," I replied. "Too bad the bill didn't go anywhere."

"Well, we actually think of it as a mini success," he said. "Typically it takes a number of years of bills being introduced and not getting passed before one makes it all the way through the legislative process. Takes time for people to get over their fears. That hearing was an important step along the way. You folks will get there eventually."

Just a few days earlier I had read a long magazine piece about Keith Stroup. It praised his leadership of this new national marijuana policy movement and described his close contacts with several members of Congress and a number of key White House staff members. He clearly had become a big league player.

He went on to say he thought the coming year was very likely to be a turning point in their national effort. The State of Washington would be pivotal, he said, and he believed our legislature, with a little help, would be ready to rethink the justice and legal logic of sending people to prison for smoking a joint.

I took a breath. Was a decriminalization bill being drafted for the next session? I had no idea.

He told me that part of his optimism had to do with what Seattle had done. An ordinance passed by the Seattle City Council in 1974 threw out criminal penalties for pot possession. With that step, Seattle became the only city in the state with such a lenient policy.

Stroup thought a case could be made that the same policy ought to be extended to all citizens of the state. "Despite what the doomsayers warned," he said, "the sky hasn't fallen in Seattle and there aren't hordes of hippies moving there. When the voters become aware of that, they'll have evidence from their own back yard that it's not such a radical step. For that matter, they'll see that it's saving them a bundle in reduced police and court costs."

He was making some good points, but I still didn't know what he wanted. There wasn't a chance to ask because he barreled ahead.

"Roger, we see you as a key leader who can shape the future of Washington State's NORML chapter. Our movement is growing like crazy throughout the country. But, just between you and me, a few of our state organizations need new leaders."

Then he told me NORML would be giving top priority to west coast states, a region with a higher percentage of progressive voters, and that he'd ask Gordon Brownell to give me a call. Gordon was in charge of NORML's west coast office and Keith described him as literally having written the book about pot lobbying.

"I know you'll like working with him. He'll give you all the help you'll need in getting your state chapter back in shape. Look, I've kept you long enough. Thanks, Professor, for getting on board. You're going to make a big difference out there." And with that, he hung up.

Meanwhile, I was still holding the phone to my ear trying to process everything that had just happened. He'd just asked me—no, not asked—*announced* to me that I was the new coordinator for the state NORML chapter. I remembered that when he testified in Olympia I had given him my business card and a note saying I was possibly interested in getting involved. But he didn't even wait for me to respond. For him, my acceptance seemed to be a given. Up until that point, I had no more considered a career in lobbying of any kind than I had considered a career as a chef.

But I let it happen. His flattery must have played a part in my decision, but what I remember most was his certainty about victory. His enthusiasm felt contagious. It seemed he thought of this as offering me a privilege, the privilege of jumping on a bandwagon that was chugging towards victory.

The timing of his call also played a role. I was still steaming after a troubling conversation I'd had a day earlier with the chairperson of the Governor's Drug Abuse Advisory Council. She had told me what recently had happened to a teen caught with pot in Okanogan County, a rural county located in the middle part of the state. This fellow was 18 years old and had been stopped at the U.S. border while returning from a trip to Canada. A trained dog detected

TOP: Royal Marine Blockhouse and Formal Garden, where the "Pig War" between Britain and the U.S. was narrowly averted. *Courtesy of the National Park Service.* BOTTOM: "A view of English Camp" by E. L. Porcher, 1868. *Courtesy of the National Park Service.*

TOP: Specialist John Mackean, social work technician, and Captain Bill Baker, the 9th Infantry Division's psychiatrist. BOTTOM: At the nearby 93rd Evacuation Hospital, Captains Jake Romo (left) and Paul d'Oronzio (center) helped me learn the ropes in Vietnam.

TOP: Bearcat, the 9th Infantry Division's base camp. MIDDLE: 1,587 people travelled from Oakland to Vung Tau Harbor aboard the U.S.N.S. *Upshur*. BOTTOM: Six of us had our hooches in this tent, with a bunker right outside in case of attack.

TOP AND BOTTOM: Medevac helicopters brought casualities to the 93rd Evacuation Hospital.

TOP: General William Westmoreland en route to visit patients. BOTTOM: The author with Vietnamese children.

OPPOSITE TOP: T.V. entertainer Art Linkletter (2nd from right) endorsed the decriminalization bill sponsored by Senator Barney Goltz (right) and Representative Alan Thompson (2nd from left). OPPOSITE BOTTOM: Dr. Feelgood. The student newspaper's spoof of a professor who wrote about how to use pot medically. TOP: I received a surprising amount of media attention while lobbying for marijuana decriminalization. BOTTOM: Magda Fric, one of many cancer patients who wanted to learn about marijuana's medical use.

ABOVE: Dr. Peter Bourne and Marilyn Dexheimer worked in President Carter's White House. BELOW: The author aboard *Aquarius*.

TOP: My brother, Bryan, at nine years of age. MIDDLE: Cheryl Richey and I were married in 1976. BOTTOM: With high school students who were visiting a science fair at the University of Washington.

OPPOSITE TOP: Drs. Alan Marlatt and Judith Gordon near their Warm Beach cabin. OPPOSITE BOTTOM: Dr. Sharon Berlin with Jessie, Teddy's best buddy. TOP: With my marijuana research colleagues, Dr. Denise Walker and Dr. Bob Stephens. BOTTOM: We recruited study participants at Seattle's annual Hempfest.

OPPOSITE TOP: Tonia Winchester worked to qualify the initiative for the ballot. 241,153 valid signatures were needed. OPPOSITE BOTTOM: Alison Holcomb, the ACLU's Drug Policy Director, wrote the initiative and led the campaign. TOP: At a press conference with John McKay, former U.S. Attorney (left), Charles Mandigo, former FBI Special Agent in Charge (middle), Alison Holcomb, and Dr. Kim Thorburn, former director of public health for Spokane County. BOTTOM: Hempfest's popularity presaged the voters' approval of I-502 in November of 2012.

TOP: 44 years later, a reunion in Hanoi with Paul d'Oronzio (middle) and Jake Romo (right). BOTTOM: Mr. Phong, a former interpreter for the U.S. Army, was our guide as we looked for where Camp Bearcat had once been located. OPPOSITE TOP: Bearcat was now a Vietnamese military facility, and these soldiers made certain we kept our distance. OPPOSITE BOTTOM: Cheryl's thoughts are with our ailing friend, Alan, as she lights incense at Angkor Wat.

Cheryl, Teddy, and the author.

marijuana in his vehicle, a total of one-half of one marijuana joint. He was arrested, his car was impounded, and he found himself in the county's district court being offered the option of paying a fine of $250 or going to jail for 32 days. If he wished, he could reduce the total amount of time spent in jail by paying his way out at the rate of $8 per day. By the time this fellow was again on the road to his home, he had experienced being arrested, being convicted of a crime, spending a week in jail, buying his way out of the remaining jail sentence with $200, paying an additional $100 to release his car from the border authorities, and paying for an attorney. He left town penniless and with a life-long criminal record.

The Governor's drug advisor was incensed and so was I. This kid had been otherwise totally law-abiding and, were he to have been caught with this tiny amount in many other parts of the state, certainly in Seattle, the police officer would have confiscated the guy's stash and given him a warning. No arrest, no record, and no coerced contribution to the county's till in order to avoid imprisonment.

That evening, I debriefed my call from Keith with my fiancée, Cheryl Richey. We had both been doctoral students at Berkeley and were independently recruited to the University of Washington social work faculty. After dating for several years, we had set a date to be married later that summer.

Cheryl was curious why I'd decided to take on the challenge of leading the NORML chapter. I began to answer her with a list of the usual arguments for reform: the punishment being more harmful than the offense, the corruption of law enforcement, and the alienation of many from society. But as I reiterated these points, Cheryl pointed out that I was stating the reasons for reform, not why I had volunteered. It occurred to me that I had a much better answer to what Cheryl was actually asking.

The egregious injustice experienced by that 18-year-old boy would be inflicted on others just like him unless the law was changed, and I might be the right person to help make that change happen. There had been other 18-year-old boys, I told Cheryl, boys turned into warriors who, after experiencing unspeakable horrors in combat, had emotionally collapsed. Or had sterling service records erased. Through my participation, albeit as a helping professional, I had played a role in what in military parlance was called "conserving the fighting strength."

I had been powerless to alter what happened in Vietnam. This time would be different.

22

PRIMARY SPONSOR

HOUSE OFFICE BUILDING, OLYMPIA, WASHINGTON
AUTUMN 1976

Representative Alan Thompson, Democrat from Kelso, was described as quiet, dignified, and laid back, but not to be underestimated. He'd served in the House for 13 years, been elected Majority Leader in the prior session, and was among the power elite in Olympia.

An ACLU lobbyist had told me, "If you can convince him to be the primary sponsor, the bill's chances will be much stronger. For three reasons . . ."

She then used her short, efficient right-hand fingers to tick off each point. "First, he's trusted by his colleagues. Second, he never publicly attacks opponents so hasn't burned his bridges with a lot of people. Third, he's perceived as non-controversial. If he agrees to be primary sponsor, the bill will benefit from his being mainstream, not someone who can be pegged as a west-of-the-mountains loose cannon radical."

So I'd court Representative Thompson and request an appointment prior to the next legislative session's start. Because to my knowledge he'd not made any public statements either way and never voted on this issue, I'd need to first check out if he was in favor of decriminalization.

In the autumn of 1976, I knocked on his partially-opened door in the House Office Building and heard him invite me in. Thompson was sitting at his desk, wearing a white shirt and bow-tie, smoking a pipe, and reading a newspaper. Tall, athletically built, and clean-shaven, my first impression of him was of an archetypical suburban dad. A Ward Cleaver kind of guy.

Bound volumes of state laws and regulations filled the shelves of his bookcases. Numerous photos of him with state and federal officials adorned the walls alongside quite a few plaques and citations.

As he stood to shake my hand and led us to a seating area in a corner of his office, I felt my anxiety cutting back a bit. He knew the general topic I'd come to speak with him about because I had mentioned marijuana policy when I phoned to make the appointment. No scowl, quick glance at his watch, or other signal that he'd want this meeting to be brief. If anything, he seemed to be quite open to both the topic and to me.

"So, a UW professor has come to Olympia to talk about changing the pot laws," he said with a grin while pointing his pipe stem in my direction. "That's surprising, you know, because the people who usually come down here to lobby for that tend to be a bit on the fringe."

I laughed, thinking it had been wise to wear a jacket and tie on this visit. I had a full beard and wore my hair kind of long, but both were trimmed. Good news, I thought. He'd decided I had credibility.

"Actually," I said, "there are now quite a few scientists, physicians, educators, clergy, and even law enforcement types who are calling for decriminalization. And," I continued with a smile, "of course there are also plenty of stoners hoping Olympia will give them a break."

I wondered how he'd react to what I'd said about stoners, but he seemed unfazed by it. I reasoned that it was better to acknowledge that reality than let it hang about as an elephant in the room. "Okay, Roger, you've got something in mind for me, so let me give you a chance to lay it out." He gestured for me to give my spiel, re-lit his pipe, and sat back, so I launched into the three-minute version of my pitch.

I began with statistics about the numbers of people outside of Seattle who were spending time in jail for pot possession while Seattle's 1974 ordinance only imposed a small civil fine. I ran down for him the rationale developed by the Shafer Commission when they called for decriminalization. That is, that pot use should be discouraged, but not with such draconian penalties that a generation of youth would be deeply distrustful of any warnings about drug dangers, no matter the drug. "Losing all credibility for valid health warnings about drugs would be disastrous," I said, not mentioning the first-hand battle my family was continuing to wage with my brother.

I offered my guess that for a bill to get passed in our state, a small civil fine for a first offense would most likely fly only if the penalty for a subsequent offense involved something more, something like a requirement to attend a drug education class. The Minnesota legislature had passed a bill with just such a provision.

He was nodding his head in agreement and writing some notes while I spoke, and when I paused, he surprised me. "Have you lined up a primary sponsor in the House yet?" he asked. "If not, I'd like to consider playing that role."

Many years later I had the opportunity to ask him why he so quickly decided to not only support the legislation, but also to put himself out front on the issue. His answer was telling. Alan Thompson was a risk taker. "I liked playing the legislative bull-fighter," he said, "feeling the horns brush by my cape."

And then he elaborated. "It was also the fact that you weren't the stereotypical stoner, Roger. I doubt that I told you this at the time, but I had already concluded that the pot laws created big problems for law enforcement. I also was concerned about young people doing jail time for pot. I thought decriminalization was the right approach, particularly with the mild discouragement provisions you talked about. But I didn't think there was much of a chance at all of a bill getting passed if the people lobbying it frightened the bejesus out of parents in our state, including parents serving in the legislature. You know, that's what happened in 1971 when Representative Mike Ross held a hearing on his legalization bill. A room full of angry shouting hippies didn't do their cause any favors."

His saying he'd consider being primary sponsor was unexpected and threw me off my pace. I still had numerous selling points to make, lists of celebrities and national organizations that had endorsed decriminalization, poll results that showed favorable public attitudes, copies of the laws in the eight states that had enacted decriminalization, and much more. But he was already way ahead of me.

"I'll phone Gary Reid in the Code Reviser's Office and let him know you're working with me. Give him a list of the provisions you'd like and he'll put them into a draft bill. That's where we should start. Once he's got a draft, I'll take a look at it. Now, let's talk about other sponsors."

He walked over to his desk and picked up a list of current House members. "I'd like you to try to balance the list of sponsors by including a number of Republicans. Talk with Ted Haley, for example. He's a physician from Lakewood. Oh, and see if you can get Scott Blair and Rod Chandler to sign on. These fellows are pretty conservative fiscally, but lean to the progressive side on a number of social issues." I told him about Rep. Blair having been one of the Republican sponsors of Richard Kelley's decriminalization bill in 1973.

He went on to suggest a list of Democrats who might agree to be sponsors. Then he turned his attention to what would be important in the hearing once the bill had been assigned to a committee. His major point was to get people to testify who'd be credible with middle-of-the-road voters. "Coach them to include in their testimony a compelling case for why the bill makes sense for families in our state and why it is not really such a radical change," he said.

This meeting with Alan Thompson had rapidly morphed into a political strategy session. Weeks before the Legislature convened, we were out of the gate and running. I had initially prepared myself for a rejection, but now it felt as if he had invited me to be on his team. My optimism bumped up a few notches about the possibility of succeeding in getting a bill passed.

Earlier that week I had met with Barney Goltz, one of our top choices for primary sponsor in the Senate. While also encouraging, that conversation had gone quite differently. A Western Washington University administrator, Sen. Goltz had been receptive to the idea of sponsoring the Senate version of the bill. He felt strongly about the right of privacy and, in his occupation, was sympathetic to the young people who were often the victims of an overly punitive law. Nonetheless, he wanted to first get input from his constituents. He'd do that and then let me know his decision.

Thompson and Goltz were quite different in their styles. Using Alan Thompson's metaphor, each had his own suiting up ritual prior to entering the bullring.

It seemed as if I, too, was in an arena. The legislators I had spoken with liked the idea of discouraging marijuana use via small civil fines and a required drug education class for repeat offenders. But the members of the steering committee I'd recruited for our NORML chapter were by no means on the same page about what we should work to accomplish, some wanting changes that seemed too radical and too soon for my comfort: full legalization, as an example.

I also knew I'd face an uphill battle on one issue with Keith Stroup. In a visit to his office, I'd told him I thought the campaign would be stronger if NORML's brochures, posters, and flyers included acknowledgment of the potential harms from pot, including dependence. "Keith, because NORML is so highly respected, we can credibly argue that these harms will be better prevented if criminalizing users were replaced by a public health approach."

No chance. He was insistent that what I was proposing was the province of other institutions such as the education, public health, and the drug treatment systems. "Look, Roger, if we include this kind of information in NORML's advocacy materials, we'll only muddy the message. Our only reference to risks," he said, "should be about the harms of putting people in jail for possessing marijuana."

I began to wonder if I'd be perceived as overly cautious by some in our group and by the national NORML office, maybe even ousted as coordinator. Somehow, I'd need to resolve my hesitancies. A campaign to undo the egregious inequities of criminalizing pot possession should not pretend there were no potential risks in the proposed alternative.

23

HYPOCRITE

"**M**aybe you'll figure it out for yourself if you tell me about the problems you're seeing." She took off her glasses and looked at me with a questioning glance. "So, what's bothering you?"

I had asked Sister Kathleen Pruitt to meet me for coffee. There were some red flags I couldn't ignore. First, a few in our group were arguing that our mission ought to be fully legalizing pot. Then, there was Keith Stroup's rejecting my wanting the campaign to more directly acknowledge pot's risks.

I feared having to make too many compromises and wanted to talk it through with someone. Sister Kathleen might not agree with me on every point, but I knew I could count on her to listen.

We met mid-morning in a restaurant near her office on Queen Anne Hill. Up on a ladder behind the counter, a waitress took advantage of the lull to tack up a string of Halloween decorations: skeletons, ghosts, witches' hats, black and orange crepe paper streamers, and bright green goblins. Every table had its own small pumpkin and an ear of Indian corn. Next to the cash register was a plastic jack-o'-lantern bowl filled with candy corn.

Sister Kathleen wore a gray modified habit and a small gold cross on a chain. Her hair had prematurely grayed. At 40, she was the oldest member of our steering committee and probably the most experienced in social activism. Several years earlier she had earned an MSW and now directed the King County Drug Abuse Program.

As a teen, Sister Kathleen had applied to a cloistered Carmelite monastery seeking a life in contemplation and prayer. The Mother Superior wisely told her she was too active to be cloistered. In later years, Kathleen would lead a delegation to the Vatican asking for a greater voice for women in church decisions, serve as a leader of Pax Christi International, a Catholic peace organization, and be jailed while protesting the denial of free elections in Nicaragua. In 1976, her decision to lobby for marijuana decriminalization while running the county's drug program was gutsy and easily could have ruffled her employer's feathers.

"First," I said, "I can't get behind the idea that we should go for legalization. The legislature would simply reject it. For that matter, a bill would never even make it out of committee."

She nodded as I spoke, quietly adding, "Maybe someday, but not anytime soon."

"Yeah, the public isn't ready for it," I said, "but neither am I. I can just imagine what it would look like, an explosion of pro-pot ads, millions of dollars in marketing exploiting teens, and even more misinformation about the drug. . . . I don't know, Kathleen, but I picture a lot of people's lives going down the drain because their pot use won't be just once in a while, but chronic and compulsive. It worries me."

I told her about Fred and Julie, two of the students who attended the Olympia hearing with me several years earlier. They had bristled at testimony from witnesses who failed to consider the possibility of harmful outcomes if marijuana were much easier to get.

"I have to tell you, it's not just what these students were saying. Some of the time when I think about what my family has been going through in the past few years because of my brother's drug involvement, all of the arguments for decriminalization that seem so rational get drowned out."

"I remember you telling me about him," she said.

"All of the talking points," I said, "the inequities of jail terms, the alienating of young people due to overly harsh sentences, the disrespect for law enforcement, whatever really makes sense most of the time for me gets obscured when I think about Bryan. I think of the 9-year-old's smile in his school photo, the life he could be living, and then there's the actual nightmare that's happening."

As I said these things, I was aware of being fearful that Kathleen would try to talk me out of being the NORML coordinator. Maybe there'd be too much internal conflict for me, a risk of emotional spillover. Had our situations been reversed, that would be the possibility I'd raise with her. But she sat with me silently. No advice and no reassurance. She just gave me time to be with my thoughts.

In a few moments, I shook off the gloom and dark cloud seeded by Bryan's struggle. I knew I'd need to find a way to see what was happening to us personally as too close for me to retain objectivity about decriminalization unless I partitioned off home and work.

In the bigger picture, families such as ours would be better off if jail terms and criminal records were no longer the front line of defense. I'd stay the course as coordinator, and hold on to my belief that pushing for decriminalization didn't mean that marijuana—or drugs as a whole—were harmless.

Kathleen was watching me. She saw I was ready to move on.

"Okay, what else?" she asked. "We're on the same page about this, by the way. I'd have to leave our group if the decision were to seek legalization. So what else is bothering you?"

I felt buoyed by her conviction on this point. It felt easier to resolve where I'd draw the line.

A waiter refilled our cups. I noticed that many of the tables in the restaurant were now occupied and was glad we were in a booth because it made it easier to keep our conversation private.

"My second problem is with the national office of NORML. We should be telling people about the possible harms from smoking pot at the same time that we're fighting to stop sending people to jail for using it. It seems to me that NORML is evasive about there being any risks." I was about to continue, but noticed Kathleen was looking doubtful.

"You're not going to win this one, Roger. As you've probably noticed, NORML's run by lawyers and their instincts are to give no ground to anything that erodes their key goal."

From the logic of what she had said, I sensed I was not going to get anywhere with these idealistic points. But I pushed on. "Look, I want people to be aware of risks to the lungs, for example. They should know about risks to the fetus if a woman smokes pot during pregnancy and the risks from driving while stoned. It seems to me that NORML should be fulfilling an educational role while working for decriminalization."

"Roger, public education about marijuana is not going to happen through our work with NORML. As much as I agree with your values, I think you've got to be realistic. The lawyers will do everything in their power to keep the focus on the injustice of criminal sanctions for pot smokers. They'll see what you're pro-posing as hobbling their efforts. Can you understand that?"

I sat in the booth with my arms folded across my chest, focusing my gaze on the half-empty coffee cup in front of me. Had anyone other than Sister Kathleen tried to convince me on this point, I'd have dug in. But here we were, two people devoting their profes-sional lives to human services and finding the battle to decrimi-nalize marijuana possession worth our time and energy. I knew she was right and that I needed to either compromise on this point or get off the bus.

I mentally checked off a list of key points. Marijuana was harmful to some people in some circumstances, but so was crimi-nalizing the user. Educating the public about marijuana's risks, including the risk of dependence, was badly needed, but a reform campaign might hobble itself if it took that task on. Voters, particu-larly those raising young children, would need to recognize that an alternative to jail terms righted a socially unjust policy while also offering protection to their sons and daughters.

Adding up the checklist made it evident there were shades of gray in relation to the nature of marijuana, how it's dealt with in the law, and the realities of politics. We had a chance to do something positive, but it required compromise.

I looked up at her and nodded.

"Anything else on your list, Roger?"

"Yeah, but here's where I'm afraid I'm going to sound like a hypocrite."

She laughed and said, "Okay, I promise to keep this between us. Nuns can't be confessors, and you're not a Catholic anyway. But trust me, my lips are sealed. You're thinking you're a hypocrite?"

"It's hard to avoid labeling myself that way, Kathleen. On the one hand, I'm heading a group that says its goal is to revise a bad law while not encouraging marijuana use. On the other hand, I enjoy getting high and I think that's fine for me. So I have to admit it feels like hypocrisy."

She was quiet for a few moments and then said, "I wonder." She looked at the pad she'd been scribbling on and then double-underlined the word hypocrite. In the margin next to the word she penciled a large question mark. She turned her pad around so I could more easily read it and then asked, "Do you really believe you need to think that way about yourself, Roger?"

Hmm. She hadn't tried to dissuade me, but clearly was encouraging me to reconsider whether the hypocrite label actually fit.

In a short while I realized that in fact the answer was evident. I looked up at her with a smile and said, "Kathleen, I think I've got it sorted out. Maybe you are a confessor."

24

UNLIKELY ALLY

SEATTLE
DECEMBER 1976

After a while, we easily could have switched places and delivered one another's speeches, we had heard them that often. In the several months prior to the convening of the Legislature in January of 1977, we had debated one another on numerous occasions before community groups about the bill's provisions.

Captain Clark Elster, Commander of the Seattle Police Department Narcotics Division, at 6'3", about 245 pounds, and with the ruddy appearance of a Sean Connery-type, right down to his bushy eyebrows and a well-honed capacity to stare down just about any adversary, was a daunting opponent. He gave no ground each time we faced off as he made a compelling case for retaining criminal penalties for possession of pot.

Despite our differences, I appreciated two qualities that Captain Elster brought to our interactions. First, he never attacked me personally, only my arguments in support of decriminalization. Second, he had a disarming sense of humor, self-effacing at times, and seemed both genuine and sincere. We could joke with one another, as we did in a number of debates held in town halls and library meeting rooms, about our "narc and hippie professor road show."

My speech usually began with an historical quote to illustrate pot's legacy of being grossly distorted. One of my favorites was a statement made by Harry Anslinger, a former director of the U.S. Bureau of Narcotics: "If the hideous monster Frankenstein came face to face with the monster marijuana, he would drop dead of fright." I'd explain that while this quote was from decades earlier, exaggerations about marijuana's risks continued to be disseminated in the schools and by governmental agencies. Coupled with overly punitive sanctions for possessing the drug, this misinformation was having the effect of making less credible public health warnings of the very real risks posed by drugs. The severe penalties were alienating many American youth from law enforcement. I'd cite statistics concerning the hundreds of thousands arrested nationally for marijuana offenses, most for simple possession, and the egregiously damaging consequences of being jailed and having a lifelong criminal record. I'd close by reminding the audience that for the people of Seattle, there was a precedent. In 1974 the Seattle City Council had reclassified possession of 40 grams or less of pot from a misdemeanor, with a potential 90-day jail term, to a civil violation, with a maximum fine of $500 and no jail time. That law had worked well, I'd argue, and had made it possible for law enforcement to attend to more serious threats in the community.

"Shouldn't all Washington citizens, not just those living in Seattle, have the same protections against overly harsh punishment for marijuana possession?" I'd ask. "Here's what will be in the bill the legislature will consider. Anyone caught possessing 40 grams or less will be guilty of a civil, not a criminal offense. The maximum fine will be $25. If someone is caught a second time, they'll have to attend a drug education class and pay for it." Then I'd sit down, knowing for certain that Captain Elster was about to do his best to dismantle everything I'd said.

"Does anyone here know how much pot 40 grams really is?" Captain Elster would ask as he stood and walked to the podium. Usually there'd be no one ready with an answer, so he'd provide it.

"You know, folks, we've been hearing that this bill is needed so that people who possess a small amount of marijuana won't be thrown into the hoosegow. Now, I don't know what a small amount might mean to you, but to me it's nowhere near 60 to 80 joints. That's what they're talking about when they say that marijuana possession should be decriminalized. Sixty to 80 joints! That's a whole lot of partying, probably by a whole lot of people. And that's only one of the problems I have with this bill. Professor Roffman makes it sound as if we're arresting, prosecuting, and jailing every pot smoker we can possibly find, but the truth of the matter is that in order to be arrested for possessing pot, someone almost always is engaging in some other criminal activity that brings them to the attention of law enforcement officers. We simply don't go looking for them otherwise."

He'd pause, put on a serious face, kind of a menacing sneer, and slowly look around the room before adding, "Now, that does not mean that if any of you fire up a doobie while we're having this chat you ain't gonna find yourselves tryin' on a pair of bracelets!" The audience always roared.

"There are several other problems with this bill. One is that it doesn't distinguish between low potency cannabis that someone might grow under lights in their basement and the really high potency stuff like Thai stick or hashish that costs a whole lot more on the street." He shifted on his feet and straightened his lapels.

"Another problem is the absolutely incorrect notion that lots of taxpayer money will be saved if marijuana is decriminalized or that greatly increased law enforcement attention to more serious crimes will be possible. The fact of the matter is that even if marijuana possession is handled as a civil offense, the police officer's time in court is just as expensive and so are the required lab tests to confirm that the seized evidence is cannabis."

He'd usually look at his watch at about this point, as if to say he was worried about the time. I knew it was a signal he was about to slam what in his view was the winning run out of the park. "I want to close by saying that from my perspective, decriminalization laws lend an aura of legitimacy to marijuana that will likely see demand for the drug increase, and incentives for dealers to increase as well. If we head down that road, we shouldn't be surprised by a whole lot more marijuana use in our communities. I don't want to overstate the consequences from getting high once in a while, but I also don't want us to overlook the serious risks from chronic use. "

Usually there'd be questions, and often a few members of the audience would go after one or the other of us for something we had said with which they vigorously disagreed. I liked it when their comments supported my arguments, but the fact that each of us took some hits during the Q & A following these debates probably kept both of us humble. That shared liability for being seen as the "bad guy" may also have set the groundwork for an unexpected diplomatic opening in our competition to win people over. From October of 1976 through early 1977, we each lobbied various groups and the battle was in full swing.

Yet all was not as it appeared to be on the surface.

Late in November, following one of our debates, I asked Captain Elster if he'd join me for a cup of coffee and an off-the-record conversation. He surprised me by accepting, and we found a booth in the rear of a nearby cafe where it was quiet.

"Clark, I'm not sure that we're all that far apart. Can I tell you where I see us sharing common ground?"

"I'm listening," he replied, and that seemed to be a good sign. He wasn't quickly dismissing the possibility that we held some beliefs in common.

"For one thing," I said, "I think neither of us wants to encourage drug use. For another, I think we both recognize that some people get into trouble with pot, but that many others—particularly occasional smokers—really don't have problems with the drug unless they make stupid decisions. Same deal as with alcohol."

I stopped, waiting to see if he'd react. But there was no argument from him about what I'd said, at least not at this point.

"Go on," he said.

"We both know there are some jurisdictions in this state where pot smokers get the maximum penalties, including jail time, while the same acts are treated very leniently in places like Seattle. I think that's the reason why this bill is so important." I told him about the 18-year-old in Okanogan County who had been caught with half a joint at the border crossing and been slammed by the fine, jail sentence, the attorney fee, and the cost of getting his car out of impound.

"By the way, how am I doing?"

Clark laughed. "As long as nobody is taking minutes of this conversation, I'll say you're doing okay."

"All right, let me try a few other points. I've been listening closely to your speeches, and I'm guessing that if some of the provisions you oppose in the bill were changed, you might think differently about it. For example, what if the amount decriminalized was an ounce instead of 40 grams, and possession of between 28 grams and 40 grams remained a misdemeanor?"

"You'd be moving in the right direction," Clark quickly said. "Any more cards up your sleeve?"

I sensed that he was enjoying this. Were we horse-trading or was this just some back and forth banter? Might our discussion lead to a compromise that would bring us together on the proposed bill?

"Well, the other point that seems to yank your chain really isn't in the bill," I said, "but rather is part of my lobbying speech. It's the comment that if possessing pot is decriminalized, police can turn their attention to more serious crimes. I'm guessing that if I dropped that, we'd see less steam coming out of your ears when we're debating."

He smiled. "Can't promise doing away with the steam, but you're finally beginning to make some sense. Not a bad thing for a distinguished professor."

I caught the barb, but knew it was intended to be friendly. We had each had two cups of coffee and the waitress was headed our way again with a full carafe. I began to believe that this conversation might lead to a breakthrough. It wouldn't hurt to try, so I put the possibility on the table.

"Clark, if I worked with the Code Reviser's Office in Olympia to rewrite the bill, and also put together a draft endorsement by the Seattle Police Department of the revised bill, would you read them? Obviously, I'd keep all of this absolutely confidential between the two of us. If the new bill doesn't adequately resolve the difficulties you have, you can tear up what I send you."

He made no commitment and got ready to leave. We both reached for our wallets and headed to the cashier. "I read lots of stuff every day" were his parting words.

When we next debated, it was as if our negotiation over coffee had never happened. We both appeared before the Seattle-King County Drug Commission, squaring off just as we had in the past. I was discouraged when I learned that the Seattle Police Chief had expressed his opposition to the bill in correspondence with city officials, guessing that nothing would come of my clandestine negotiations with Clark.

But Clark did read both the revised bill and the draft endorsement I had sent him several days after our conversation. Then, without his telling me in advance that it would be happening, I read in the newspaper on January 25th that the Seattle Police Department had issued a press release endorsing the "improved" Marijuana Education and Control Act pending in the Washington State Legislature. It was gratifying to realize that the Chief's endorsement incorporated much of the wording I had suggested. A few weeks later, the Chief testified for our bill in a legislative hearing and his appearance greatly boosted the bill's chances for passage.

Years later, thinking back about the steps Clark Elster and I had taken to find common ground concerning a very small piece of legislation about a relatively minor issue, recalling our stealth as negotiators brings a smile. Underlying the stereotypes of the police "narc" and the "hippie professor" were commonly held values, and we had taken the time and chanced the risk of failure in seeking and finding a compromise.

25

FORK IN THE ROAD

ABERDEEN, WASHINGTON
MARCH 1977

Like so many of the talks I had given to service clubs around the state, the monthly meeting of the Aberdeen Rotary Club was held during the noon hour in a hotel private dining room. The Nordic Inn was the venue for this talk and about 125 people were present.

I usually felt confident that I'd be received well, even if some disagreed about decriminalizing pot. This one might be different, though. A NORML member who lived in that city warned me that this club was a particularly conservative Republican stronghold. I wondered if anyone at all in the audience would think favorably of the proposed change in the law. Even if they did, would they publicly say so?

Baked chicken, string beans, a mixed salad, and chocolate pudding topped with a dollop of Cool Whip were served after the

Program Chairman welcomed the crowd, introduced some visitors, and made a few announcements. Later, as the dishes were being cleared, he began what I expected would be a routine introduction.

Not this time.

"You know, folks, it's not every day that we get to have a chat about pot. Usually, in a town like ours, it's a subject that stays under the table."

At that moment, he reached under the table and ceremoniously held up an enormous paper mache doobie that must have been three feet long. "I thought that while our speaker enlightens us about a bill being considered in Olympia, we ought to do a little homework to be sure we really understand what it's all about. Has anyone got a match?"

The audience roared with laughter. I noticed that a few of the young waiters had stopped bussing dishes to watch this bit of drama unfold.

"So don't be shy as I pass this around," he said. "Take a deep toke and hold it in for a minute. Don't worry. We've got some medics standing by to resuscitate you if you pass out. Who wants to be first?"

Someone shouted, "Why don't you show us how it's done, Steve?"

Amid laughter, someone else said, "Yeah, Steve, don't worry about Sheriff Dan. He'll look the other way."

Without missing a beat, a uniformed officer sitting at a table near the back of the room began walking toward the head table with a menacing look on his face, brandishing a set of handcuffs, and saying, "You have the right to remain silent. Anything you say can and will be used against you in a court of law. You have the right to speak to an attorney."

As the sheriff recited the Miranda warning, Steve feigned a look of horror and quickly thrust the prop joint into my hands, pleading, "It belongs to him! Honest! Arrest this Seattle hippie, Sheriff."

With that melodramatic warm-up, my apprehension about speaking before this conservative group lightened up. It seemed that these folks were enjoying themselves. Perhaps they'd even be a little more receptive to my talk.

This was one of dozens of talks I gave around the state to garner support for the bill. Program chairs for Rotary, Elks, Kiwanis, and Lions clubs usually were more than happy to oblige when I sought invitations to speak before their groups. Each had the responsibility of lining up luncheon speakers, and they often found themselves short of options. I was rarely turned down.

When planning each of these speaking trips, I also submitted op-ed articles to the local newspapers and asked for appointments with the editorial page editors. Frequently, there'd be the chance to also give a talk at a local community college and be interviewed on a radio station. To cut expenses, I usually stayed the night with a local NORML supporter when the commute back to Seattle was too far.

I had a canned speech, with the bullet points typed out on fifteen 5" x 8" index cards, each of which had a topic label such as how marijuana works, its effects on health, the prevalence of use, and how many people were being arrested for possession. One card included examples of egregiously long prison sentences given to people who simply possessed pot for personal use. Those cards made it easy for me to tailor my talks to be appropriate for each audience and to quickly find answers to questions.

I'd quote Dr. Robert DuPont, the Director of the National Institute on Drug Abuse who said marijuana was less of a public health problem than cigarettes or alcohol. He favored a small civil fine and no jail term for possession.

I'd read from an Ann Landers column in which the popular advice columnist responded to an Indiana woman whose

20-year-old son had been given a one to ten year prison sentence for possessing thirty grams of pot. Ann Landers replied, "It's time Indiana joined Illinois, Colorado, Alaska, and the other enlightened states. Possession of marijuana should not be a crime."

While speaking to the Aberdeen audience, I was aware of several people whose facial expressions and shaking heads signaled they were unhappy with my comments. Just after the Ann Landers quote, one of them, a man whose shave-tail haircut made me wonder if he was a drill sergeant, had had enough. He shouted out, his voice dripping with sarcasm, "Maybe Indiana has got it right, professor. You know, young man, that boy's friends will see him doing hard time for pot and they might just think twice about flouting the laws. You start getting permissive and soon you'll lose a generation of young people."

I felt the heat rising in my neck, and as his eyes bored into me, I imagined what he might be thinking about my long hair and full beard. Seeing some others nodding in agreement, I braced for more angry remarks.

Before I could reply, however, a woman on the other side of the room took him on. "Jim, maybe you'd be okay seeing your son go to prison if he got caught with pot, but that's not what I'd want for mine. My kid is the same age as that Indiana boy. I don't want him to use marijuana, but if he does, for heaven's sake I don't want to toss him on the garbage heap."

To my relief, even more people in the audience were visibly agreeing with this woman. Steve, the Program Chairman, stood and asked everyone to hold their comments until I had finished. His intercession seemed to work, and I moved on to an anecdote I'd first heard from Professor Jerome Skolnick, one of the Berkeley faculty members with whom I'd studied. My goal was to stimulate people to question some of their common assumptions.

"I'm just about finished," I said, "but first I'd like to tell you about another drug being used by young people today. At this point, it's still legal. It causes a heightened pulse rate, facial flushing, sweating, an elevation in adrenal activity, and in many cases a loss of breath followed by dizziness and nausea. There have even been reliable reports of death following its use.

"So, from what you've heard so far about this clinical picture," I asked, "would you want to discourage the use of this drug? Maybe make it illegal?"

As expected, lots of people nodded in agreement. I waited a moment and then dropped the other shoe.

"Many of you agree. Well, I've got an admission to make. I've lied to you. These effects aren't from use of a new drug. They're what happens when a person plays tennis."

I paused for a moment. "Again, the symptoms include a heightened pulse rate, facial flushing, sweating, increased adrenal activity, loss of breath, sometimes dizziness and nausea, and even cases in which the player died."

I heard a few groans. But most in this audience were apparently willing to play along and consider the point I was trying to make.

"I've played a trick on you to show how, when taken out of context, a set of consequences can be misconstrued. So let me list the consequences that people experience for a few hours when they're stoned: an increase in heart rate, a reddening of the eyes, impaired short-term memory, and an altered time sense.

"Does my tennis example shift your thinking a bit?"

A few people laughed, while others looked thoughtful. Some were not amused. I closed by asking, "Maybe my trick has backfired. Anyone think playing tennis should join smoking pot as a crime punishable by a jail term?"

I was tempted as I asked this to look over at the man who reminded me of a drill sergeant, but decided that might be too provocative. For the next fifteen minutes, the questions and comments from this audience gave me the sense that quite a few people were open to the idea of decriminalizing pot possession. This crowd turned out to not be the solidly opposed bastion of conservative thinking I had anticipated. Or maybe some minds had been changed.

Through trial and error, I gradually improved in my ability to shape each talk for specific audiences. One of the big challenges, however, was dealing effectively with people who expressed their disagreement with personal attacks. "Do you use pot?" was the most common, closely followed by "Do you have any children?" and "What kind of a role model do you think you are, professor?" Getting defensive or trying to evade these questions never succeeded.

Over time, I became more comfortable in simply responding honestly and directly. "Yes, I do from time to time." The questioner might not be satisfied with my answer, but I had the sense that approach helped me be more credible with many in the audience, and sometimes even the questioner lightened up just a bit.

Skeptics often raised another issue. "Isn't this the first step toward legalization?"

I was asked that question while a guest on a weekly television interview program hosted by John Komen, an editorial writer for the *Tacoma News-Tribune*. I knew he had serious reservations about decriminalization. For that matter, he had written an editorial opposing its enactment. But I had hopes that he could be convinced, so when he asked me to be a guest on his program, I took the risk.

The television studio was located on the campus of a vocational college. Students operated the three cameras while another served as floor director. The host and I sat on opposite sides of a table and as he waited for my answer, he glanced down at his highlighted pages of notes. I took a breath and did my best to calm myself.

"No, John, it certainly is not, in my judgment," I replied. "If, after decriminalization is enacted, there would be a move to legalize marijuana, other things being equal, I would be there opposing that move."

He had a doubtful look on his face, but was giving me time to answer more fully, so I pushed on. "My background is not to be a lobbyist first and foremost. I'm a faculty member at the University of Washington and I specialize in alcoholism and drug abuse. And I don't need to tell you as a journalist what costs our society pays from the abuse of mood-changing chemicals. The estimates are that alcohol abuse costs amount to $42 billion each year and the abuse of drugs like heroin $17 billion."

He parried with a question I expected. It had happened this way many times. "So why do we add another problem by decriminalizing marijuana?"

"I don't think we would be adding another problem, John. The horse is really already out of the barn. Marijuana is being used now by more than 40 million Americans. The current marijuana law doesn't seem to deter people. What it does do, however, is promote a great amount of disrespect for law enforcement and it undermines the credibility of what drug educators such as myself are saying about risks. And if the law is bad because it has those consequences, then I think that the law needs to be changed."

I had noticed that he was repeatedly capping and uncapping his pen, and wondered if it was a sign that he believed he was losing the contest. Or was he preparing to pump up the pressure on me? It quickly became evident he was not going to back down.

"Isn't it true, however, that the National Organization for the Reform of Marijuana Laws really wants more than decriminalization? Really wants more than just civil penalties for the smoking of marijuana?"

"I'd be lying to you," I replied, "if I said that there are no members of NORML who want legalization. But they're in the minority in the organization and the organization is advocating decriminalization, not legalization."

He wouldn't let go. "As a first step, I think. And as I've watched its history, it looks to me like NORML will do anything it possibly can and accept anything it possibly can in the way of legislation that decriminalizes or reduces the criminal penalties in any fashion in order to gain that first foot in the door toward legalization. Now, Roger, isn't that a definition of what NORML wants?"

The cap was flying on and off his pen, and the fervor of his insistence flashed through his eyes as he tried to stare me down. I felt the heat of the accusation as well as from the studio lighting and wondered if the cameras were picking up perspiration on my face. I needed to get it right. The ball was back in my court and I swung.

"NORML is a coalition, John, and I'll simply say to you that in that coalition there are a number of physicians, attorneys, government officials, academicians such as myself, as well as hippies. That coalition will break apart if NORML does move in the direction of legalization. A lot of people who are scientists or who are drug educators are saying we want to find a better way to discourage use without such terrible consequences for so many people. I can simply tell you if NORML moves in the direction of seeking legalization, it will certainly lose me."

Point and set. He was finally ready to move on, although every subsequent question raised yet another problem with the decriminalization idea. I held my own, though, and the time flew by. I was surprised when I heard him thank me for being his guest and end the show. We'd been talking for thirty minutes, but I'd have guessed we'd only talked for ten.

When it was over, I didn't have the opportunity to ask him about a hunch. It had seemed, as he challenged me on one topic after another, that he had ever so subtly let me know, by a brief smile or a nod of his head, I had done well. I might not have changed his mind about the marijuana law, but we apparently had made good television.

The months I spent in 1977 lobbying the bill and giving talks around the state were quite heady. I often saw my name in print and received lots of praise from NORML leaders such as Gordon Brownell in San Francisco and Keith Stroup in Washington, D.C. John Komen's program was among many television and radio programs on which I was interviewed.

All of this attention was a big ego boost. One letter, however, helped me to remember the virtue of humility. It arrived about a week after I appeared on a live morning television program in Seattle.

Dear Professor,

This morning my family watched the Seattle Today show and saw you being interviewed and answering questions from the audience. To be honest with you, we don't agree at all that pot should be encouraged, and that's of course what would happen if the law eases up on these people.

You're supposed to be a drug expert and you should know better. We don't need another legal drug that'll tear apart families. We've already got booze for that purpose and it's doing just fine.

But that's not why we're writing.

My 4-year-old son, Ryan, came into the room while you were on and suddenly pointed at the tv set and shouted, "There's Marco!" At first, my wife and I didn't understand what he meant, but then we doubled over. We must have laughed for at least ten minutes. You see, Marco is our 7-year-old Airedale, and with your beard and moustache you look just like him.

So, that's why we were glad we saw you on the program.

I don't think Cheryl and I have ever seen an Airedale since then without one or the other of us exclaiming "There's Marco." I got a new nickname.

—✂—

On February 11, 1977, I read the morning newspaper while having coffee in a Spokane hotel's restaurant. Suddenly, I discovered I had a golden opportunity to make a point about misinformation being common when the topic is marijuana.

I had testified for the bill the previous day at a House Judiciary Committee hearing in Olympia, and then flown to Spokane and stayed overnight. In an hour, I'd be speaking to the Spokane Chamber of Commerce at their breakfast meeting. This audience was made up of approximately 75 business and political leaders.

In most respects, my presentation was identical to many of the others. But when giving several historical examples of unproven beliefs about pot that found their way into books and newspapers— that it caused users to become violent, to become insane, or to be propelled on to heroin addiction—I made a point of saying that in a few minutes I'd have a current example of news media distortion in stories about marijuana.

As I came to the end of my talk, I returned to the issue of distortion. "There was a hearing in Olympia on the decriminalization bill yesterday. Is there anyone here who attended it?" I asked. As expected, no one had.

"Let me read to you how the hearing was described in this morning's *Spokesman-Review*." I heard a few people laughing as I said that, but at the time it didn't register why.

"The headline reads EX-ADDICT OPPOSES MARIJUANA BILL. And here's how the story reads."

"Marijuana use is a life-wrecking habit," a former drug addict told legislators Thursday. "It's a shameful day for our country when an ex-drug addict has to stand before the public asking you not to decriminalize marijuana, making it simple for our youth to destroy themselves as I nearly did," Brent Ebinger of Longview told lawmakers. The House Judiciary Committee is studying a bill that would make the possession of small amounts of the drug a civil violation instead of a criminal offense. Committee action on the measure is scheduled for next week.

Ebinger told the panel his 14 years of drug addiction, including marijuana use, tell him decriminalization of the drug is wrong. "I agree we have a problem in this state with marijuana and other drugs," he said. "But we don't solve that problem by compromising and turning our backs to the whole situation." Members of the committee have grilled dozens of persons offering testimony at two hearings on the proposal. Testimony ranged from emotional horror stories to pure statistics.

"I won't take the time to read the last few paragraphs," I said. "They simply summarize both the proposed bill and the current state law. So, do you think you have a pretty good idea about what happened yesterday at that hearing in Olympia?"

Again there was some laughter, but this time I noticed a number of people looking in the direction of one man who held his hands up in a shrug.

I relished the opportunity this story was giving me. "I flew here last night after attending that hearing," I said. "If you had been there with me, you'd have heard the Bellingham Chief of Police testify in favor of the bill. You'd have heard the head of the Seattle Police Department's Narcotics Division read a letter of support for the bill from the Seattle Chief of Police."

I wasn't finished, but the laughter in the room was growing in volume and I raised my voice to be heard. "You'd have heard the

Chairperson of the Governor's Advisory Council on Drug Abuse testify in favor of the bill. You'd have heard an official from the State's lead drug abuse division express support for the bill. You'd have heard me speak in favor of the bill. Oh, and yes, you'd have heard Brent Ebinger talk about it being a shameful day for our country."

I stopped and the laughter continued. The man who by now just about everyone was looking at signaled his surrender by waving his handkerchief. As he was given a round of applause, the Program Chairman leaned over and whispered, "He's the publisher of the *Spokesman-Review.*"

I felt triumphant. While I always hoped my canned speech would win converts, nothing like this anecdote, an irrefutable example of misinformation about pot, could make the point as powerfully.

—⁂—

While the questions asked by proponents and opponents began to be predictable, there was one issue I hadn't expected to be raised in the furtive, almost apologetic way in which it tended to come up. It usually happened after I had finished delivering a talk. The person would linger, waiting for a private moment.

"Can someone get addicted to pot?" The questioner was most often a male in his twenties or thirties, and as he asked the question he'd usually avert his eyes and look decidedly uncomfortable. Quite clearly, this was a personal dilemma.

I understood the need to wait for a private moment. While it was important to me that my presentation about marijuana's effects was balanced, many of these speaking events, particularly those held on college campuses, had the feel of a rally. Prior to my talk there'd be lots of laughter while the *Reefer Madness* film was playing, a number of people would be wearing marijuana leaf-emblazoned t-shirts, and through their comments and questions, members of the audience would bolster one another's views that most of the warnings about pot were simply propaganda. In that environment, publicly asking if pot was addicting would not have gone over well.

A letter I received from a woman who had heard me speak captured just such a concern. Her husband's pot use had become a thorn in her side.

She wrote, "I quit smoking seven years ago when I became pregnant and have tried it only once since. I became so overcome with paranoia that I have had no desire to use it since. My husband has always been a heavy daily user. If I suggest that he quit or not smoke on some occasion, he gets irate and refuses. He says there is nothing wrong and that he doesn't smoke that much anyway. It reminds me of an alcoholic's denial of their alcoholism. I often wonder what he would be like straight. Sometimes I even wish he would get busted so that he would have to get treatment. But that is only in my dreams. I wouldn't want my children to be affected that way. We can't seem to become close to anyone who is a non-smoker, and whenever the doorbell rings, I have to look around and make sure it's all put away. I have told him if I ever left, it would be because of his pot use, but I really don't think he believes me. I suppose that leaving is easier to say than to do. Thanks for letting me put it in writing. Having to remain anonymous irks me too. Good luck."

My best answer to people expressing this personal concern was that little was known about marijuana dependence, that most experts in the field believed pot was not physically addictive, but that it was possible for heavy users to become psychologically dependent. Often, the questioners were surprised at that answer, having thought pot addiction was simply a myth contrived by drug abuse zealots. Then discovering first hand that their use had become compulsive was confusing.

In 1977 when the question came up, there were no research findings on how to effectively treat dependence on this drug. Seven years later, having heard so many anecdotal reports while delivering talks around the state, I first applied for federal funds to conduct just such a study. Designing and testing marijuana dependence counseling approaches then became a major focus of my academic career for decades to come.

Before that could happen, however, I would come to a fork in the road and have to decide which way to turn. In 1974 and in the several years that followed, I got high increasingly often, so often that I began to negotiate with myself about limits. Only on the weekends, I'd tell myself, and then the definition of weekend became hazy. Not while needing to prepare a lecture or grade student assignments I'd say, until short-cuts and rationalizations eroded that rule as well. Never daily, I'd resolve, until crossing that line happened once, then again, and yet again.

That letter from the wife of a compulsive pot smoker could have touched a nerve, prompting me to take stock of the similarities in what her husband and I were doing, kindling a sensitivity to how that woman's frustration might in fact be what Cheryl was experiencing. But this writer's message never hit home for me. I worked at keeping my defensive shield engaged.

I didn't want to acknowledge that the road ahead was divided. Needing to quit and yet not doing so wasn't at all compatible with how I saw myself—a university professor whose ideals about justice were the foundation for his advocacy.

Perhaps that image was still accurate. But, as I was slow to admit, just as had been the case in the one-sided *Spokesman-Review* article about the Olympia legislative hearing, there was much more to the story.

26

ART LINKLETTER'S ADVICE

spent several days each week lobbying in Olympia, keeping track of legislators who intended to vote "yes" and those who were unalterably opposed. While I felt disappointed when someone said they'd be voting against passage, most were courteous when letting me know where they stood. Some even acknowledged they believed decriminalization made sense, but that voters in their district would toss them out of office if they voted in favor. I appreciated their honesty.

My meeting with a long-term legislator from eastern Washington was a memorable exception. Based on his voting record, I expected he'd be against the bill, but wasn't at all prepared for how he'd let me know just how strongly he felt. Less than a minute after entering his office, handing him a summary of the bill's provisions, and beginning my lobbying spiel, without speaking a word he tore up the summary, dropped it into his wastebasket, pointed to the door, and turned his attention to some document on his desk. I stood there for a moment, astonished that a state senator would act in such a rude manner. My audience had ended, though, and as I later learned from other lobbyists far more experienced than I, he had been relatively mild with me. Nevertheless, that unspoken rebuke stung.

The "undecided" legislators were the biggest challenge. When told that they hadn't yet made a decision on the bill, I asked if they had specific concerns, hoping that I might be able to pull together some information that might turn them around. I also had learned that the most successful lobbyists knew a great deal about who listened to whom. Mickie Pailthorp, the ACLU lobbyist, often had insider information about who might be able to influence someone still on the fence about decriminalization. I'd then ask that proponent to pass along a favorable word to their colleague. Sometimes it worked.

As the weeks passed, passage looked promising in the House, but it would be a closer call in the Senate where there'd be considerable opposition. Yet another formidable challenge would be Governor Dixie Lee Ray. Both during the campaign and as Governor-Elect, she had responded to questions about marijuana laws indicating that she supported lowered penalties. Now, however, she was expressing reservations. In a talk to a community group, she said, "I'm not saying all drug addicts begin by smoking marijuana, but a significant number admit they started with marijuana and it soon became insufficient to satisfy their craving. Making it a small thing such as a parking ticket—sorry, that's no way to control it."

The Governor had been trained as a scientist, so presumably she could be convinced with data that "the stepping stone hypothesis," the notion pot users are somehow compelled to graduate to using harder drugs, was false. But she was also a politician, and I suspected her apparent backsliding on decriminalization was based more on political considerations than science.

I began to realize that winning over opponents would take more than research findings, logical arguments, statements by experts, and editorial endorsements. Even favorable public opinion polls would have a limited effect in bringing converts to our side.

There had been a sea change during the 1970s in how decriminalization was perceived, and the active support of parents was going to be vital if this bill were to become law. When the decriminalization movement began in the late 1960s, the plight of adults who had been imprisoned, some for decades, for possessing small amounts of pot raised a compelling question about proportionality. The key rationale for decriminalization in the 1960s was that excessively punitive penalties violated civil liberties.

By the mid-1970s, however, marijuana use had increased dramatically among young people, head shops had proliferated, and magazines such as *High Times* clearly promoted getting high. When decriminalization was argued, concerns about adult civil liberties were shunted aside by many in the public. Now the key issue was protecting youth. Therefore, parents' voices needed to be heard, and those voices needed to argue that decriminalization would indeed protect, rather than harm, their children.

It occurred to me that one highly popular entertainer, if he could be persuaded to support the bill, would have enormous credibility as a spokesman for parents. Art Linkletter, the much-loved host from 1952 to 1970 of the television program *House Party*, was best known for his hilarious interviews with children, many of which would undoubtedly be YouTube sensations today.

Linkletter's credibility would be all the greater because of his having had a major change of attitude concerning drug laws. In the years just after his 20-year-old daughter, Diane, committed suicide in 1969 by jumping out of her sixth floor kitchen window, he had adamantly opposed any thought of leniency for drug users. He believed her suicide was caused by an LSD flashback. But in a 1975 article in *Good Housekeeping* magazine, he wrote that prevention first and foremost requires open and honest communication between parents and children. Decriminalization now made sense to him.

I knew he had recently spoken in California and Ohio in favor of legislation similar to our bill. Might he come to Washington for the same purpose? I put a letter in the mail to his Beverly Hills office, guessing that the chance of his responding was highly unlikely. To my great surprise, however, he not only responded but also said he'd be coming through Seattle on March 28th on his way to Aberdeen where he'd give a talk the following day. While his schedule would be tight, he was open to meeting with me. When I asked if he'd hold a press conference at Sea-Tac Airport just after his arrival in order to support our proposed law, he agreed.

Along with a small entourage of airport security and public relations personnel, I awaited his arrival at a Western Airlines gate. He was the first passenger off the plane, and as we shook hands, he was as warm and enthusiastic as his TV persona. A number of people in the terminal called to him or applauded as we walked to the airport's small press room.

Before taking questions from the half dozen reporters in the room, he said a few words about his family's personal tragedy. "I was introduced, as you know, to the drug scene in a very violent and agonizing way when my daughter took her life some seven or eight years ago while experimenting with LSD. I was just an average middle-American as far as drug abuse was concerned, knew nothing more about it than most people, and launched out into a series of lectures in which I made a lot of statements that I later regretted."

A reporter asked why he had changed his mind. Linkletter said, "I spent a lot of time with kids who were smoking pot. I didn't read about it from some clinical viewpoint, or some statistical angle. I went out and was with the kids. . . . They thought that the tremendous criminal sanction of a felony against pot was a most unfair thing and helped to promote the so-called generation gap. . . . And to send a kid to jail and cause him to be a felon, it didn't make sense, and so the kids didn't buy it. So in spite of the fact that they all knew what the laws were and the arrests were mounting up into the hundreds, and hundreds of thousands across the country, and doubling almost every year, they went right ahead and tried pot because they didn't believe what they were hearing. So, I thought, if that was happening, which brought about a disregard for law, they didn't believe anything we said. If we said these things about pot, then they didn't believe what we said about heroin. And I changed."

Just as the news conference was winding down, Andy Reynolds, a reporter for KING-TV, stage whispered, "It's not only kids that say the darndest things." The rest of us laughed and one of his colleagues retorted, "I bet you've waited all night to say that."

I felt like jumping up and down with excitement. I'd make sure that Governor Ray and all of those in the Legislature who were opposed or undecided received clippings about this event. Maybe, just maybe, this would be the year in which decriminalization would be enacted.

It was getting late and after a few more questions, the press conference ended. I then drove him to Aberdeen where he'd speak the next day. Along the way, we talked about the risks of being seen as pro-drug when advocating reduced penalties.

"You've boosted our chances in the Legislature," I said, "but I want to thank you for giving me something that's personal."

"Tell me about it."

"Well, while lobbying for this bill, I've sometimes met with some pretty cynical reactions. One representative got really angry with me, demanding to know why I wasn't in the classroom since that was what I was being paid by the taxpayers to do. In a committee hearing, another legislator said I was a lousy role model for young people. And every once in a while I'll get mail that's about as hateful as you can imagine, writers telling me that I'm destroying their children's future. Sometimes I wonder if I'm doing the right thing."

"Roger, you're not ever going to make everyone happy. You're sticking your neck out for a controversial issue. You know, a few years ago, I might have written a letter like that to you, and it wouldn't have been nearly so nice."

We both laughed, and I told him how his having held this press conference boosted my resolve. "You hit the nail on the head by saying excessive punishments undermine the credibility of parents, teachers, and scientists. Kids stop listening. You gave me a needed reminder about why this is important."

"It took me a long time to recognize how wrong I was," he replied. "You know, some parents get so frightened by drugs that they banish the topic, refusing to talk with their kids, just laying down the law and assuming that's all that's needed. Some pay a horrible price when a child experiences a crisis, sees no way out, and commits suicide."

He looked out at the passing scenery and we drove in silence for a few miles. "Since Diane's death, I've flown all over the country to spend time with some of those parents, people whose souls are in torment because they've lost a child. I've not wanted to talk about it publicly, but it's the most important work I've ever done."

I had continued to grapple with doubts and disappointments while lobbying for the bill since my talk with Sister Kathleen five months before. That night, however, I couldn't have felt clearer about the value of this effort.

27

FINAL PASSAGE

WASHINGTON STATE LEGISLATURE
WINTER/SPRING 1977

The Marijuana Education and Control Act of 1977 was introduced as HB 257 in the House on January 17th, and as SB 2330 in the Senate on January 27th. In both chambers, the bills were referred to the Judiciary Committees and it was at that point that we faced our first major hurdle. Would the chairpersons schedule public hearings? It was not at all uncommon for a bill to languish in obscurity, never even being discussed, because a committee chairman chose to kill it.

There would be no sudden death, at least not yet. As January 27 approached, the date when the House bill would have its first committee hearing, our team was at full throttle with daily commutes to Olympia to lobby individual legislators and strategize with the primary sponsors. During this period, we lined up people to testify, continued to present talks about the bill to community groups around the state, and occasionally drafted correspondence for members who sought our help in replying to criticisms from constituents.

It was an intensely invigorating experience, at times like a spine-tingling ride on a roller coaster. A legislator would tell me he or she intended to vote "aye," or an endorsement would be announced, or a key person would agree to testify in favor at a hearing and I'd feel the thrill of a contest we'd surely win. An unfavorable editorial would be published, a legislator would chastise me for not doing my job by staying in the classroom, or I'd learn that an amendment was going to be introduced to gut the bill of its most important provisions and my optimism would plummet. Surely, we were going to lose.

Alan Thompson did his best to be a leveling influence, reminding me that twists and turns were inevitable. At times, I could take to heart his advice to calm down, to not let each mini-defeat become demoralizing. At other times, the wisdom of that guidance eluded me and it was a bumpy ride.

It became evident that many of the same issues brought up in testimony four years earlier at Representative Kelley's hearing were still very much on the minds of people who opposed decriminalization. Some claimed that replacing a misdemeanor penalty with a civil fine would send the wrong message, particularly to young people. Others believed marijuana's harmful effects argued against softening the penalties. And others warned law enforcement would still be hobbled by this new policy which would not necessarily allow them to devote more attention and resources to other more serious crimes.

One of the most persistent opponents was Representative Claude Oliver, a 31-year-old first term Republican representative from Kennewick, a city in the southeastern and traditionally more conservative part of the state. Rep. Oliver tried repeatedly to derail the bill, at one point moving for indefinite postponement. When it seemed that the bill would not die, he moved to lower the amount to be covered by the civil violation category from 28 grams to five. None of his efforts succeeded. Then, on the day when the House took up the bill for third reading, he put a fake joint on each House member's desk, claiming nonsensically that because dealers cut marijuana with other materials, many pounds of pot could be covered by the 28 gram limit.

I let his claws sink into me, feeling angered by his largely bogus claims and even resenting the sound of his voice as he fired volleys of buckshot at the bill's provisions. He and I were both in our thirties, but as I watched him sarcastically swat every which way at the bill, I felt just as I had when watching a scuffle during junior high school, taunts and all. I don't believe he helped his cause, as surely I was not the only one to see through his ruse, but nevertheless I could feel him getting under my skin.

At times during the debates the mood in the room became somber as people told of personal tragedies. Susan Roylance said that her brother had been a pot smoker and was killed in a car crash after falling asleep at the wheel. Brent Ebinger, the ex-addict whom the Spokane Chamber of Commerce members heard me speak of, pleaded that pot use leads to an "I don't care" attitude that ultimately wrecks young people's lives. A woman testified that two of her son's friends used marijuana and subsequently died in accidents. Representative Alex Deccio told of a near-accident of a school bus on which his daughters were riding. It was later learned that the driver—and the students—had unknowingly eaten marijuana-laced brownies.

Listening to these individuals brought to mind the turmoil my family had experienced as my brother, Bryan, became deeply drug involved. I believed decriminalization was the right answer to undo injustices in our drug policies and the collateral damage criminalization and incarceration caused. But what then were the answers for people like my brother who dug themselves into deep holes by misusing drugs? I didn't have an answer, and it was a question that would continue to bother me for years to come.

The stories of personal misfortunate were compelling. I suspected that if the bill failed, it would not be for want of expert testimonials, endorsements, data from Seattle or the eight states that had passed similar legislation, or favorable public opinion poll data. If the bill failed, the fears evoked from these very personal accounts would have carried the day. I was by no means alone in having a loved one whose drug experiences frightened me.

When the House Judiciary Committee voted seven to two in favor of recommending passage by the House, I was elated. We had overcome numerous hurdles in the Committee and our tally of how members planned to vote made it evident that succeeding in the House of Representatives was possible. It would be close, but there was every reason to not give up.

Then on March 31, when the bill was up for third reading and final passage, I watched as the momentum that had been building from all of our earlier successes came to a crashing halt. As the last few lights turned on in the "aye" and "nay" columns on the electronic tote board, I was stunned. Forty-six had voted in favor, forty-seven opposed, and five members were absent. We had lost, and Alan Thompson had inexplicably joined those who had voted "no."

In our projections, we had concluded the bill would narrowly pass, but we had failed to consider the possibility that some members whose votes we were counting on might not be present. What a mistake. Five members were absent that day and every one of these individuals had said they would vote for our bill.

My great disappointment was compounded by my ignorance of parliamentary procedure. A moment after the vote count was announced, I saw Alan walking toward the cloak room just off the House floor where I had been watching the proceedings. The smile on his face utterly confused me. I was relieved when he explained that in order to move for reconsideration, he had to have voted on the prevailing side. His changed vote from "aye" to "nay" had preserved his right to make sure the bill could be brought back for another vote.

So it wasn't over yet. But one issue was very clear. We'd need to account for each supportive representative's whereabouts every day in order to be assured that Alan did not move for reconsideration until everyone whom we were counting on to vote "aye" was present.

It took four days. On Wednesday, April 6th, he made the motion and demanded an oral roll call vote.

I tallied the "aye" and "nay" votes as the roll call progressed, trying to focus both on the cumulative totals and whether each legislator was voting as we had predicted. It was more than I could handle. In a few moments, before I was able to add the numbers, hearing applause from the public gallery made it clear we had won. Fifty-two "ayes," 43 "nays," and three people absent.

Alan once again walked over to where I was standing along with several steering committee members. He shook our hands and congratulated us for the roles we had played in achieving this success. Mickie and Frank were effusive in thanking him for his leadership.

For the moment, I hung back. I was speechless.

—⁂—

The Senate was next and, as it turned out, passage of the bill in the House was a game changer in another important way. The chairman of the Senate Judiciary Committee had decided to not bring the bill up for a vote. For all intents and purposes, SB 2330, the version introduced by Senator Goltz, was dead. But when the House passed the amended HB 257 and sent it to the Senate, the assignment bypassed the Judiciary Committee entirely. Alan Thompson's bill went to the Social and Health Services Committee.

Once again, the possibility of decriminalizing possession had been rescued from what otherwise would have been a dead end. When Alan had tried to prepare me for the many twists and turns that can occur during the legislative process, I guess this type of maneuver was an example of what he had in mind. I never learned how the decision to bypass Judiciary was made, but suspected Sen. Goltz had had a quiet conversation with the Senate President.

My NORML colleagues and I worked the members of the Senate every bit as diligently as we had worked the members of the House. Our informal tally of how senators were inclined to vote made it evident that we faced an uphill battle. Too many said they'd definitely vote against the bill or were tentatively planning to do so.

However, the "do pass" vote by a majority of the members of the Social and Health Services Committee gave us hope that the bill might also succeed in that chamber. A number of senators would speak forcefully in favor of passage during floor debate.

First, however, there was another obstacle to overcome. The bill would not come to the floor unless the Senate Rules Committee voted to move it ahead. Fifteen senators sat on that Committee and in our informal tally only four were strongly in support. Eleven members were either solidly against the bill or undecided. The bill was again at serious risk of being stopped in its tracks.

Over time it became evident we were truly at the end of the road. We'd not get the majority vote in Rules. A very long game of chess had been played and there were no moves left to be made.

We wondered why the end came in the Rules Committee. Had Governor Ray's negativity toward the bill in her press interviews worked against us? It was well known that her relationship with many in the Legislature was highly contentious, yet might a likely veto have dampened the willingness of some to expend political capital by voting in favor of our controversial measure?

All the questions I had couldn't prevent the inevitable, though. It was over. Before I could get too discouraged, however, Keith Stroup reminded me that in the long run, bills such as ours succeeded only after a series of tries. In his view, we were much more likely to win passage next time because of how far we had come before further movement was stymied.

We'd gear up for another full court press in the 1979 session, I thought, skipping the 1978 short session when state budget issues would likely push aside most other business. It might take two more years, but removing criminal penalties for marijuana possession was still achievable in the near future, and perhaps over the next two years, the social taboo of marijuana would lessen even more for some of the more conservative members. But it was not to be.

28

TOPPLING DOMINOES

**HYATT REGENCY HOTEL, WASHINGTON, D.C.
DECEMBER 1977**

The half-eaten lemon meringue pie landed harmlessly on the Hyatt Regency Hotel ballroom dais. Out of a corner of my eye I had noticed a heavy-set bearded man walking briskly up the aisle and then breaking into a jog as he closed in on the speakers' platform. Six hundred of us in the audience, most undoubtedly as confused as I was, then saw him suddenly hurl his gooey missile toward the man at the lectern. His aim was off, however, that fateful Sunday afternoon in early December of 1977.

The pie assassination had failed, yet less than a year later, like the tipping over of the first tile of a phalanx of dominoes poised to challenge a world record, the tossing of that $3 pie was the opening salvo in a string of linked events that brought to their knees both NORML and the marijuana reform movement.

At the pinnacle of its influence, NORML had thousands of dues-paying members and a slew of volunteers in active chapters throughout the country. At the organization's annual conference held each December in Washington, D.C., hundreds of policy advocates received chapter-building and lobbying training in an array of skill-building workshops. Another set of seminars offered training to attorneys on strategies in defending clients charged with marijuana offenses.

It seemed incongruous to me that NORML's annual meeting could be held at a major conference hotel, more generally the venue for conventions of business and industrial groups as well as legal and medical associations. Both day and night, the whiff of pot was pervasive in the hallways on the upper story hotel room floors. Security staff had clearly been told to "stand down," a rather unique example I thought of special accommodations.

National and international reform leaders fueled our enthusiasm in the conference plenary sessions. *Yes, the day will soon come when no one will go to jail for smoking a joint. Look to the Netherlands for an example of a rational and humane marijuana policy. Keep the pressure on your state legislators and governors, making sure they know that Ann Landers, Art Linkletter, the Shafer Commission, President Carter, the American Bar Association, and a host of other luminaries and professional organizations endorse decriminalization. It's only a matter of time before they'll see the light. Perhaps your state will be the next to fall in line!* The optimism about succeeding was palpable. I was part of a rapidly growing movement and felt carried along by the swell of contagion in the conference hall.

By then, eleven states had decriminalized pot possession, and several more were expected to soon follow suit. Keith Stroup, NORML's founder and leader, counted dozens of Congressional and White House staffers, a number of leading scientists specializing in cannabis research, and numerous elected and appointed high-ranking government officials as both professional colleagues and friends. NORML had clout.

That political influence, however, virtually dried up as an inside-the-beltway soap opera unfolded involving cocaine snorting and dope smoking by lobbyists, politicos, and journalists at NORML's annual party a few blocks from the Capitol, a pernicious leak to a nationally syndicated columnist, a rebuke of NORML's leader by the White House, and the defaming and eventual forced resignation of a senior member of the president's staff. By that drama's final curtain, I and several other state volunteers had resigned from NORML, its director had been censured and would soon depart the organization he had founded, and the formerly open doors of official Washington had slammed shut to advocates for marijuana policy reform.

The beginning of the movement's unraveling, Act 1 in this play, occurred in the Sierra Madre of Mexico in 1975. There, peasant farmers who grew pot had been enjoying a healthy boost in their $200 average annual incomes. Some were now bringing home as much as $5,000. Now, they suddenly faced a dire threat to their livelihoods. Mexican drug enforcement agents, flying American-supplied blue and white Bell & Howell 206B helicopters, had begun spraying marijuana fields with a pesticide known as paraquat. Three days of exposure to the sun caused a chemical reaction with the leaves' surfaces, removing all moisture, turning the leaves yellow, and destroying the crop.

The campesinos, however, quickly devised a solution to their problem. Within minutes after the helicopters left, they harvested the plants and immediately shielded the produce from the sun, thereby stopping the catalytic process. Then the contaminated leaves and buds were mixed into the approximately three to five thousand tons of Mexican pot smuggled each year into the U.S.

The possible consequences of all this were alarming. Ingesting as little as one-tenth of an ounce of liquid paraquat would be lethal to humans. But would smoking pot that had been sprayed endanger the user's health? Might we end up with thousands of dead or seriously injured marijuana users? Although this supply eradication effort was being conducted by Mexicans, the U.S. was funding the operation. Should that funding be immediately halted, at least until more could be learned about the risks? In early 1978, three years after the paraquat spraying had begun, those questions landed squarely on the desk of President Jimmy Carter's Special Advisor on Health Issues, a psychiatrist by the name of Peter Bourne.

Bourne found himself being pressured by several competing constituencies. Keith Stroup, NORML's Director, called for an immediate cessation of all U.S. funding of paraquat spraying. Diametrically opposed were a number of senior federal law enforcement officials. In their opinion, no efforts were warranted to protect the health of marijuana smokers since they were violating the law by using the drug.

Bourne was also very much aware of President Carter's views about the eradication program. Preventing drug abuse by stemming the supply was one objective. Another was addressing the destabilizing impact on the governments of Mexico, Colombia, and other countries where the underground drug economy was contributing to massive corruption and the rise of cartels. President Carter, despite his support for decriminalizing marijuana possession in small amounts, would not easily be swayed to lessen his administration's commitment to stop illicit drugs from entering the U.S.

Then there was the rapidly growing anti-drug parents' movement called Families in Action. With its roots in Carter's home state of Georgia, its leaders mobilized to turn around the increasing rate of drug experimentation by children and adolescents. They first set their sights on curbing the proliferating drug paraphernalia sales industry. Those involved in the movement would have reacted strongly had the Carter administration backed down in its international drug control policies. Clearly, there would have been a political cost.

Finally, Bourne had his own medical ethics to consider. He realized that if smoking tainted pot caused damage to the user's lungs, some might claim that the harm, however inadvertent as a consequence of paraquat spraying, was iatrogenic. *Primum non nocere* is a key ethical standard in the Hippocratic Oath. First, do no harm.

I had come to know something of his philosophy several years earlier in the summer of 1974. At the time, he was deputy in charge of treatment programs in the Nixon administration's newly established White House Special Action Office for Drug Abuse Prevention. Marilyn Dexheimer, a friend I had known since our days as undergraduates at Boston University, headed SAODAP's congressional liaison staff. The two of them flew out to the University of Washington to present at a drug policy conference I had organized.

The conference ended mid-day and before they returned to the capitol, the three of us went for a sail on Puget Sound. A brisk wind filled the sails of *Aquarius*, our Norwegian double-ender cutter, and the snow-capped Olympic Mountains, Mt. Rainier, and the city's skyline were picture postcard perfect. We zipped smartly along, Dex and Peter taking turns at the helm.

The boat heeled way over as the sails caught a large gust of wind and Dex shouted "Yahoo," holding firmly to the tiller, her long hair a nautical weather vane. "This is almost as good as galloping across a meadow on Tequila. Not quite, but close."

Peter looked over at me, smiling, and I winked. We knew full well that few if any creatures in Marilyn's life, human or otherwise, could challenge the preeminent status held by her cherished palomino.

For the next few minutes, no one spoke. The sound of the boat's hull racing through the waves offered a musical interlude in our conversation, a pause abruptly interrupted by an unexpected laugh from Peter. For the moment, despite our questioning looks, he kept the reason to himself. Then he let us in on it.

"Roger, Marilyn told me about your Vietnam tour in 1967. Did you know that I was there a year before you?

I hadn't known. Had he gone over as a division psychiatrist or as a member of an evacuation hospital psychiatric team, I asked. Neither was the case.

"No, actually I was a pee collector." He waited, enjoying my look of puzzlement.

"Okay, let me be a bit less mysterious," he said. "I went over as a member of a Walter Reed Army Institute of Research team that conducted studies on the biology of stress, and we did that by analyzing urine samples. I laughed a moment ago because it suddenly occurred to me that this afternoon's sail has been the most stress-free experience I've had for a very long time indeed."

"It's therapeutic, isn't it," I said. "Do you suppose it's biochemical? That as the land recedes, leaving behind all of one's responsibilities and anxieties, the open sea beckons where there's only a horizon and whatever lies beyond, and that the sailor experiences this as a dose of imaginary Valium?"

"Precisely," he exclaimed. "It's all about brain chemistry. Our research in Vietnam explored what happens in the soldier's brain while facing an imminent attack."

Peter told us about cortisol, a hormone released by the adrenal gland in response to stress, and about a compound called 17-hydroxycorticosteroid, or 17-OHCS, that is produced by the liver to break down cortisol. By measuring the 17-OHCS level in the urine, it's possible to determine how much cortisol has been released: in other words, how stressed the individual has been.

"We wanted to know what happens biologically when soldiers are chronically exposed to high levels of danger," he said. "To answer that question, an enlisted technician and I lived for three months with a 12-member Green Beret team in an isolated camp near the Cambodian border. We were in Viet Cong-controlled territory, by the way. The team's mission was to monitor the flow of Viet Cong from the Ho Chi Minh Trail into the Central Highlands."

"I'm trying to picture this, Peter, but it strains my imagination," I said. "You got these troops to pee into cups while in that setting? While facing the possibility of attack at any time? How did you possibly get them to cooperate?"

Dex laughed, adding, "You must have kept the key to the beer supply to get them to go along."

"Actually, Marilyn, getting the troops to agree was easy," he said. "The really hard part was getting permission to do the study from the brass in Saigon. While I was fighting that prolonged battle with the bureaucracy, I analyzed samples of my own urine and, not unexpectedly, my 17-OHCS values were sky high."

We roared. "I can imagine what those fellows wrote home to their families," she said. I blurted out, "Just one more reason for referring to that region as the Golden Triangle."

Peter shrugged, saying something about how this study seemed to inspire people to make pee jokes. He told us of his surprise in finding that the enlisted men in this unit had very low 17-OHCS values, even when they had been alerted that an attack was imminent. He concluded that their tight cohesion as a unit gave them an enormous sense of group support, with a corresponding lowering of stress.

I asked if he thought of his current work in drug abuse as detouring him from a research area for which he obviously had passionate interest. To the contrary, he replied. He saw a direct connection. Many people who use illicit drugs, he said, even more so those who use them chronically, are likely self-medicating for high stress whether or not they think of it that way.

The key to drug abuse prevention, he said, was to prevent the progression of emotional distress as early as possible. He also strongly believed in preventing the induction of new drug users by those who are experienced by making treatment for current users immediately available when and where they want it.

Peter reminded me of LTC Lloyd, the psychiatrist in the Army Surgeon General's Office who got me out of hot water. He, too, was far more interested in understanding the human needs drug use served, why some people felt drawn to them and not others, and far less in relying on punishment as a universal deterrent.

Might Peter be interested in an academic appointment? I wondered. The directorship of the University's Alcohol and Drug Abuse Institute would soon be vacant, and I thought he'd be an ideal candidate. He let me know though that he hoped to be headed in a different direction. Governor Jimmy Carter, for whom Peter had set up a state-wide drug treatment program, was now thinking about making a run for the presidency. Peter was encouraging Carter to do so, and if Carter ran, Peter would work on the campaign.

Knowing that he favored a public health approach to substance abuse and removing criminal penalties from pot possession, I had the sense that the University's loss would be the country's gain. Were Carter to be elected, Bourne would likely shift the focus of national drug policy in a new direction, one that I heartily believed in.

In early 1978, several years after our idyllic sail, Bourne was on President Carter's staff and faced the paraquat dilemma. It heated up immeasurably when two events occurred just days apart. First, Secretary of Health and Human Services Joseph Califano, a long-time anti-smoking crusader, issued a warning to pot smokers that irreversible lung damage might occur if an individual smoked three to five contaminated joints a day for several months. Second, NORML filed suit seeking a court order for the government to conduct an environmental impact study of paraquat's effects, both to the smokers of pot and the farmers whose crops were sprayed. NORML also asked for an injunction that would immediately stop U.S. funding to Mexico for paraquat spraying.

Bourne, taking a more conservative course than Keith Stroup had demanded, decided to commission two studies. One would approximate how much contaminated pot was getting into the U.S. and the other would find out if Califano's warning was indeed accurate.

In the meantime, media coverage of the possible risks had users in a panic. Toxicology labs in various parts of the country were swamped with requests to analyze samples. In Washington State, however, no labs were offering this service. Moreover, two of the three local television stations, when covering the story, refused to provide viewers with the name and address of a lab in California that was accepting mailed samples for analysis.

I was concerned, and this threw me into a new focus. The urgent issue now was saving marijuana smokers from the dangers of toxins.

Might a local lab be interested in filling the gap in our state? I found myself at the door of Dr. Vidmantas Raisys, a University faculty member who both directed the clinical laboratories at Harborview Hospital, a medical center affiliated with the University, and served as Washington State Toxicologist.

Dr. Raisys' small office was lined with shelves crammed with journals, piles of manuscripts, and a good many books. He wore a jacket and tie, was clean-shaven, and had a conservative haircut.

That environment, so much about clinical science rather than hot political issues, was formidable. What would his reaction be, I wondered, to the request I was about to make?

I approached our meeting with some trepidation. It seemed all too easy to vilify marijuana smokers based on a stereotyped image of them as irresponsible, flaunting a disregard for the law, and enjoying lifestyles that made no contribution to the community. I often had heard that perspective expressed when debating the merits of decriminalization and it was troubling. I'd soon learn whether these views would greet me in the State Toxicologist's lab.

"I'm here to ask for your help, Dr. Raisys. I've been lobbying to change the marijuana possession law. Just recently, quite a few people in the state have become alarmed about paraquat poisoning. I think there's a potential public health emergency here." I stopped, wondering what would follow.

He had heard about the issue, and picked up a newsletter from his desk. "I know a little bit about this," he said. "Let me read something to you." He looked through the newsletter and found the item he had been seeking. "Here it is. 'The PharmChem Research Foundation in Palo Alto has already processed 5,000 samples. Just to keep up with the demand, they've hired twenty-two new employees.' By the way, Professor Roffman, they reported last week that 28% of their samples were positive for paraquat."

He looked at me with a troubled expression as he read this item, but I wondered if that indicated he found the whole matter distasteful. Or could it mean he believed the health risk potential was a valid concern? I got right to the point.

"Might the State Toxicology Lab help determine how big of a problem this is locally?" I asked. "Could your lab test samples from around the state?" I held my breath, half expecting this meeting was about to end.

"No, I'm afraid we couldn't do that. The law is quite clear that the Toxicology Lab can only function on behalf of medical examiners, coroners, and law enforcement agencies."

He saw the look of disappointment on my face and took a few moments to ponder the issue. I was about to ask if he might refer me to a local lab in the private sector when he surprised me with a question.

"Look, Roger, help me to understand how this might work. How would you obtain marijuana samples?"

"Well, I've got a mailing list of several hundred NORML supporters from many parts of the state. I could publicize the need for samples and instruct people to send them anonymously to the NORML post office box with a serial number from a dollar bill as an identification code. I could also give them my phone number to call in order to find out the test results."

"Wouldn't you be taking a big risk here?" he asked. "I mean, what if you were caught with marijuana when you removed the mail from your box?"

I wasn't sure where he was headed with these questions, but it was much better continuing the discussion than the alternative. I hoped he'd perceive my answers as reasonable.

"I'm sure you're right," I replied, "but I think I'd be able to offer a compelling defense if I were arrested by explaining the purpose in what I was doing. My wife and I have talked about it and we both think it's a risk worth taking." He looked away and was quiet for a few more moments and then took a risk of his own.

"Okay, Roger. I'll do the testing, but it'll be entirely separate from the official work of either the Toxicology Lab or Harborview Hospital. I'll run the tests myself." He paused for another moment, glanced out the window, and muttered to himself, "I'll need to find someplace to store the marijuana and decide how to dispose of it after testing."

He seemed to come to some conclusions about these issues and then looked over at me, smiling as he watched me exhale. "If you and your wife are willing to go down this road, I guess I can meet you part way. In my mind, the lung damage that these young people might experience would be quite unfortunate. Let's see if we can't do something to prevent that."

I was touched by his willingness to put others' welfare ahead of his own. Over the years, I had met many people who made such a choice, and they were inspiring.

Within a month of our meeting Dr. Raisys had analyzed 35 samples users had sent to the NORML post office box. Only three of the 35 were positive for paraquat. I wasn't sure whether to feel relieved or alarmed because there was no way of knowing if those 35 samples were representative of all pot being smoked in the state. At least we now knew some of it was tainted.

At the national level, the fact that the U.S. was continuing to fund Mexico's spraying program in the spring of 1978 angered Keith Stroup. As he saw it, Peter Bourne, an official who was supportive of marijuana decriminalization and had the power to set things right, now was the enemy. Despite their close relationship, Keith obsessed about Bourne's failing to aggressively move to stop endangering pot smokers' lungs. Before long, Keith's vendetta with Bourne about the government's support for paraquat spraying spurred the demise of NORML and the reform movement.

—⁂—

As the curtain rose on Act Two in this drama, that lemon meringue pie was sailing toward a speaker at the annual NORML conference in December of 1977. The target was Joe Nellis, Chief Counsel of the House Select Committee on Narcotics Abuse and Control. He was one of several Congressional and White House officials comprising a panel on international marijuana control policies.

Nellis was not being well received by this audience. He had asserted that the U.S. was obligated to keep marijuana illegal because we were a signatory to the 1961 Single Convention, a treaty which, in Nellis' opinion, trumped local, state, or even federal laws. Moreover, he believed that de facto decriminalization, in other words officials choosing to not enforce marijuana possession laws still on the books, was a treaty violation. A number of people shouted their disapproval and several others lined up at the floor microphones to take him on.

And then the pie was thrown and chaos ensued.

The thrower was a member of the Youth International Party, radical anarchists better known as the Yippies, and his name was Aaron Kaye. As his pie headed toward them, the panel members scurried to avoid its path and in the process knocked over a pitcher of water, some of which splashed on Nellis. In the midst of this disruption, Marc Kurzman, a University of Minnesota professor serving as chairman of this year's NORML conference, dropped a bombshell. He took the microphone, denounced Keith Stroup, NORML's director, for having paid for the pie and encouraging this assault, and apologized to the panel members and the audience. At that point, several people began shouting their disapproval of Kurzman and it felt as if the Yippie Party's purpose of promoting anarchy was being achieved.

Later that afternoon I learned from Marc more of what had happened. He had heard prior to the international policy panel that Kaye was itching to pie someone. Keith had told Kaye that Joe Nellis was no friend of the movement, so Kaye had his target. But he didn't have any cash and hit Keith up for the cost of a pie. When Kurzman got wind of the plan, he sought out Kaye and thought he had dissuaded him from carrying out this prank. Indeed, Kaye had decided to call it off. But when Nellis began to get heckled by the audience, Kaye locked and loaded. He decided he'd do his part to express the audience's anger at Nellis.

This incident, I thought, was a serious blot on NORML's credibility as well as my own as a state NORML coordinator. I felt particularly discouraged because Nellis was there at my suggestion. I had met him several years earlier at a Seattle drug policy conference and he had had dinner with Cheryl and me in our home. I knew he didn't favor decriminalizing pot, but hoped his coming to the conference and having a dialogue with those who felt differently might make a difference in how he thought. That hope, needless to say, turned out to be a nonstarter.

I wrote to Nellis expressing my regret about the incident. He replied, saying, "I sincerely hope that the moderates and those who see the necessity for working within the system will henceforth repudiate street tactics since, if these are continued, no responsible member of government will risk embarrassment by being seen with anyone from NORML."

In the several weeks following the conference, tensions rose within NORML's leadership. Several were calling for Keith to step down as director. Strain also became evident between NORML and the White House. Bob Angarola, one of the members of the panel Nellis was on, served as General Counsel for the White House Office of Drug Abuse Policy. He wrote a letter of admonition to Keith:

> There is no doubt in my mind that the marihuana reform movement has matured over the last six or seven years, largely because of your own patient and able leadership. The gains registered and the support received were in great measure a function of your work in obtaining for NORML the credibility it deserved. I was

therefore upset to learn that its National Director condoned, and in a sense encouraged, such an irresponsible act against one of the organization's invitees. This can only prove counterproductive to your and NORML's most worthwhile efforts. It also must call into question the advisability of participating in future conferences which you sponsor.

Keith fumed about the letter, particularly the fact that it was printed on White House stationery and distributed to all of the other panel members. He shot back a response two days later, writing that he considered the matter trivial, but offering an apology to anyone who felt differently. He concluded with his own admonition:

I feel obliged to remind you that it is not our style, or even our personal conduct, that should be at issue; rather, it is the substantive drug policies of this country that have provided us an area of common interest and concern. While you appear preoccupied over a procedural matter, I am concerned about your apparent support for such policies as the use of highly toxic herbicides to eradicate marijuana fields in Mexico and other foreign countries. At the end of this decade, were one to look back and analyze our mistakes in an objective fashion, which do you think would be seen as the greater mistake: my involvement in the pie-throwing incident at the NORML Conference, or your involvement in and support for a program that resulted in paraquat-contaminated marijuana being smoked by young people in the United States? I would hope your sense of outrage could be redirected.

Keith took one additional step in response to having been rebuked. He let it be known that Peter Bourne needed to repudiate

Angarola's letter. If he did not, Keith would release to the press information that Peter would find damaging.

Within just a few days, Bourne obliged Keith in a letter that reaffirmed "the very high personal regard in which I hold you and the remarkable leadership that you have provided to NORML under conditions that I know have not always been easy."

What shoe was Keith threatening to drop? For that answer, we return to the annual NORML conference party, the venue for Act Three.

—⁊⁊—

Act Three: For all intents and purposes, the December 1977 NORML conference party at the elegant Stewart Mott mansion just off DuPont Circle was both a celebration and a demonstration of the organization's political chops. Mott, who inherited a fortune amassed by his father, the largest holder of General Motors stock at one time, was deeply committed to protecting constitutional rights. The party he threw for NORML was lavish, with live music, a spectacular buffet, and waiters carrying trays of both canapés and fat sinsemilla joints circulating through the packed crowd of the beautiful and the famous.

Journalists, White House and Congressional staffers, scientists, and activists hobnobbed, drinking liberally from the open bar and swapping gossip, shouting to be heard over the band's throbbing rock music. Some of the celebrities I spotted included Hunter S. Thompson, Ed Bradley, the CBS news reporter, and Christie Hefner. It was a bash.

A little after ten there was a buzz of excitement near the door. The president's drug advisor had arrived. Keith quickly escorted Peter upstairs to a fourth floor inner sanctum. What happened in that room turned out to be of historical significance.

After making certain that all in the room were committed to this event being off the record, Keith invited Peter to do a few lines of cocaine and Peter accepted. There were about ten people present, several of whom were journalists. But, once again, an agreement had been made and it would have been perceived as professionally unethical to violate the terms.

That secret most certainly would have been kept had it not been for two critical occurrences. One was Keith's increasing resentment of Peter as the paraquat problem heated up in the winter and spring of 1978. The second was an unwise decision Peter made when a White House assistant asked for his help.

The dominoes were still standing. A pie had been thrown, cocaine had been snorted, letters of rebuke and reprimand had been sent and received, a threat had been made, a conciliatory letter had been written, and the paraquat controversy had been festering.

Then the first domino toppled.

On July 20, 1978, I read the following headline in the *Seattle Times*: CARTER AIDE TAKES LEAVE TO 'CLEAR HIS NAME.' In this Associated Press story, the lead paragraph summed up the highlights:

Dr. Peter G. Bourne, the White House advisor on drug abuse, began a paid leave of absence today after conceding he wrote a prescription in a phony name for an emotionally troubled employee who wanted to keep secret that she was getting the much abused sedative Quaalude.

The story went on to explain that a druggist tried to reach Peter to ask which of two dosage levels were intended, found that the phone number on the prescription pad was out of date, and determined that the name on the prescription was not the name of the person at the counter. He called the police.

I suspect Peter would have been able to weather the storm of adverse press over the next few days. Perhaps he'd have been charged with a misdemeanor, but I believed he'd retain his White House position.

But, homing in on fresh blood, one of the reporters who had been at that NORML party, although not in the inner sanctum, pleaded with Keith to confirm the rumor that Peter had snorted cocaine. Keith, in an act of what I thought to be incredible hubris, responded that he would not deny the accuracy of the rumor.

Learning that he was about to be outed, Peter immediately resigned. The next morning the *Washington Post* headline read: BOURNE USED COCAINE, SAY WITNESSES.

Seven months before he signed the illegal prescription that led to his resignation from the White House yesterday, Dr. Peter G. Bourne publicly used two illegal drugs, cocaine and marijuana, at a party given for 600 people by the National Organization for the Reform of Marijuana Laws.

I felt sickened as I watched what happened to Peter, and then outraged when I became aware of the role Keith had played. In a letter to him, I wrote:

Threatening to ruin a person's career is tantamount to blackmail. Bourne had been a friend of NORML and a strong ally to many in the field of drugs and alcohol who were seeking major changes. But even if he were not as fully supportive of reform objectives as we would have liked, the tactic of disclosing his actions while a guest at a NORML party is simply poor ethics. Because of his position in

the White House, there was no question but that such a disclosure
would result in his fall. Because of the seriousness of this matter, I
urge you to consider stepping down as NORML Director.

I sent copies to NORML's Board of Directors and each of
the state coordinators. For a short while, Keith stood his ground
in defiance of the calls for his resignation. When it appeared that
he'd succeed in keeping his position, I resigned. In a letter to our
supporters in the state, I wrote that my resignation represented a
belief that until the National Director was replaced, the organization was more of a problem than a solution to those of us working
in the states for reform.

In early August, the Board formally censured Keith. A few
months later he indeed did step down.

The dominoes had fallen, the doors of official Washington had
slammed shut, and the marijuana decriminalization movement
would be dead in the water for the next thirty years. What an
incredible waste of the huge accomplishments the movement had
made, I thought. The bottom had fallen out because of the poor
choices made by an individual, not because the movement's goals
were any less desirable. I felt cheated.

Yet when one door closed, another opened.

29

16 POUNDS OF POT

A COTTAGE NEAR SEATTLE'S GREEN LAKE
WINTER 1978

The journey began gently, with a playful flute mimicking a twittering songbird while accompanied by plucked notes from a single violin. Magda stood next to the stereo, eager to introduce Cheryl and me to *Vltava*, an orchestral movement from Smetena's *Ma Vlast*. She wore a lilac-colored skirt, a blouse fringed with lace, and a loosely fitted matching cardigan. It was apparent that she was wearing a wig, and her skin had a pallid translucence that gave evidence of the illness she had been battling.

"Imagine," she instructed us, "that we're on a skiff. We're in the Bohemian Forest at the place where the waters of the Vltava River begin flowing."

As she painted the picture she wanted us to see and feel, it was evident the scene was vivid in her mind's eye. "Here the water is shallow, the stream moves slowly, and this light and sweet tune tells us that the start to our journey is unhurried and calm."

"Look over the side of the boat," she said, and at her urging, we both looked in the direction she was pointing, no longer a baseboard heater in their modest home. "You see, even the fish are not in a hurry to get anywhere."

Then the tempo began to increase, with several flutes and violins swirling in melodic dance. "Can you feel the current flowing more quickly now? Can you see the trees at the river's banks and the inland pastures passing by more quickly?" We nodded in response to Magda's expectant smile. She was clearly enjoying our company in the experience she was narrating.

Now in her 70s, Magda retained from her childhood training the fluid expressiveness of a ballet dancer. Her hands sculpted the imagery of the river's ripples and whirlpools.

Soon, the full orchestra had entered, with pounding timpani and bass drums conveying an ominous alarm. "There are rapids ahead," Magda warned. "Hold on. I don't want you to fall in." I pictured the boat beginning to buck, and in their tiny Green Lake bungalow in Seattle where Magda and Tony had lived for the past twenty-five years, we were on a virtual river adventure in a country neither of them had seen for decades.

Smetena's iconic work is deeply symbolic of Czech identity. In sharing it with us that evening, along with Magda's delicious apricot koláčky pastries and Tony's super-strong coffee, our hosts were beginning our education about their homeland. On each of our visits with them we also were learning of the grief they still felt for the fate of a country they had fled when the communists took over in the mid-1940s.

Now, in 1978, they were facing yet another catastrophic loss. Magda had been diagnosed with breast cancer, had begun chemotherapy, and feared that the severity of the treatment's side effects would be more than she could endure.

A nurse at her oncologist's office had phoned me. Would I visit with the Frics? They had a question. Might using marijuana help her endure the side effects of cancer treatment?

―᙮―

Several months earlier I began to appreciate the dilemma faced by patients urgently seeking information about marijuana. Within a short period of time, a secretary at the university, a professor, and another professor's wife—all being treated with chemotherapy—approached me independently to ask if there was any truth to the rumor that it could reduce the accompanying nausea and vomiting.

I made copies of a 1975 article published in the *New England Journal of Medicine* for each of them. Dr. Stephen Sallan had found that synthetic tetrahydrocannabinol capsules, available at that time only to FDA-approved researchers, were effective as an antiemetic. Since tetrahydrocannabinol (THC, the main psychoactive compound in marijuana) worked when administered orally in a research lab, my university colleagues wondered if the THC in marijuana joints would produce the same effect when inhaled.

They had many other questions as well. How much marijuana would be equivalent to the 15 mg. administered to Sallan's subjects? How often should marijuana be inhaled? Might it be harmful? Could it produce hallucinations? Is it addictive? What if you can't inhale? Can the THC in marijuana be extracted and then consumed in food? What about the legal risks?

There were lots of counterculture books offering guidelines for growing pot, as well as recipes for marijuana brownies, tea, and other foods. Moreover, there was a growing body of scientific literature, articles, and monographs about the drug and its effects written for researchers in the field.

None of the three people who approached me had any familiarity with either the science journals or the magazines and books written by and for drug users. Finding a publication that would tell them how to "clean a lid" or "roll a joint," much less cook a batch of marijuana-laced brownies, wouldn't have been easy. Evaluating the accuracy of the information contained in such publications would have been even harder, so I decided to help them find what they needed. My UW colleagues read a lot and asked even more questions. Subsequently, each of them smoked marijuana prior to chemo treatments with the knowledge and support of their physicians. Each found that it eased the treatment's gastrointestinal side effects.

A trickle of calls from other people came in and then the number increased. Patients, their family members, and occasionally oncology nurses contacted me to answer questions about pot's medical use. I began visiting people in their homes or hospital rooms, bringing along a brief mimeographed summary of the information I had pulled together for my university colleagues.

Many of these visits were deeply moving. A husband sitting with his wife of forty years, flickering glimpses of fear in their eyes as they invited me in, leading me to wonder if they first were struggling with making a decision about me. Was I credible, or might I be a snake oil salesman? The responsibility I had taken on felt greater than any I had held before. If I were going to do this, I would act as I'd want someone to act who visited my mother or father, were either of them to have cancer.

I experienced an emotional toll from these visits, often with patients whose desperation was palpable, and I carried the pain of their plight home with me. On some of those evenings, Cheryl simply sat with me when I returned, my arm around her neck and her head resting on my shoulder. No words. I was visiting with patients two or three evenings each week.

I had no answer, however, for one question nearly all of them asked. Then, in mid-1978, I received a most unusual phone call that resolved that very big problem.

—∿—

"I'm trying to reach the head of the NORML Washington chapter. Are you him?" the caller began without identifying himself. My first thought was that he probably had just been arrested for a marijuana offense and was hoping NORML would pay his legal costs.

I explained that he'd reached the right person, but that I was no longer the Coordinator for the NORML chapter and a replacement hadn't yet been named. I started to give him the address for the national NORML headquarters, but he cut me off.

"Um, actually I'm not really calling about that. There's something else. Uh, what I'm calling about is. . . ." He paused, and then said, "Look, can you promise me that our conversation will be kept private?"

I began to wonder if he might be in the military or perhaps in some occupation where pot smokers could face even more serious consequences if their use were made known. Fairly often, people who called me about pot let me know they were worried that my phone line might be bugged.

"Okay, I understand. You don't have to worry about your privacy with me, but if you're concerned about the phone lines, you could call me from a pay phone."

"Yeah, that's what I'm doing. All right, here's what's going on. My dad had cancer and died a few months ago. He smoked pot and it really helped him with the chemo. The docs and nurses at

Swedish Hospital looked the other way and we were grateful for their attitude."

I wondered if this caller's dad was one of the patients I had visited in the past few months. Was he calling to thank me? But that wouldn't explain his being so jittery about his privacy. My confusion was about to be cleared up.

"So, here's the deal. I grow pot, a lot of it, and I want to donate some to cancer patients, but I don't know how to do that. I mean, I thought about delivering a stash to Swedish and some of the other hospitals, but it's just too risky for me. I thought you might have some ideas."

My God, this was hard to believe. I was meeting dozens of cancer patients every month, most of whom had no idea how to buy pot on the street, and here was this guy, growing it and willing to give it as a gift! Yes, I did indeed have an idea. Might I be the intermediary between this caller and the patients? Would Cheryl go along with the risk I was thinking of taking?

She would. Three nights later, in the parking lot of a closed dry cleaning shop, the caller and I met. In his mid-twenties, tall and with long hair tied in a ponytail, he could have been one of thousands of students on the UW campus. Perhaps he was. In any case, I never learned his name. It was better that I didn't know. That night he gave me a cardboard box filled with sixteen pounds of pot and promised to check back with me periodically to see if I was ready to be resupplied.

We stored it in our basement. That much pot brought up the image of Scrooge McDuck's money bin, brimming over with gold and jewels. There was enough in that box to supply more than 250 patients with an ounce each. And he had said there'd be more when I needed it. I'd struck a gold-bearing vein, or rather it had struck me.

Each time I visited a patient, I brought with me a baggie filled with the grower's donated pot. If, after answering their questions about marijuana and its medical use, the patient asked how to acquire pot, I took the baggie out of my briefcase and told the story about the source. Often, the patient or family member wanted to offer some payment, which I refused, explaining that the pot was intended by the grower to be a gift. I might have added that I was quite sure I'd spend even *more* time in prison than I was already risking if I ever received such a payment. On the other hand, sitting down for a cup of tea and a piece of homemade honey cake seemed a harmless way of accepting the patient's appreciation.

This was an extraordinary time for me, a time when I felt gratified for being able to make a difference for people who were suffering. In a way, I was repeating a role I had played once before. While in the Army in Vietnam, I believed in the importance of what I was doing as a social worker and for the most part avoided the larger question of the war's legitimacy.

A decade later, I had become a marijuana dealer of sorts, once again helping people caught up in a war, but this time the war against marijuana. I was putting one foot in front of the other, believing in what I was doing, and detaching from the larger question of the drug's illegality.

I eventually wrote a manuscript for the lay reader. Its title was *Using Marijuana in the Reduction of Nausea Associated with Chemotherapy*. George Murray, a Washington State senator who had been a co-sponsor of our decriminalization bill, owned the publishing house that issued the booklet. He had responded very positively when I told him about the need for a publication for patients that would translate both the scientific and street drug literatures.

It included guidelines for the novice on using pot and the experience of feeling high. Also there were recipes for preparing foods and tea with marijuana. For people whose nausea kept them from holding down anything taken by mouth, I added instructions on making marijuana suppositories. A professor of pharmacology contributed the suppositories instructions, having learned the process from a nurse who had served in Vietnam and now worked in the burn unit at University Hospital.

Two professors of oncology at the School of Medicine were generous with their time in writing sections and reviewing the draft for errors. In his foreword, one of them foreshadowed a key controversy about marijuana's medical potential that would remain unresolved for decades ahead:

It is, in some sense, unfortunate that such a publication need to be written at all. It would be better if THC were treated as any other new, potentially beneficial drug and not surrounded with myth and mystery. This is especially important because it is finding use in the treatment of patients with cancer. Cancer itself is often treated as a mystery and causes thoroughly old-fashioned kinds of beliefs, superstitions, and dread. A surprisingly large number of people with cancer find themselves being shunned by relatives and friends. Anything that can be done to decrease the myths surrounding cancer and its therapy will be of tremendous service to an enormous number of people. I believe this publication will help dispel a few of those myths.

Despite the involvement of my oncology and pharmacology colleagues, I was very much aware that publishing the booklet had its risks, not the least of which was giving readers untested instructions about an unapproved drug, all of which was far from my area of expertise. But who else would take this on?

Conventional wisdom held that because marijuana was unapproved, the government had no responsibility to disseminate information on which patients could base a decision concerning its use. All well and good as a general principle, I thought. But what of the many patients ill with cancer who, having heard that the drug might help, were desperate for information?

Whether or not the drug was approved, these individuals were going to take actions in their own best interest. I wrote to the Commissioner of the Food and Drug Administration: "To cancer patients, indeed to those with many diseases, the health care system is denying what some people would argue ought to be a basic right: full, understandable information on which to base a decision, even if the decision might be to use an unproven substance. The most appropriate distributor of such information is the Food and Drug Administration."

Dr. Jere Goyan, the FDA Commissioner, disagreed, writing, "Efforts to publicize unapproved therapies, no matter how sincere, subvert the vital process of new drug testing." I thought that if patients suffering with illnesses such as cancer, glaucoma, and spasticity never yielded to the temptation to medicate themselves, perhaps the Commissioner's opinion would make more sense.

—◊—

The music came to an end and so did our trip on the Vltava River. We were back in Magda and Tony's living room, sitting quietly and savoring echoes of the final strains of Smetena's extraordinary tone poem. Magda had taken us on a journey, visiting a place she would never again see yet remained intensely alive in her memory.

I had come to know Magda during her final journey, one that also involved moments of calm interspersed with the hazard of turbulent rapids. For her, using marijuana had been a figurative life jacket while on that river.

PART 4

DEPENDENCE

30

I WANT YOU BACK

A fire was burning in the Franklin stove, its heady odor enhancing the rustic feel of the living room in our friends' vacation home. New Orleans jazz was playing on the stereo, and a platter of barbequed salmon had been set next to the bowls of sweet corn, asparagus, and salad on the dinner table.

Earlier, while visiting with our friends Alan and Judith, the four of us had climbed down the long steep staircase behind their cottage to the Warm Beach mudflats, where we walked along the shore, pausing from time to time when one of us would point out crabs, sea urchins, snails, and other creatures in the tide pool habitats. Two blue herons foraged in the shallow water nearby and a bald eagle circled for a time overhead, each on the watch for its next meal.

They were a distinctive looking couple, Alan with a full salt and pepper beard and cherub face, a twinkle in his eyes, and Judith whose long, very curly hair reminded me of Cher. We had toasted our friendship just as the sun set and watched the sky's changing patina, a quiet moment among friends. Some years earlier each of us had been unmarried when we individually found our way to the University of Washington. Discovering we were both becoming romantically involved, Alan and I frequently compared notes about this courtship business, sometimes sharing laments when we hit similar bumps on the road.

While the salmon was cooking, Alan lit a joint and we passed it back and forth, Judith and Cheryl both deciding to stick with the wine. It was time to eat, and as we pulled our chairs up to the table, illuminated both by the fading light above Puget Sound and three taper candles, I had no premonition of what was about to happen.

Thinking about that evening a few days later, I remembered that we had been talking about academic freedom and the occasional hot letters of protest sent to the University of Washington president demanding that someone on the faculty be fired. One of them was Dave Beatty, a professor of social work. He had been lambasted in a KIRO television editorial for offering a course on working with gay and lesbian clients, a blatant misuse of taxpayer dollars according to the station's general manager.

I had said that while I didn't think I had yet been singled out in a protest to the president, a letter that showed up in my mailbox several weeks earlier had shaken me up. Sent by a Seattle pediatrician who knew that I had been lobbying for marijuana decriminalization, the writer argued that smoking marijuana had "maimed young souls." He had ranted about Timothy Leary's encouraging people to get high and ended his letter with a chilling curse: "For

all the horror Leary and you have caused, may you roast in hell."
He had adamantly demanded that I not reply.

We laughed as I told this anecdote, but it was a letter I wouldn't
forget. Its sting lasted, I suspect, because I would never have the
chance to talk with him, try to change his mind about my intentions,
convince him that criminal penalties were not protecting young
people, or help him see why decriminalization was a step in the right
direction. I was by no means on a quest to "maim young souls."

Alan commiserated with me and described the heat he had taken
for having studied moderate drinking as a possible treatment objective for adults with alcohol use disorders. He was dumbfounded by
the erroneous but seemingly persistent rumors that he wanted to
encourage abstinent alcoholics to resume drinking. He shrugged,
saying this misunderstanding seemed to come with the territory,
and told us the advice he had been given by a senior professor in his
department. That professor had received many angry letters after
local media described the raw honesty with which he taught his
highly popular undergraduate courses on human sexuality and race
relations. He said he kept the letters as a reminder that he must be
doing something right to rouse that sort of emotional response, and
encouraged Alan to do the same. I decided I'd take this advice as well.

The conversation must have shifted, but as I looked back a few
days later, I couldn't recall the new topic. What I did remember,
however, both vividly and painfully, was what had been happening
to my body part way through the meal. All of a sudden I had
become aware my heart was pounding, pounding so loud that I
heard it. I felt a tremendous wave of fear and my breathing became
labored. Under the table, my hands felt numb and shook with a
tremor, and I was surprised that no one seemed to notice. How
could they not know and not hear the drum? Simultaneously, I had
the thought that if I said anything about what I was experiencing,

I'd only make the symptoms worse by giving them attention and then needing to deal with how Cheryl, Alan, and Judith would respond. I looked at the front and then the back doors, thinking that I needed to escape from this room, fearing that I would lose control and do something frightening if I stayed at the table. But if I stood up, would I run to the back of their lot and jump from the steep cliff just to end this torment? My God, I can't stand this, I thought. And it seemed to be getting worse, my imagined escape fueling the storm in which I was held prisoner, hurtling, although in reality I hadn't moved. It was a terrifying condition to be in and it seemed endless. Please, God. . . .

Gradually I became aware, perhaps five or ten minutes later, that my heart rate had slowed, the tremor had stopped, and my breathing was more normal. Somehow, and to my great relief, my ordeal had escaped notice by the others and I had survived and was able to return to the conversation. We ate dessert and a short while later Cheryl and I packed up the car for our return to Seattle.

I drove, and that 90-minute trip required all of the concentration I could give to staying alert and awake. Cheryl suggested we play "Name That Tune" and I was grateful for the distraction. When we pulled into the garage and began unpacking the car, Cheryl commented that I had seemed quiet at dinner and wondered if I was okay.

"I'm feeling better now, but it's been a terribly uncomfortable evening. I had a panic attack while we were eating and I thought it would never end."

She was furious. "Why didn't you tell me? I can't believe you drove us home. I could have driven. No, I *should* have driven. Roger, it's frightening to think about how much danger you put us in."

I knew she was right, but at that moment I needed to sleep and promised that we'd talk about it the next day. It was going to be a difficult conversation, one that I knew was overdue.

—*m*—

"I want you back. It's as simple as that."

We had agreed to talk about it after dinner the next night, and during the day I had been mulling over what I'd say and anticipating the feelings Cheryl would likely express when my pot smoking was on the examining table. But I hadn't expected what I had just heard. I started to say something, but Cheryl held up her hand in a gesture that said stop.

"Look, I know this is going to be tough for you, so I've been thinking very carefully about what I want you to understand." She unfolded a sheet of paper on which she had written notes, looked up at me and paused for a moment before continuing. "Give me a few minutes to tell you what I've been seeing and how I've been feeling about it, and then you can reply. Deal?"

I nodded. In the four years we'd been together, some of our difficult patching ups had got off on a sour note, with one or the other of us finding something to object to in the other's words or tone. No such detours tonight, at least not at the outset. I was listening.

"Look, I think you're in over your head and I'm worried about you. You're getting high much more often than you used to, and I think you're paying a huge price for it, and so am I."

In my mind, I was already drafting the script for what I'd say when my turn came. It'd include the fact that I only smoked in the evenings, that it wasn't every evening, that we both had fun when we got high together, that I knew what I was doing and was on top of the situation, that . . . But, she had said she was paying a huge price, too, and that stopped me. I didn't understand.

"I've watched you become stressed when you've decided to get high instead of preparing for a class session, and then setting the alarm for 4:00 A.M. so you'd have time to get ready. That hasn't been easy on you, and I know you've sometimes beat up on yourself for it, for thinking you could do your class prep while high and then realizing that was just not going to happen."

She saw that I was squirming and wanting to reply, but she didn't stop. "That worries me. And what if you don't make tenure when we're up for review next year? It's not just your class prep that's getting short shrift, but also your writing. What'll happen to us if I'm promoted and you have to look for another job?"

I was adding to my script, wanting to talk about the writing projects I had planned or had underway. Surely she'd see there was no need to catastrophize about our careers.

"But even if these things weren't a problem, there's another issue that I need you to understand. It's about us. I feel you've abandoned me, that the person I married—even when you're sitting next to me on the couch when you're high—is not there." She was beginning to cry, and my plan to explain, reassure, to promise more self-discipline dissolved. I began to feel terrible, recognizing in a visceral way the painful ordeal she was describing. She was revealing an aching loss.

"Your mind goes to a different place, and talking with you when you're stoned is really frustrating. I can't help think that if you really cared about me, you'd want to be with me. You, not the stoned you. I feel rejected by you and it hurts."

She had stopped and was folding up the piece of paper. We were both quiet, and the only movement in the room was Popoki, our Maine Coon cat, jumping up to settle on Cheryl's lap. My script was in shambles, and her having said I had abandoned and rejected her was reverberating in my mind. I stood up and went to the window, searching for the right words. I wanted to say, "I love you and I'm sorry," and soon would do just that. But at the moment, I was filled with awareness of what I had become.

31

DEPENDENCE

SEATTLE
SUMMER 1978

This wasn't the first time that my getting high had come between us. Two years earlier, in the summer of 1976, we attended a party given by a friend on the faculty. Afterwards, Cheryl complained about my barely making it into our house before collapsing on the bed and falling asleep in my clothes. As she saw it, there was nothing social about being that wasted. Rather, it was akin to being dead drunk, and my being in that condition was no fun for her. She let me know she was anxious about my increasing preoccupation with being stoned.

When we began dating, getting high every once in a while was frosting on the cake of a new love affair. Smoking pot while sailing on *Aquarius*, having a picnic in a park, attending a concert, or before making love wonderfully enhanced the sensual pleasures of these experiences. That is, it did for me. Cheryl got high only on rare occasions and found that the novelty quickly wore off. She eventually stopped altogether. Marijuana was just not her cup of tea. I was headed in the opposite direction, however, particularly in the weeks after quitting smoking cigarettes.

It made sense at the time to chalk up my increased use as just a short-term replacement for the oral gratification from inhaling tobacco smoke. I thought I'd surely return to a more occasional use pattern after satisfying this temporary need. But I really was dodging the more likely explanation of what was happening.

My career as an academic was in trouble. I wasn't publishing enough and was under the gun to increase my scholarly work before the "up or out" decision when being reviewed for tenure and promotion. Moreover, because I had been appointed to the faculty without having completed the doctoral degree, my unfinished dissertation loomed as a near certain basis for being denied tenure. If that happened, I'd be looking for a job while Cheryl, whose publication rate was impressive, would become an associate professor with tenure. Just thinking about that possibility was distressing. Would our relationship survive?

When Cheryl first voiced her objections, I made promises and intended to keep them, just so long as there wasn't an ultimatum to quit. I'd reduce the frequency of smoking pot and would be more careful about how stoned I got. That was the plan and it worked for a while, until it didn't.

The truth of the matter was that I was walking straight ahead into marijuana dependence while looking sideways, keeping the reality of where my behavior was taking me just outside the periphery of my vision. In a word, I was perfecting the art of procrastination. It didn't happen all at once, of course, and the exceptions, the instances where I completed a manuscript or made progress with the dissertation, reinforced the myth, a delusion really, that I was engaged, productive, and succeeding as a scholar.

In that period I spent a great deal of time working to support decriminalization. I suspect that becoming an activist served a number of purposes. I believed in the cause, of course, but my intense absorption in the movement had two additional effects. It put me with people and in places where regularly getting high was the norm, leveling the playing field as I calibrated and then recalibrated what was acceptable for me. Being an activist also gave me a compelling rationale for further delaying the concentrated effort I needed to devote to research and publishing. Achieving decriminalization was important, a really worthy goal, and I told myself that as a university faculty member, I was in a unique position to bring credibility to the movement. The conclusion to this line of reasoning was also a recalibration of sorts. I persuaded myself that my faculty colleagues would value the lobbying I was doing and I'd soon have the time to catch up with publishing and research. And whenever these rationalizations seeped through my consciousness as being just that, notions that were heading me for deep water, getting high was a soothing distraction, an escape.

By the summer of 1978, nine years had passed since I first listened to Roberta Flack's sultry voice. While lying on the carpet of my friends' home in Berkeley, the music filling my head through earphones, my eyes were opened to the sensual pleasure of being high. I loved it and over time I graduated from being a non-user to an occasional smoker to a compulsive one.

The personal stories of marijuana dependence I occasionally had heard after delivering decriminalization talks around the state brought home to me the fact that dependence on the drug was real. Until now, however, personal accounts told by others were abstractions. I knew about marijuana dependence, but only on an intellectual level.

Now, Cheryl had confronted me, saying that she felt abandoned because I was choosing to be high so frequently. I tried to convince her to think otherwise. We were spending lots of time together, I argued, and even if I was stoned, we still were enjoying one another's company. Cheryl stood her ground, though, and reiterated that I wasn't the same person when I was stoned, not the person she wanted to be with.

I eventually not only heard her, but fully recognized that what she was enduring was not going to disappear. If anything, it would continue to worsen. Realizing that my actions were causing her to feel rejected and hurt shifted my awareness from my head to my gut. And so I quit.

I was 36 years old, my activism with NORML recently had ended, and my relationship with Cheryl and earning the right to keep my job both urgently needed attention. It was time.

But could I do this on my own? Over the last several years when I had tried to put limits on my use, committing to following certain rules, drawing lines that I'd pledge to not cross, I had eventually given in to temptation every time. Could I be successful now? As I saw it, there was a strong disincentive to seek help. I felt that if I disclosed my dependence on marijuana, it would tarnish my reputation and I didn't want to pay that price.

Also, I reasoned that I had never tried to completely quit, only to take brief marijuana abstinence holidays. Maybe closing the door completely to any future pot use would leave less room for the corner-cutting that had been part of the slippery slope of each previous relapse.

I decided I could do it. On a warm late summer evening I flushed the last half ounce of pot down the toilet. I tossed my clips, pipes, and papers into a garbage bag and deposited it in a dumpster at the gas station two blocks from our house. Finally, I called the guy from whom I had been buying pot, told him I was quitting, and asked him not to cooperate with me if I succumbed in a moment of weakness. He'd heard this before from other customers and, I suspect, put the odds at 50-50 that I'd be calling him again before long.

Cheryl rewarded me by cooking up a batch of hot fudge and making banana splits. Because her father had died just a few years earlier after struggling with alcoholism for most of his adult life, she knew all too well what it was like to intensely wish for a loved one to change and live with the disappointment when it didn't happen. For her, the steps I had just taken offered hope, albeit hope tempered with cautious optimism. For me, the beginning steps of quitting felt freeing. It was no longer a "some day" or a "just for a while" idea.

Looking back, I think it took about a year before I realized that at some point along the way I no longer missed being high. In the early weeks and months of abstaining there were so many cues that stimulated a thought about smoking pot, often much more than a thought. Cravings showed up when I was up and when I was down, in the evenings and on the weekends, and when I was with people with whom I had frequently been stoned. When Cheryl and I argued, I'd have an intense longing to get high. When I became frustrated with a challenge at work, feeling stuck while writing, or facing a stack of student papers that needed to be read and evaluated, vivid memories popped up of how quickly and easily a toke or two would transport me to a far happier mood. Resisting these temptations, finding some way to distract myself or just endure the unfulfilled desire, was hard. It seemed as if getting through this period was something like the healing of an open wound, new tissue slowly granulating in to fill an empty space.

I came perilously close to having a slip about six weeks after quitting. Cheryl had flown to Spokane to conduct a three-day assertiveness skills workshop. Knowing that she'd not return until Saturday and that a friend was giving a party Friday night, a party where undoubtedly people would be getting high, set in motion the wisps of a furtive plan. No, it wasn't really a plan because consciously acknowledging what I was conjuring up would have created a crisis and forced me to either take action to prevent a slip or admit that I was choosing to let it happen. So I purposefully kept the anticipation of the opportunity Friday night would bring in the shadows of my thinking, too obscure to pin down, the images only partially formed and therefore not real. As Friday grew closer, the desire and the not-really-a-plan simmered.

Then, it was 8:00 P.M. on Friday night and I had been home for a few hours, had a pizza and a Coke, and was watching a television sitcom. It would be many years before one could watch two programs simultaneously, with the picture from one channel being superimposed on the picture from another. Yet that night, I was flipping between two scenes. The sitcom was hardly drawing any of my attention as I constantly monitored the time, pictured people arriving at our friend's party, and felt the growing insistence of an impulse to join them. Wanting to feed the building hunger, I poured myself a scotch and sipped it until the program ended. Then, without really making a decision I abruptly jumped up, found my keys, put on my coat, ran down the stairs, got into the car, and put the key into the ignition. Then I stopped, feeling my heart racing and even the beginning of a buzz in the anticipation of where I was headed. I sat there. Time ticked by and I teetered on the edge, torn by indecision. Minutes passed and I felt terribly alone. I walked back upstairs and dialed the number of the Spokane hotel where Cheryl was staying, wanting to just hear her voice.

She answered. I poured out the desperation I had been feeling and told her what had nearly happened. That emotional connection with her brought me back from the precipice, a place that had for a while felt quite frightening. I had leaned way over the edge and peered straight down.

The open wound eventually began to heal. Over days and then weeks and then months of not getting high, I relearned how to live a straight lifestyle. My confidence in being able to sustain what I had begun gradually became stronger. The moodiness and swings of emotion that marked the beginning of leaving marijuana—and any dependence—behind gradually calmed down. I also began to notice improvement in my memory and concentration, changes that made evident two of the adverse consequences that chronically getting high had caused.

I was on my way to leaving pot behind when a former student dropped by during office hours. Before long it became apparent that I'd get as much if not more benefit from talking with her as she'd get from me.

—⁂—

Kay had taken an addiction counseling course from me the previous spring and was one of my favorite students. She wrote well, often volunteered for role plays in which counseling methods were demonstrated, and impressed me with the questions she asked. Upbeat and energetic, Kay was also a popular member of her class, one who was particularly respected because of all that she was juggling, being the single parent of an eight-year-old boy and holding a part-time job while attending school.

But today, when she came to my office door her first words were "Roger, I need help." She was obviously distressed. The redness in her eyes made me think she had been crying. Her long brunette hair was tied back with a rubber band and she wore jeans, running shoes, and a purple University of Washington sweatshirt, an outfit common among the thousands of students on the campus each day. However, I had never seen Kay dressed this informally. Something was wrong.

I closed the door to my office and sat opposite her. She was looking down and for a few moments wrung her hands without speaking. She was clearly conflicted about something. I waited as she composed herself. In a few moments, she was ready.

"I need to quit pot and what's really upsetting me is I'm frightened I can't do it." She paused and looked up.

"Tell me about it," I said.

"I'm making all of the excuses that we read about in those case examples last spring," she said. "I'm really ashamed to tell you this, but I've been a daily pot smoker for four years, ever since my husband and I split up. When we talked about the diagnostic criteria for drug dependence in your course, I just couldn't deny the truth any longer. I'm feeling overwhelmed and really discouraged, Roger."

She'd earned a high grade in the class and, as far as I knew, was on track to graduate. Her disclosure caught me by surprise. What had happened, I wondered? She answered that question and told me a lot more as she talked non-stop for the next several minutes, occasionally reaching for a tissue from the box on my desk and dabbing at her tears.

"I feel like I'm doing a lousy job in every aspect of my life. I'm cutting corners with raising my son and he deserves so much better than having a pot head for a mom. I'm terrified that if my ex-husband finds out the truth, he might use it against me in a custody hearing." Tears were running down her cheeks as she spoke. "If I lost him, I'd want to die." She gripped the arms of her chair and had a look of desperation on her face. "I can see disaster coming."

As I listened, I felt the heaviness of the dilemma she was experiencing. By getting stoned to allay her fears, she was aiding and abetting the very dangers that haunted her. Two tracks were playing in my mind as we spoke, one attentive to her and another yet again tuning in to a question that had doggedly persisted over a number of years. Will decriminalization open Pandora's box? Will a more liberal marijuana policy, no matter how many problems it solved, force far more people such as Kay to their knees? Were the heroin addicts I spoke to nearly a decade ago right all along?

"I'm barely keeping up with course assignments," she said, "and even then I know I'm not doing the work I'm capable of doing. I see clients at my practicum who are struggling with addiction and I feel like a fraud because I'm just like them, except I'm in the closet about it. How can I possibly help anyone when I can't help myself?"

She began sobbing. As she heard herself inventory the ways in which she was disappointing herself and risking losing her child, the impact she felt was overwhelming.

"You know, there's one conclusion I've come to after lying to myself for so long and after failing miserably to handle this. I can't do it on my own. To be honest, I'm frightened that I can't do it period."

"I get it, Kay," I said, and thought for a few moments about what I might do. "You're feeling stuck. Can I help?"

"Roger, would you? If you really mean it, I've got an idea and it's the one thought that is giving me some hope."

She glanced over at my bookshelves and then stood and took down one of the texts we had used in the course. "The recovery skills that we read about in this book make a lot of sense and I think they might work for me, but I've got to have someone to do this with."

She flipped through the pages and found the chapter on ways people commonly sabotage themselves. Half a dozen case examples described people who fell off the wagon within weeks of getting started with abstinence. Hanging out in places where others are drinking or getting loaded and keeping a hidden supply close by in case of an emergency were just a few of the many scenarios in which people tripped themselves up. The book's author followed each case example with some strategies the person might have used to prevent a slip.

"I can't afford to go into treatment. The only way I can stay in school is by keeping my job and I don't have any savings. Anyway, I'm doubtful I'd get any real help in one of those programs. I can just hear the counselors saying, 'It's just pot.' They wouldn't take me seriously. So I wondered if you'd be willing to meet with me weekly for a few months. I'll re-read this book, I'll write a contract and make a commitment to quitting, and I'll have you here to keep me accountable. I'll pay you a fee for each session, although I'll need to make it kind of a token payment. Hopefully, you'll let me pay off the balance over time after I've graduated and am back working full time."

As she talked, several thoughts were going through my mind. It had been ten years since I had worked with a client, my schedule was already jammed, and I wondered about the ethics of being a counselor to a student I had taught. Also, what about the ethics of working with someone grappling with the same issues I was?

But I also remembered the adage that the best way to learn something is to teach it to others. Might helping Kay be a way I could help myself stay the course in my own abstinence? I needed time to sort out these issues.

"Kay, I'm not sure I can agree to this," I said, "but let me have a few days to think it over. I'm really glad you've let me in on what's happened. One way or another, we'll find a way to get you through this."

She teared up again and thanked me. After she left, one more student came by with a quick question about an assignment. Then when office hours were over, I grabbed my coat and took a walk on the campus to mull this over. It was brisk, but the sun was out and the sight of snowcapped Mt. Rainier drew me toward Drumheller Fountain, dubbed Frosh Pond generations ago, where I found an unoccupied bench and watched half a dozen ducks vying for pieces of bread several students were tossing in their direction.

Two issues seemed easy to identify and resolve. I wouldn't accept any money if I held these meetings with Kay and I'd disclose my own dependence on pot. Less clear was whether it would be ethical to be a counselor to a former student. My profession's code of ethics said social workers should not engage in dual or multiple relationships with clients where there's a risk of exploitation or potential harm. The code emphasized that when a dual relationship occurred, the social worker was responsible for establishing appropriate boundaries. To me, that meant in order to be ethical, I'd need to be very clear when I was being a teacher and when a counselor. Was that possible, I wondered? At the very least, I thought, there'd be no risk of a grade being compromised since she was no longer studying with me.

Their paper sacks now empty, the students headed in the direction of University Hospital and the ducks circled over to the other side of the fountain, probably hoping to find more folks with left-over lunch. I sat there for a few more minutes, jotting some notes to myself and weighing the pros and cons. I wanted to agree to Kay's request, but might I regret it? I suddenly realized that one possible reason for telling her I couldn't work with her was self-protection. If I started getting high again, I'd not want to admit it to her. With a jolt, it became clear that part of my thinking at that moment was actually a first step on the road to returning to smoking pot.

As many people who live in the region would say, Mt. Rainier was "out." Very little haze obscured the mountain's peaks, feeding an illusion that it was actually much closer to Seattle than it looked on days where haze heightened the perception of distance.

My flash of insight evaporated the remaining haze in my thinking. I had come to a decision.

—⚬—

Kay and I met weekly for four months. When I told her that I was walking on the same path, she was all the more enthusiastic, hoping I'd have insights from my own experiences that might point the way for her.

We began by re-reading the book from my addiction counseling course and discussing how each chapter might apply to Kay's circumstances. Then we talked about the various steps she'd take in preparing to quit. We moved on to strategies for getting through the initial days of abstaining, avoiding slips, and learning alternatives to getting high, like regularly exercising. We talked about the people in her life she might count on for support and those who might intentionally or unintentionally undermine her.

In our meetings, the focus was on Kay, yet inevitably I found myself thinking about the reasons why I had stopped getting high, the situations in which I was most at risk of slipping, and how I was keeping myself from giving in to temptation. We weren't really a support group because all of our attention was devoted to Kay. Yet both of us were benefiting.

Kay quit to be a better mother and to live up to the high standards she set for herself as a professional. I stopped to save my marriage and achieve tenure and promotion at the University. Kay recognized she was at highest risk of slipping when she'd been drinking or when in the company of two specific friends who continued to get high. For me, the storm warning flag waved in the evenings between 7:00 and 10:00 P.M. and when Cheryl was out of town.

While these weekly sessions were about her, our meetings provided a safety net for me. When having a thought about getting high, I could easily set it aside. I knew that in just a few days we'd meet again, and if I had had a slip and told her, it would likely bring us both down, and the thought of that outweighed any compulsion to smoke that had crept in. We were roped together on this climb.

The case examples in the book stimulated our discussions. Completing the exercises pushed Kay to problem-solve how she'd handle temptations to get high and what she'd say to herself when she began rationalizing about the possibility of being a moderate smoker. Another exercise called for detailed plans on how she'd quickly get herself back in line in the event that a slip occurred.

Our conversations revolved around her life, her challenges, her skills, and her successes. Even so, the route I was taking in overcoming marijuana dependence was becoming clearer through the vicarious learning that took place in our sessions.

After meeting for four months, Kay was ready to continue on her own. She was more certain than ever that the decision to quit was the right one and she was more discerning in gazing down the road and anticipating the rough spots, what we jokingly referred to as the "pot holes." Kay reveled in how the positive changes she was making in her lifestyle were boosting her self-image. I felt confident in her succeeding with the longer-term work of overcoming marijuana dependence.

Those months of working with her also planted a seed in my mind. As I thought about it, Kay was right that many staff working in drug abuse agencies underrated marijuana's addiction potential, dismissing the possibility that marijuana smokers could experience major adverse effects. That attitude, if conveyed to people seeking treatment, would be extraordinarily discouraging.

Another treatment barrier was embedded in the pot culture. Specifically, there was the popular perception that pot smokers were laid back, peace-loving, and otherwise law-abiding members of a politically astute counter culture, while true drug addicts, the people for whom treatment programs were established, were antisocial, criminally inclined, apolitical, and were using drugs like heroin or speed. Stereotyping fed these perceptions, of course, yet these "us" versus "them" notions prevented pot smokers who'd become dependent from believing that the clients and counselors in addiction treatment agencies would be people with whom they might resonate.

I began to consider setting up a part-time private practice specializing in counseling marijuana dependent adults. The University of Washington permitted faculty members to devote up to one day each week to outside income-generating activities. Some on the faculty consulted with industry or government. Two psychology professors I knew had private practices, one specializing in the treatment of migraine and another, my friend Alan, in the treatment of alcohol abuse. Several in the School of Social Work did outside work counseling families.

If I hung a "Marijuana Dependence Treated Here" shingle on my office door, would there be any takers? Based on my personal struggle with marijuana, the work I did with Kay, and the private conversations I had with a number of people after my decriminalization talks, I was fairly convinced that there'd be potential clients waiting for me to open my door.

Indeed there were. Beginning in 1981, I saw clients one day a week in sublet office space overlooking Seattle's scenic Elliott Bay. Networking with mental health and addiction specialists in the region led to a steady stream of inquiries. I had some concern that my having been an activist for decriminalization, a position I still held, might deter some treatment professionals from referring clients. Perhaps it did with some, but clearly not with many others who either agreed with my views or believed they didn't matter.

Working with clients over the next few years made it evident to me that research was needed on how to most effectively support adults who were dependent on marijuana. No one in the addiction field had studied this issue. Consequently, the counseling approaches I used were largely "borrowed" from treatment protocols designed for and evaluated with problem drinkers.

When I submitted a grant application to the National Institute on Drug Abuse to conduct a controlled trial of marijuana dependence treatment, the application was rejected. Data available from treatment agencies across the country made it appear to the reviewers that the only people who met criteria for dependence on marijuana also met criteria for dependence on at least one other substance. And, since models of treatment already were being designed and evaluated for poly-drug dependence, there was no need for a marijuana-specific treatment trial.

I was convinced otherwise. As Kay had said, people who worked in drug treatment agencies were unlikely to take seriously anyone seeking help in quitting pot, and pot alone.

Now I needed to prove my case.

32

UNMET NEED

UNIVERSITY OF WASHINGTON SCHOOL OF SOCIAL WORK
DECEMBER 1984

t was almost noon and I was feeling discouraged. Not one call had come in. Three of us, each facing an oppressively silent telephone in a small office in the School of Social Work, repeatedly looked up at the clock as the hours slowly passed. Stacks of photocopied blank questionnaires were piled on our desks and our pencils were sharpened. We were ready and had been sitting there waiting for three hours. Would anyone respond?

Two months earlier I had grappled with the question of how to demonstrate to the National Institute on Drug Abuse that a population of marijuana-using adults existed who were experiencing symptoms of dependence, were not dependent on alcohol or other drugs, and who wanted help in quitting. The ideal research approach, a survey of a representative sample of adults living in Seattle, would be expensive and I didn't have funds to cover the costs.

An alternative approach seemed feasible. Even better, it could be done without any money. I'd borrow some office space at the School and recruit and train a group of student volunteers to staff the phone lines for two weeks. Then I'd put out a call for adults who smoked pot and had concerns, asking them to phone for a brief interview. The University's public relations people would issue a press release about our study that hopefully would be picked up by the daily and weekly newspapers. I'd ask local radio and television stations to run free public service announcements and I'd seek opportunities to publicize the study by being a guest on talk shows.

The publicity would describe the project as an anonymous survey and would make it clear that this was not an offer of counseling. There'd be no monetary incentives for people who agreed to be interviewed. The goal would simply be to learn about what people were experiencing.

At noon, two new volunteers arrived to take over for the next three hours. Just before leaving to drive to KIRO radio where I'd be interviewed, I told the students who'd just arrived that they'd probably have lots of time to do homework. So far, at least, the anonymous survey idea seemed to have been a dud.

Jim French was a Seattle radio icon. Each day his popular show's guests included a variety of newly published authors, actors and musicians currently performing in our city, and representatives of various causes seeking publicity just as I was. His interviewing style was friendly and he seemed genuinely interested in what I had to say. I told him these anonymous interviews would help us better understand whether adults who smoked pot had concerns about their use, and if they did, what was bothering them.

He offered a guess about what we were going to find. "Professor, isn't it likely that the concern at the top of the list will be the risk of getting arrested?"

"You know, I wonder if that one will be the most common," I said. "Something tells me that people who smoke a lot might actually be less worried about that than how it affects their quality of life. We'll see. This kind of study hasn't been done before with marijuana smokers, so we'll learn a lot."

Ten minutes after the interview began he thanked me for dropping by and began running an advertisement. A staff member came to escort me to the building lobby.

While the dialogue with Jim French had gone well, I felt let down as I drove back to the University. I had expressed optimism about the survey during the interview, but was actually wondering why I had ever thought it would work. It seemed unlikely any calls would come in and I felt stymied about how to refute the NIDA grant reviewers' conclusions. I also realized how important this project had become to me and felt bad that I had failed.

As I walked into our borrowed office, the sight that greeted me turned my growing pessimism on its head. Both volunteers were on the phone conducting interviews and there were twelve filled-in questionnaires in the "Completed" box. As I was taking off my coat, the third phone line rang. The two volunteers simultaneously gestured to me, letting me know my shift had begun.

For the next two weeks, the phones were rarely silent. Just as someone hung up after completing a call, the phone would ring again. The floodgates had been opened with other local media following KIRO's lead in publicizing the study. By the end of the two weeks, we had completed interviews with 225 people. What they told us clearly supported the existence of the marijuana-dependent adults whom I had sought funding to study.

The typical caller was an employed male in his early thirties who had first smoked pot at age 17. Four years after their first experience with pot, 78% had become daily users. All but nine had experienced problems associated with their marijuana use at some point, the most common of which were difficulties with thinking or memory, lowered self-esteem, concerns about health, and stresses in family relationships. For 74%, marijuana was their only substance problem. Sixty-eight percent said they'd definitely be interested if a counseling program tailored for marijuana dependence became available.

While the nature of this survey made it impossible to estimate how many people fit the profile of adults dependent only on pot, these numbers spoke volumes about an unmet need. And they countered the conclusions the reviewers had drawn from descriptions of clients being served by drug treatment agencies across the country. Using our newly acquired survey data, I applied once again to NIDA for funding. I'd need to summon up a lot of patience as the application went through the six-month review process before a decision was made to accept or reject it.

This time it was successful. NIDA awarded three years of funding to support the first-ever controlled trial of marijuana dependence counseling. I was elated.

On the day the notice of grant award arrived, Cheryl and I splurged by dining at Ray's Boathouse, a Seattle favorite overlooking Puget Sound. Having a bird's-eye view of the parade of boat traffic heading to or from the Ballard Locks, a link between Puget Sound and the fresh water of Lake Union, was one reason for the restaurant's popularity, as was watching the sun setting behind the Olympic Mountains.

Just after the sun had gone down, a waiter walked along the narrow outside deck and used a long pole to crank open the window awnings. Cheryl and I shared a crème brûlée and sat qui-etly watching as fish leaped to feed on the insects swarming just above the water's surface. As I mused about that day's good news, I realized that being able to conduct this study offered one more benefit than those I had thought about. My sessions with Kay six years earlier had given me a safety net that reinforced my early abstinence from pot. Doing this research with marijuana-dependent adults, I realized, would provide more of the same, important even this far into leaving marijuana behind.

I felt safer.

33

WE'RE NOT ZEALOTS

GREEN LAKE
SEPTEMBER 1986

A t about noon on a sunny and unseasonably warm early autumn Saturday, Bob Stephens and I drove to Green Lake, a Seattle urban park that on a spectacular day such as this drew thousands. Some were picnicking, others walking, biking, or running along the 2.8 mile path around the lake, while still others swam in the indoor pool or played sports on one of the park's many fields and courts. Dozens of paddle boats, kayaks, and canoes were out on the water. Along the lake's banks a number of men were fishing, their dinged-up coolers and worn folding camp stools telling signs that they were old hands at this.

We found a parking spot near the community center and set out for a walk. On a crowded day, observing the arrows on the paved two-lane path was a wise idea. Runners and bikers were to go counterclockwise in their lane while walkers had the option of going in either direction in theirs. Regulars to the park knew that walking in the runners' lane risked an occasional frown or even a bruise from a collision.

In order to take a one year psychology internship, Bob and his wife Amy had moved to Seattle from Florida where he completed his doctoral studies. He later accepted a post-doctoral fellowship with my friend Alan Marlatt who was an alcoholism and addiction researcher in the psychology department. When I told Alan about the grant award and that I'd need to hire a project director, he suggested I talk with Bob. Describing his excellent methodological training and some of the professors with whom he had studied, Alan offered an insight about Bob that heightened my interest: "He doesn't realize how good he is."

Bob and I had first talked in my office at the University a week earlier. Our meeting had gone well, I thought, and today we'd have another chance to discuss the project and the prospect of working together.

Twenty-nine years old, standing 6'4", with a muscular build and shoulder-length hair tied back in a ponytail, Bob would not likely be seen as an easy mark by anyone looking to pick a fight. Yet, as I soon learned, he was a sensitive man. It was easy to talk with him and feel heard. Alan's perceptiveness about Bob seemed accurate. People were drawn to him, in part I suspected because of his humility.

As we passed the boat launch area, three kayakers were getting ready to set off while a sculler was waiting for dock space to haul out. Just then we both laughed as we caught a familiar whiff, realizing that two skaters who had rolled past must have been smoking a joint. Jokingly, Bob suggested we chase after them to see if they might have an extra. The lingering scent and our banter about the skaters offered a segue to the conversation I'd hoped we'd have that afternoon, a conversation about our personal philosophies. As it turned out, he had some of the same questions in mind.

While the design of the study, the timeline, and the eligibility criteria for subjects had been specified in the grant proposal, would Bob and I see eye to eye about other issues? For example, would we care what prospective staff members thought about pot smokers? Would we be on the same frequency when writing the recruitment ads? Would they imply a "just say no" message, Nancy Reagan's solution to the drug problem? That would trouble me. What would we want interested callers to experience when first contacting our office and later when coming in for an assessment interview with a staff member? As we began to explore these issues, we found ourselves disclosing parts of our lives that don't typically get talked about in a job interview. Each of us began learning where the other person was coming from.

"For me, doing this study is personal," I said. "I had to quit getting high because it became a compulsive thing. I'd probably have lost Cheryl if I didn't and I'd never have been promoted." As I said this, I wondered if he'd jump to a conclusion that down deep I thought pot smoking was a bad idea for anyone, even him.

He nodded as we walked along, waiting to see if I had more to say. I appreciated the space he was giving me.

"When they call our office, I want people like me to feel that we get what they're going through, even the likelihood that they're not completely sure they want to quit. I want them to know we understand that it's really hard."

I told him I wanted our clients to realize we're not zealots, that we don't believe pot smoking is necessarily bad, and certainly not because it's illegal. I added the fact that I had lobbied for decriminalization in the 1970s.

Bob was clearly listening. "I've been thinking the same way," he said, "and by the way, I also think it should be decriminalized, maybe even legalized. Look, the fact of the matter is that I get high and from time to time have to reel myself in when I'm doing it too much. So at least I can tell you that I know what it feels like to be on the other side of the line. I can't say I know how you felt, though."

As I listened to him, it seemed as if the gold bars were lining up one by one in the slot machine window. He, too, had had the experience of smoking too much and was willing to tell me about it. Even more important, he knew not to make assumptions about another person's struggle.

We were passing the Bathhouse Theatre and through an open door could hear actors rehearsing a play. On a nearby lawn some people had set up a badminton net. An errant shuttlecock flew in our direction. Bob jumped and caught it, handing it to one of the players who had run over to retrieve it.

"You know, Roger, we'll need to make clear that in trying to help people who've become dependent, we're not condemning all use. For that matter, I'd want to hire staff who are fundamentally okay with pot smoking, whether or not they get high themselves. That fit with your thinking?"

I told him it did. But then, just as I was sensing we were in total alignment and how good it was to hear him talking about "our study," he took what I feared would be a 180 degree turn.

"Having this conversation reminds me of one of the qualms I've had about this job. It's not about you, but about some inadvertent conclusions people could jump to because of the nature of this study."

I felt apprehensive as he said this. Were there some harms the study could cause that I'd completely missed? Was he about to tell me he'd not accept the job if I offered it?

"Let me see if I can explain what I mean. The first implication I worry about is an assumption that if someone's life is somehow messed up and they smoke dope, that dope is the cause of their problems in every case. I think it'll be all too easy for subjects to add it all up that way because it'll make sense to them. They might misattribute the cause to pot when something entirely separate in their lives is the real cause, something like depression, or perhaps anxiety, or maybe fallout from a traumatic event that happened at a critically important time in their lives.

"And then there's a second risk," he said. "It's that some people who will want to join the trial would actually be better off if they didn't quit, even though they're dependent on pot. In other words, their getting high is actually a better alternative than what they'd face if they stopped. I wonder if in fact we could harm them."

He was thinking about people who self-medicate with marijuana, whether or not they'd call it that. Taking away something that helps ameliorate physical or psychological problems without offering a replacement could be more damaging for some people than leaving it alone.

I realized he was absolutely right and told him so. We continued our loop of the lake, neither of us talking for a few minutes. I wondered if procedures in the counseling protocol could be designed so that the problems we'd just identified were minimized. I asked what he thought.

"Yeah, I think we'd want to build these points into the training we give to our counselors," he replied. "There might be times when subjects in the study will want to talk about these issues and the counselors should be ready if they come up."

He looked over at me as we continued walking and added another thought. "But I guess I also want to tell you I'm glad we're both seeing these as risks. It makes a big difference for me."

I couldn't have agreed more and felt relieved that we'd grapple with these issues together. I held out my hand and we sealed the deal. This was the person I wanted for the project director position and he wanted the job.

That first grant was followed by numerous others, all focusing on counseling for adults or adolescents with marijuana problems. We continue to work together on these studies close to thirty years later.

The data we've collected from well over a thousand study participants have deepened our understanding of the human experience in becoming dependent, the consequences of heavy pot use that concern people the most, and the life circumstances most difficult to deal with when learning to be abstinent. Doing this research is inherently rewarding, in part because of the successes achieved by many who enroll in these studies, and in part because the failures of others compel us to take on remaining mysteries inherent in understanding human motivation and capability.

34

HEMPFEST

U pwards of 200,000 people came to this stunningly beautiful waterfront park on Seattle's Elliott Bay to participate in what since 1991 had become an annual event. Quite unlike the celebration of all things musical at Folk Life and Bumbershoot, festivals held in this city each year on Memorial Day and Labor Day respectively, Hempfest was first and foremost a weekend celebration of marijuana. Local and national activists gave speeches urging reform of the marijuana laws, live bands performed on multiple stages, and dozens of booths where hemp products, a variety of paraphernalia items, and snacks were sold dotted the park's five acres.

A testament perhaps to Seattle's culture of tolerance, the scent of pot smoke wafted throughout the park. Most who got high were discreet. Only one person was busted that weekend, evidence I thought that the police were clearly looking the other way whenever possible.

A banner spanning the front of one of the many booths read "Marijuana Studies at the University of Washington." A sign just below the banner advertised free lemonade. Our research team had rented the space in order to publicize a study evaluating an intervention called the Marijuana Check-Up. Thousands of pot smokers would see the booth and we hoped a number of them would be interested in enrolling. At the least we'd help them quench their thirst.

The counseling approaches Bob and I previously tested were for adults who wanted to quit or cut back. The check-up was different. It was tailored for people who had concerns about their use but were ambivalent about whether to continue getting high. We described it as an opportunity for someone to take stock of their experiences with pot and think through their options. There'd be no pressure to change and it would only involve two sessions.

Along with several of his doctoral students, Bob had flown to Seattle from Virginia to help our Seattle crew staff the booth at Hempfest. Well over a thousand people stopped by during that weekend, totally depleting our supply of lemonade and the flyers about our latest NIDA-funded trial.

When we first talked about renting the booth, I wondered if we might find ourselves being confronted. I envisioned indignant pot proponents tearing into us for focusing on people experiencing problems with pot when what really needed to be done, I pictured them saying, was proving once and for all how beneficial the drug was and that it caused none of the horrors deserving of its "reefer madness" history.

It happened, but only a few times. During one of my shifts at the booth, I noticed a fellow who was waiting patiently, but with a serious, maybe even angry, look on his face. When his turn came, he got right to it.

"I want to know where you get your funds," he demanded. "I know what the banner says," pointing to the front of the booth, "but tell me the truth. Is the DEA funding you?" He was referring to the Drug Enforcement Administration, a federal agency concerned more with putting dealers out of business than with counseling. He was wearing a Rasta Jamaican knit beanie with bright bands of red, gold, black, and green, and a white t-shirt sporting the NORML logo. My questioner looked to be in his 50s, and had a bushy salt and pepper moustache. From the outset, I got the sense that he was on a mission. Before I could tell him we weren't funded by the DEA, he shifted the topic. "Forget that. You wouldn't tell me even if you were on their payroll. So, have you ever heard of the Indian Hemp Commission or the LaGuardia Report?"

He was asking about two investigatory panels, one in the late 1800s and the other in the 1940s, both of which had largely exonerated marijuana as causing insanity and horrific violence. I indeed had heard about them, but it was impossible to get a word in edgewise.

"By the way," he continued, "the proper term that should be on your banner is cannabis, not marijuana. If I had time, I'd explain why." Without taking a breath, he was on to another charge. "You probably don't know that the Seattle City Council gave cannabis a clean bill of health in 1974 when it threw out jail penalties and it threw out giving people a criminal record for possession." He was almost spitting his accusatory words. "There's no way they would have done that if smoking cannabis had any of the deadly effects that you want people to believe happen."

"Give me a chance to answer," I began to say, but he quickly cut me off.

"Do you really believe that you can convince all of these people who, by the way, are only coming over because of your free lemonade, that cannabis is addictive? Why don't you tell the damned truth, for Christ's sake?" At this point, he shook his head with a look of disgust and walked away.

I was not about to chase after him. On the few occasions when we were confronted, we listened. Listened and did our best to steer clear of any arguments. More often our staff heard how cool it was that UW professors were interested in learning about pot. From time to time, people of various ages came up and told us they had been in one of our studies as subjects. Quite a few who visited the booth took us up on the offer to learn about our new check-up study. All in all, there was a surprisingly positive reaction to our being at Hempfest.

And then there was a question we had heard again and again over the years. Was it true that a particularly potent strain of cannabis was being grown for research purposes in a closely guarded lab on the UW campus? The questioners had heard that a small number of favored grad students and professors got to have access to it and they wanted to know if they could get in on the deal, maybe volunteering in a study that required getting stoned with this dynamite dope. We've never learned how that rumor got started, but it's a myth that persists to this day.

Early in the afternoon, with our staff handling the flow of visitors to the booth, Bob and I took a break and found a spot to sit on the park lawn. From a distance we heard a crowd's applause. I wondered if the cheering was for a band that had just finished a set or a speaker who had the audience pumped up.

When we first sat down, we watched a fully laden cargo ship being guided to open water by two tugboats. Now under its own power, it was steaming north where it would pass through Puget

Sound and proceed out to sea. Closer to shore a speedboat headed into Elliott Bay, and another, trailing a long line attached to a parasail, was returning its rider to the dock. Sailboats, some ocean worthy and others just dinghies with sails no larger than a bed sheet, were out in great numbers. Seattle at the apex of summer is spectacular.

At one point, Bob nudged me and pointed at three people, two female and one male, all likely in their early twenties, sitting about 15 yards from our spot. It was evident they were passing a joint, and we heard their laughter.

"Rog, I look at people like these kids and sometimes think what we really ought to study is how people can get the most enjoyment from pot while avoiding any of the downside."

"Learning to be a cannabis connoisseur," I quipped. "Wouldn't that turn the addiction treatment field on its head? If we could test ways of teaching novices moderate pot smoking skills, we'd probably prevent a lot of people from running into problems."

"That's exactly what I was thinking," Bob said. "You know, we should be teaming up with some folks in Amsterdam and open a Dutch-style coffee shop at the University and turn it into a research lab."

For alcohol researchers on campus, there actually was such a lab. It was located in the Psychology Department. Called the Barlab, this fully equipped cocktail lounge was set up by our colleague, Alan Marlatt. The equipment in that room permitted covert audio and video recording of how people behaved under a variety of circumstances. For example, researchers could determine if people tend to drink more quickly if there's loud music playing, in greater volume if they've purposefully been drawn into an argument by a research assistant serving as a plant, or at a slower pace if there are fewer people around them. Studying marijuana use behaviors in a similar way would be groundbreaking.

"Open a coffee shop in Seattle? Starbucks would run us out of town, my friend," I said. We laughed at the impossibly unrealistic idea we were coming up with. In truth, though, we enjoyed dreaming up trials that would contribute new knowledge to the field if the political barriers could somehow be overcome.

―⁓―

This idea was just one of many that we discussed and sometimes debated over the years of working together. By the time I retired from the University of Washington faculty in 2009, we had conducted nine federally funded trials of marijuana interventions over more than twenty years. Well over a thousand people had participated, both adults and adolescents.

We had published a book, *Cannabis Dependence: Its Nature, Consequence, and Treatment*, that summed up the findings of the studies we had completed as well as research on marijuana dependence conducted by others in the U.S. and internationally. We'd also published with several other colleagues a treatment manual, *Brief Counseling for Marijuana Dependence: A Manual for Treating Adults*. Over the years we'd received lots of positive feedback, but one individual's anonymous comment got right to the crux of what overcoming drug dependence is all about. This individual wrote: "Thank you for giving me my life back." I got it.

If only I could have done that for my brother.

35

ETERNAL INTERMISSION

"**R**oger . . ."

It was 6:30 A.M. It was Friday, May 5th, 2006.

No, not again. Seven years before, also at an early hour, I had heard my sister Arlie's voice, with the same heaviness, a quiet urgency. Then she was calling me from the east coast to tell me that our mother had died.

Now, just hearing my name spoken in a way that had imprinted in my memory was ominous and foreshadowed what she was about to tell me. The only question was: who?

It was our brother, Bryan. He had died a month short of his 51st birthday. His wife, Christina, found him lying on a couch when she woke and phoned 9-1-1 when he was unresponsive. My niece, Meredith, kept her 7-year-old brother, Bailey, occupied while the EMTs tried to resuscitate their dad. Our sister, Sherry, quickly arrived and held on to Christina as they watched the medics carry Bryan out to the ambulance, still working on him, an oxygen mask on his face. But he was gone.

Bryan had been receiving treatment for a rare form of cancer called leiomyosarcoma. My first thought was that if cancer was the cause of his death, I had no idea the disease had progressed so far.

Damn, I should have known. But Bryan and I hadn't spoken for at least two years. The silence between us went on and on, unattended yet festering. That morning, as Arlie told me what had happened and what was known at that point, I felt flooded with remorse for the part I could have played, but didn't, in reconnecting with him. He had cancer, for God's sake.

But something else stood in the way. Bryan's on-again off-again struggle with addiction had been very much on-again in recent years. From my sisters I heard he was playing one physician off another in getting multiple painkiller prescriptions, and then using these medications not just to stem the cancer pain but also to stay loaded, and by selling a portion of what he had been prescribed to make money that would go back into getting more pills.

Throughout his adult years, each time Bryan stepped away from his recovery and again became a player, a screen descended between us. When we talked, I felt an intense aversion to his "used car salesman" image, a packaging of himself that was a barrier to authenticity between us and, during our infrequent conversations, made my jaw ache. Life was going well, extremely well, he would have me believe, when I knew better. He undoubtedly felt the vibes of the judgmental attitude I had about what he was doing. Now, in this latest period of no communication whatsoever, I knew his cancer and/or his drug abuse could potentially kill him. Yet I did nothing.

Not long before he died, I later learned, Bryan feared Christina might leave him. She told me she'd reached the end of her rope trying to cope with his heavy abuse of and dealing drugs, his inability to keep a job, and the impact these were having on her and their children.

It wasn't the cancer. Bryan had died of a drug overdose. There was no note and we didn't know if it was accidental or intentional. We'd never know.

What I believe, however, is that he must have felt terribly desperate on that final night of his life, desperate and alone.

—∞—

Another flight to the east coast, going home. First Dad, then Mom, and now Bryan. It took a little more than five hours to make the non-stop trip from Seattle to Boston, yet there was a separate time dimension to this journey, a blurring of vision, the present dissolving to the past. I sat in a window seat, peering into the clouds. Scenes began to unfold.

One reel, grainy black and white, only much later in color, camera held in shaky hands, sudden blots of light-damaged film, an archive to record we were there, we were a family. One after another of the four of us as newborns, held up by Mom nuzzling a tiny face as Dad filmed. Cousins playing with us in the sand at the Point of Pines beach house, toddlers and puppies being gently dunked into the shallow surf. Both sets of grandparents and even Mom's grandparents, Zade and Bubbe, the formality of their dress carrying forward the conventions of their time. And birthday parties, lots of them in a family with four children. The youngest asking the four questions at a Passover seder; "Why does this night differ from all other nights?" Light moments, laughing and playing, mugging for the camera.

There, there I am, bundled up on a sled Dad's pulling in the snow outside our Dorchester three-decker. And there, the original Teddy, a cocker spaniel, first a puppy, then grown, and in later scenes his once brown and then white muzzle making it evident he was old. Sherry, then Arlie, from infancy to early school years, feeding the deer and giraffes at the Franklin Park Zoo, an elephant ride at Benson's Animal Farm in New Hampshire, a family vacation in Miami, Dad posing with parrots on both shoulders and arms.

And there's Bryan, maybe a few weeks old, and Mom is letting me hold him carefully. For a few seconds we hold one another's gaze. Brothers.

Now nine years old, Bryan posed for a grammar school photo, my wallet size copy inscribed "From Bryan to Roger with Love." His blond hair carefully combed, his checkered shirt buttoned up all the way, and he's smiling, a bit of a gap between his upper front teeth, a moment captured in which his happiness seems genuine. It was, wasn't it?

So . . . why? It wasn't supposed to have been this way.

Another reel cut in, not from among the family photo albums but rather formed in my mind's eye, standing in stark contrast with the earlier images. Defiance, violence, vandalizing, quitting school, getting thrown out of the Army, and then the anger and recriminations as our parents differed about what to do, what he needed, how not to enable him, all of those unanswered questions and fears.

From my clients I knew that families sometimes break when a parent or a child tramples on the values that form the walls, floor, and ceiling of its culture, its rules, and aspirations. Then again, one member's acting out can be a clarion call, a signal to uncover and begin to heal a family's hidden dysfunction. And then there's the mythical dybbuk, in Jewish tradition a soul possessed by the spirit of one who is restlessly wandering, seeking to expiate his sins. What had happened to Bryan?

At 35,000 feet, somewhere over middle America, I found my explanations careening from one cause to another. The easy resolution to my uncertainty was labeling him a sociopath. The more likely was that a confluence of factors, some out of his control, had set him on a trajectory that closed a door, then another, then still more.

Labeling was not just easy, it also fed my desire for vengeance. He'd caused our parents, his wife and kids, all of us, enormous pain, seemingly with a total lack of empathy. Let him pay for that. Labeling, particularly with this label, was striking back at him. Even today, much of the time I hold onto that belief about him. It's accompanied by imagined shouted challenges. "Why couldn't you have tried harder? Didn't you care what you were doing to the family? To me?"

Alongside the darker blame and shame I harbor when I think of Bryan is an awareness that I had the extraordinary good luck of timing. Bryan and I, thirteen years apart in age, book-ended the kids generation in our family. I was an adolescent in the 1950s, turning twenty in 1962, and getting through the most vulnerable time for a young person's social development just as the placid Eisenhower era was ending. Coloring within the lines was unquestioned.

Bryan, in contrast, experienced being a teen during the mid-1960s to mid-1970s when massive upheavals in social norms were taking place. Just when I was sitting on that court martial board in Vietnam and surveying GIs about pot use, Bryan was twelve years old. That was the year Tim Leary uttered the famous phrase, "Turn on, tune in, drop out." During Bryan's teenage years, defiance was embedded in the anti-war, civil rights, and women's rights movements, the drug culture exploded, and the notion of coloring within the lines just because they were there was pounded and pummeled.

I needed to give him a break. Sure, we both had the benefits of family heritage pictured in those grainy film clips, and the privilege that came with our family's financial means, the communities in which we were raised, our being white. I don't know what set Bryan onto a different path than I took, but I wonder. Had he been the oldest and I the youngest, who would I have become?

Then another thought suddenly occurred to me, sufficiently vivid to make my heart pound. It once again raised the question of what might have happened had I been an adolescent during the flourishing of the drug culture.

When I was on the cusp of being a teenager, 12 years old and in the seventh grade in 1955, Cantor Lebow at Temple Israel was preparing me for my bar mitzvah, the religious coming of age for Jewish boys when they turn thirteen. For months I'd been learning the portion of the Law, the five books of Moses, which I'd recite at a Saturday morning religious service.

This milestone was a reminder of my place in the continuity of the Jewish people and that year ought to have been a highpoint for me. As the date for this ceremony approached, in a sense I was being carried along by a community made up of my parents, the cantor, Hebrew school teachers, and several other boys also preparing for their bar mitzvahs.

But something else was happening that year. I experienced it entirely alone and filled with shame. Awaiting me on the way home from school, sometimes also in the corridors between classes, were stinging epithets, biting words intended to wound. Being taunted, fighting, and getting beat up propelled me into hiding. Yet hiding offered only short-lasting protection as there'd be a next day of danger, with no end in sight.

I kept it secret and, as I later realized, because of that there wasn't the possibility of supportive adults and classmates helping me to get through this. No classes, capped by a Saturday morning ceremony, on this part of becoming a man. I was being bullied and I felt entirely powerless.

What happened back then remained all too close to the surface for a number of years, eventually receding. Except, while traveling home for Bryan's funeral, the realization of what might have been hit me hard. Had the option of getting high been available to me in that painful time of my life, would I have taken it?

—∞—

As we had arranged for each of our parents, the funeral was held at the Stanetsky-Hymanson Memorial Chapel in Swampscott, just a few miles from where we had grown up, and the burial was in the family plot in the Chevra Mishna Cemetary in nearby Lynn. I spoke at the funeral, saying things about my brother that were intended to be comforting, particularly for Bailey, Meredith, and Christina, but really for all of us. His love for his children, the joy he experienced when Meredith gave birth to his granddaughter, Kendall, his skillful game of golf, his special relationship with Sherry, the delicious noodle kugel he made, his passion for boating—I found a number of his qualities and memories of our earlier lives to weave into my talk. I suspect some heard my meaning when I said I was grateful that he was finally free of the immense pain of these last years.

—∞—

Bryan had smoked a lot of pot, and people don't die from marijuana overdoses. That was clear. His heart and lungs quit working because he had exceeded his tolerance to opiates, drugs like oxycodone.

But, on the day of his funeral and continuing to today, I wonder: Might his pot use have played some part? Did he find himself in a ditch too deep to climb out of, not due to any one drug but rather from the combined effects of whatever he took to stay loaded, and the price this way of living cost him with his family, in his ability to work, and in his feelings about himself?

One conclusion seems clear. Some who become players will travel down a path of self-destruction, and those who are on the sidelines—people like me—will likely feel angry, sad, helpless, remorseful, ashamed, and stuck in an eternal intermission.

PART 5

ACTIVISM RENEWED

36

CHEECH AND CHONG

WASHINGTON, D.C.
30 DECEMBER 1996

Ten years earlier, several senior officials in the Clinton administration sought to stem an unfolding crisis.

"This is not a medical proposition. This is the legalization of drugs!"

The speaker was retired General Barry McCaffrey, the nation's drug czar. He shook his head with a look of disgust. "This is not medicine. This is a Cheech and Chong Show!"

He held up a handful of newspapers, waved them in front of the cameras, and picked out one from the pile. Pausing to look out at the reporters before continuing, as if to underscore his point, he went on. "Here's what the medical advisor in the state of California saw as potential uses of marijuana: forgotten memories, cough suppressant, Parkinson's Disease, writer's cramp." He sounded incredulous as he read each item on the list.

McCaffrey was clearly fuming and I felt my pulse quicken. This was going to be even worse than I had feared.

It was Monday morning, December 30, 1996. I had stayed at home to watch this much-anticipated news conference. Alongside McCaffrey were the Attorney General, the Secretary of Health and Human Services, and the Director of the National Institute on Drug Abuse.

President Clinton had rolled out the heavy artillery. It appeared this was about to become the latest barrage in the war against marijuana.

A month earlier the voters in California and Arizona had chosen to exempt from prosecution patients whose doctors had recommended they use the drug. That is, they'd be protected under state law. Marijuana possession under federal law would remain a criminal offense. The stage was set for a confrontation.

Janet Reno came to the podium. Tall, wearing the oversized round frame glasses that were her trademark, and speaking in the measured cadence for which she was well known, the Attorney General threw down the gauntlet. "DEA officials will review cases," she said, "to determine whether to revoke the registration of any physician who recommends or prescribes so-called Schedule 1 controlled substances."

I was appalled. Without a DEA registration, physicians would be greatly limited in the drugs they could prescribe. In essence, they'd be prevented from practicing medicine.

She continued with her ominous warning. "We will not turn a blind eye toward our responsibility to enforce federal law and to preserve the integrity of the medical and scientific process to determine if drugs have medical value before allowing them to be used."

"But what about people like Magda Fric," I wanted to shout at her. "Can you be that uncaring about people desperately seeking some relief? Would you turn a blind eye to their plight?"

I felt my jaw clenching. As I watched the four officials at the podium, noting the stern expressions on each of their faces, I wondered if they'd take the same position if it became personal, if a member of their own family were ill and could potentially benefit from marijuana. I had debated medical marijuana policies with people who insisted that no exceptions could be justified to the FDA-mandated testing for safety and effectiveness. Quietly, after those debates had ended, several very privately acknowledged that if they or their loved ones were suffering, they'd consider using pot.

"Of course you would," I thought. I felt discouraged by the Attorney General's heavy-handed insensitivity. "Damn, where are you coming from?"

Just after the news conference concluded, I imagined how it might have gone if these federal officials had seen the two new state laws as an opportunity. In my mind's eye, a very different scenario would have unfolded. I made it up, putting words in their mouths. I relished what they might have said about what the California and Arizona voters had done. If only it had happened like this. . . .

The drug czar would have spoken first. "Let me welcome you this morning." No stern disapproving looks. For that matter, his very tone of voice would be compassionate. "We recognize that some physicians believe their patients will benefit from using marijuana." The others at the podium would have been nodding their agreement, even Janet Reno. "We understand that a majority of voters in California and Arizona want this decision to be between doctors and their patients. Therefore, today we are announcing a modified federal strategy concerning marijuana's medical use."

In my fantasy of what might have happened, the Attorney General would then have reminded everyone that while the federal prohibition of marijuana stood, the recent elections in California and Arizona called for an accommodation. She would announce that she had asked the U.S. Attorneys in those states to not prosecute individuals whose physicians recommended marijuana use for medical purposes. Not the patients and not the doctors.

Then Donna Shalala, Secretary of Health and Human Services, would have come to the microphone. Her accommodation would have involved directing the Food and Drug Administration to issue information about marijuana similar to what we commonly find on package inserts with prescribed medications. Sure, it'd be incomplete since the research evidence was still scanty. Yet the goal would be to help doctors and patients to be as fully informed as possible.

I was on a roll. Next, I imagined her saying that the DHHS soon would fund two new research centers devoted to studying the therapeutic potential of marijuana. Finally, Alan Leshner, Director of the National Institute on Drug Abuse, would announce a new public education campaign. He'd say this campaign would be tailored to help young people understand the difference between marijuana's medical benefits and the risks of its recreational use.

Of course all of what I fabricated was pure fantasy. Yet why couldn't it have happened this way? I hoped many others might think about this as I did. Would submitting an op-ed piece to the *Seattle Times* in which I'd lay out my imagined scenario be worthwhile? I wanted a friend's help in thinking this through.

Alan Marlatt, the psychology professor who had set up a fully equipped bar in his department to study drinking behavior, listened patiently as I ranted about the Attorney General's threat. We met at Ivar's Salmon House, a replica of a Northwest Indian longhouse. Its commanding view of Lake Union and the downtown Seattle skyline, the ceremonial racing canoes suspended from the ceiling, the dozens of historical photographs of Native Americans, and its open-pit alder barbecue made it a tourist favorite. For years Alan had frequently held lunch meetings there and he was well known among the wait staff.

He commiserated with me when I lamented the coldness of those government officials, but laughed when I told him what they ought to have said. "Rog, any idea what would have happened if they'd said those things?"

I knew he was going to rain on my parade, but I persisted, summoning up an attitude of indignation for my soapbox speech. "Yeah," I said. "They'd have been praised for respecting the will of the voters." I ticked each point off on the fingers of my left hand. "They'd have been applauded for having compassion for seriously ill patients, for respecting the integrity of the medical profession, and for giving the public credit for having common sense."

He was patiently listening, and I finished with a flourish. "And, Alan, they'd have stood tall in the eyes of anyone with an inkling of how much hysteria typically follows any acknowledgement that marijuana can be beneficial."

I sat back in my chair, my arms folded across my chest, almost daring him to refute any of these points. He wasn't disagreeing, of course, and I knew he wouldn't. He smiled at me, slowly shaking his head, and giving me a moment to exhale. We both watched a Kenmore Air seaplane descend and land, somehow dodging a number of nearby sailboats and yachts dotting the lake.

"You're dreaming," he finally said. "If they'd said what you wanted to hear, conservatives in Congress would have pounced. I can just imagine Newt Gingrich tearing into Clinton for being 'soft on drugs.' The Republicans would have used that again and again as a weapon in every campaign ad from now until the next election.

"But that's not all," he added. "If reformers, people like you and me, praised the administration for its accommodations to the state initiatives, our endorsements would be one more nail in that 'liberal' coffin. Clinton would be accused of getting into bed with the radical left." He must have seen that my face had reddened. He stopped and waited for my reaction. We were friends and I appreciated his frankness, but his reality check was hard to hear. But what made it hurt the most was that I knew Alan was right. It was inevitable that the White House would try to derail the initiatives, just as it was inevitable that Surgeon General Jocelyn Elders would be forced from office when she called for rethinking the nation's policies concerning drugs and risky teen sex.

There's a postscript. The ACLU filed suit, claiming that the threat against physicians constituted an infringement of their First Amendment rights. The courts agreed. The initiatives would stand. For the time being, the problem of federal interference was resolved.

But there was a hitch waiting just around the corner. Other states would soon follow California and Arizona by enacting medical marijuana laws that bypassed the federal prohibition. Deep tectonic plates of marijuana prohibition had shifted and a tsunami had begun surging in our direction.

37

COMPASSION

S *our Diesel, Purple Kush, Train Wreck, Jedi, Cat Piss!* The question I found myself baffled by was: "Why didn't I see this coming?

These were names for various cannabis products, each purportedly having its own unique formulation of cannabinoids to best fit specific medical conditions. *Nectarine* was said to be good for relieving hip pain, giving the patient a sense of joy while not causing sedation. *Purple Kush* had a grapey taste with an immediate pain relieving effect, while also decreasing anxiety and depression. A bit of web surfing revealed the existence of a detailed Wikipedia-like pharmacopoeia concerning a large variety of strains of pot derived from two cannabis species, indica and sativa.

And then there were the dispensary ads that filled page after page of alternative weekly newspapers in states where the laws had been changed. The marketing images and messages in these ads were clearly tailored for people quite unlike the older cancer patients I had once visited. One ad showed Jane, a sexy young woman with a stethoscope around her neck standing in front of a display cabinet that included six-inch marijuana starter plants and jars filled with buds. Jane held a clipboard that listed the prices for an ounce of *Charlie Sheen* ($170), *Blue Dream* ($300), or the top-of-the-line *Cherry Bomb* ($320). The ad noted that tinctures, edibles, and clones were available at this dispensary where walk-ins were welcome.

When California and Arizona jump-started the populist medical marijuana movement in 1996, it had been nearly twenty years since I had quit smoking pot. And I was that much older, long since having any social involvement with friends who got high.

On the other hand, I was conducting research on marijuana dependence counseling and also working privately as a therapist, primarily with marijuana-dependent adults. I was steeped in the subject. Yet the fact of the matter was that I didn't see any of this coming.

An enterprise born out of compassion for seriously ill patients gave rise over the next decade to a new populist marijuana movement. Between 1996 and 2012 seventeen states and the District of Columbia adopted laws that protected medical marijuana users and the providers who, acting as caregivers, became their source of supply.

I doubt, however, that many who supported these new laws anticipated the massive gray market that was evolving. As in the California gold rush of the mid-1800s, the ranks of marijuana growers exploded. Medical marijuana dispensaries were opened, a handful at first, soon numbering in the thousands. Known colloquially as the Green Rush, the enormous growth in the industry was due in part to Attorney General Eric Holder's 2009 announcement that the Department of Justice would not prosecute those in compliance with state medical marijuana laws. Just the kind of progressive White House response I had wistfully fantasized back in 1996 when, instead, the Clinton administration threatened to punish physicians who recommended marijuana's medical use to their patients.

The floodgates flew open. In Denver, within nine months of Holder's decision, more than four hundred dispensaries were in business. In another year there were nearly 1,000. Eighty thousand Colorado residents soon held physicians' authorizations, with state officials estimating the rate of increase at 400 applicants per day. A Berkeley professor of law referred to the evolving medical marijuana scene, in many respects a side door approach to quasi-legalization, as "slouching toward Amsterdam."

Many who would benefit were in reality cheating the system. Medical marijuana laws became a form of back door legalization for buyers, many of whom had no valid medical need. And the provisions of these laws offered a gold mine for those doctors who indiscriminately sold their signatures, and growers who, under the guise of being the primary caregivers, crossed way over the line in claiming their crops were solely for patients.

I had once championed the cause, passionately believing that bypassing the federal prohibition of marijuana's medical use was rational, compassionate, and quite separate from the effort to decriminalize non-medical possession. In my mind, it was all about people like Magda and my three university colleagues, each of whom struggled with cancer, and the many patients I had visited to help them learn about marijuana and clandestinely supplied with that anonymous grower's gift.

Over time, however, as the truth about this new industry became apparent, I found myself feeling discouraged, discouraged about the scamming, yet also ambivalent. After all, notwithstanding the unsavory aspects, relief was becoming more readily available to many who were truly ill.

Thirty years after I had led the State of Washington chapter of NORML and lobbied for decriminalization, I felt alienated by people leading the reform movement. This new generation of activists was riding the medical marijuana bandwagon, believing this was the way to eventually gain public support for entirely ending the prohibition of pot. I also realized that I missed being on the bus. I had liked being on the front lines. I still believed in reform, but I felt out of synch with those trying to achieve it in this way.

Did I need an attitude adjustment? Might some cheating be a price worth paying to make marijuana accessible for those who really needed it? I remained undecided. Then, twelve years after the California and Arizona initiatives started the ball rolling, a conversation with a friend helped me better understand my disquiet.

Just after Labor Day in 2008, Cheryl and I packed the car, loaded our Australian Shepherd, Teddy, in the back seat, and drove north to Mukilteo where we'd catch the 1:00 P.M. ferry for a twenty minute ride over to Whidbey Island. Sharon Berlin, a friend for more than thirty years, had recently retired from the University of Chicago social work faculty and, after spending summers in the village of Langley on the island, now lived there year round.

Often during our visits we spent time at Double Bluff Beach on the southern tip of Whidbey. A favorite for seashell collectors, the beach offers spectacular views of Mt. Rainier, the Seattle skyline, the Olympic Mountains, bald eagles, and container ships traversing Puget Sound. We particularly enjoyed going there because Teddy and Jessie, Sharon's Labradoodle, had free run of a long stretch of the beach that was designated an off-leash area. There was something deeply satisfying about seeing them having so much fun at the ocean.

The dogs and I had been playing while Cheryl and Sharon talked. After a while, Cheryl went looking for artistic pieces of driftwood and unusual stones, and I took a turn walking along with Sharon, tall and lithe with short brown hair.

"Have you read that *New Yorker* article that I gave you?" she asked. Sharon had loaned her copy of the magazine to me a month earlier. In the "reporter at large" section of the July issue, David Samuels had contributed a piece titled "Dr. Kush: How medical marijuana is transforming the pot industry." Samuels spent six months researching the topic, having been taken behind the scenes in California by a friend from their undergraduate years. The friend, his moniker Captain Blue, was now a marijuana broker, earning six figures annually connecting upstate growers with retail dispensaries.

I took a minute to think about how to respond. We'd just passed a rustic shelter constructed of driftwood, tree stumps, and planks of lumber. This part of the beach, ever changing with the ocean's new deposits of debris, offered the potential for adventures. The tide was out and because it was easier walking on the sand than on the rocks, we headed toward the surf. Up ahead a woman shouted, letting her kids know they'd climbed high enough on the steep bluff. The kids yelled back that they had just a few more yards to go to reach a dug out spot that to them probably looked like a cave.

I had looked forward to having this conversation. Sharon would be a good sounding board. It's not that she lacked opinions on this subject. She had always let me know what she thought, even if we disagreed. Nor was my expectation shaped by her being a good listener, although that was undeniably one of her qualities. I suspect that the main reason I wanted to talk with her was because Sharon readily disclosed her own uncertainties, sometimes with a tongue in cheek lament of "God help me" as she expressed her doubts, always with a touch of humor and a good deal of humility. In our conversations uncertainties were permitted. Sharon was willing to be vulnerable while reflecting on the layers and facets of tough issues.

"To be honest," I said, "I got angry reading the article. It seems to me that the movement has been taken over by greed."

She nodded in agreement and added, "A whole lot of people apparently are terribly ill in California."

I glanced over to see if she was serious and she laughed.

"Yeah, I think that's what bothers me more than the money," I said. "As I see it, the compassionate intent of the voters is being mocked by healthy guys in their twenties who have a wink-wink nod-nod five-minute chat with a totally unethical physician about their supposed suffering with pain or anxiety. Money changes hands, a form is filled in, a fake patient gets legal cover never intended for that purpose, and everyone's happy."

All of this just felt sleazy to me. I was letting my resentment pour out, knowing as I did so that I was sounding self-righteous. I'd not be this candid with most people. While these thoughts and feelings were genuine, I realized they also conflicted with values that had led me to marijuana reform activism in the first place. I still believed criminalizing use was wrong.

"Even as I hear myself saying it, Sharon, I feel conflicted. I don't know. I'm not against people who want to smoke pot being protected from getting convicted of a crime, but I don't like this way of getting to it." I felt discouraged about what had begun to sound like whining. I really didn't fully understand what was driving my negativity.

We gingerly stepped across a ledge of slippery rocks to explore pools exposed by the minus tide and spent several minutes looking at a colorful mélange of mussels, urchins, and anemones. Four gulls impatiently hovered. For them it was grazing time and we tourists were an annoyance.

I bent down to take a closer look at a red sea urchin, and then had another thought. "You know, it feels good to vent. But on the other hand, I can't imagine saying this to people growing pot and running dispensaries who really believe what they're doing is contributing to healing." The article had described a pharmacist in her fifties who for decades had worked in a hospice. She said that in their final days, because smoking marijuana made it possible for patients to avoid strong narcotics, they had the chance to interact with their friends, share with their families, and be present until the final moments.

"Thirty years ago, their values were my values," I said. I wondered. Had I changed, changed that much?

"What bothers you the most?" Sharon asked. "Is it the profit-making? The subterfuge? Something else?"

That must have been just the right time to ask that question because the answer came to me readily. "Yeah, I think I understand what I've been resenting. It boils down to two issues. First, the blatant scamming that's embedded in what's intended for medical purposes taints the whole enterprise. I end up feeling judgmental, kind of hyper alert and full of scorn, about all of the growers and dispensary owners and authorizing physicians and supposed patients. It doesn't leave me room to react like I'd like to, and that is to totally champion the legitimate help that genuinely ill people are receiving."

I noticed Sharon nodding and felt relieved that I'd been able to articulate part of what had been festering in my reactions to the article. "The second problem is that if marijuana is going to be legalized, it should happen through the front door, not the back. We should say what we mean when we put non-medical legalization on the table. And when we do that, we should also acknowledge that some people can be harmed, some can become dependent, and some, especially young people, can get in way over their heads and pay a huge price. It's not a consequence-free endeavor. And then we need to come up with the money to pay for programs to deal with these risks, to prevent kids from abusing pot, and to provide services for those who will need it. Legal pot should be taxed enough to pay the bill."

My heart was racing. I felt clearer. Sharon capped the moment. "Sounds right, Roger. I think you've hit the nail on the head."

Cheryl was up ahead sitting on a felled tree trunk, the two dogs resting nearby on the sand. We joined her and Cheryl showed us a handful of keepers, rocks streaked with minerals, and a gnarled chunk of driftwood. "Anyone hungry?" she asked. We snacked on some crackers, slices of cheddar cheese, and red grapes. The three of us and the dogs sat quietly for several minutes, watching a freighter make its way north and a heron, its wings extended, gracefully land on a sandbar several yards from where the frothy water disappeared into the sand.

Cheryl asked, "What did I miss?" I laughed, telling her that I'd had a free therapy session. I described the clarity I'd discovered in what had been so murky.

"In a way," Sharon said, running her hand through her hair, "I've had kind of a similar struggle."

"What's been happening?" Cheryl asked.

"It's about the volunteering I've been doing, preparing lunches for Whidbey Island kids. Back when we started this, the program was serving perhaps fifteen or twenty families who were in need, but in the last several months the number of parents who've applied for free weekend lunches keeps jumping up. The other day one of the volunteer leaders was going on about how great it was that we were reaching so many more people, but in the dark recesses of my mind I wondered how there could be so many families who couldn't provide lunches for their kids and whether some people were just taking advantage of the program."

Sharon shook her head. "Even having this thought, I feel like one of those old-time prim and grim social workers who only wanted to serve the 'truly needy.' But it still hasn't been an easy thought to shake. It takes a lot of effort to raise the money needed to buy the food, and maybe some of it could be going to better use for people who are really in need."

"Yeah," I said, "I've not liked the prim and grim thoughts either."

"Well, I think I'm coming around to thinking that it really is beside the point if a few people might be getting a free ride. It doesn't really matter. I'm realizing that there actually is a lot of need in this idyllic place, and anyway, who would want to try to set some kind of criteria for who deserves lunches, to have to discern who was 'poor enough?' That would be horrible. I think the answer is simply open-handed generosity. Giving freely, no questions asked. That's the answer."

Cheryl and I smiled. Sharon's resolution was simple and right, and it fit with what we knew to be values deeply held by our friend.

"Ready to walk back?" Sharon asked. The conversation shifted and we headed for the car. Back at Sharon's house we barbecued some lamb, made a salad, fed the dogs, and settled down at the dining room table. Then a quick packing up and saying our goodbyes when I realized we'd need to hustle to make the next ferry.

On the trip home I replayed that conversation in my mind. Might I, too, conclude that it just didn't matter? I envied Sharon for being able to have her doubts about legitimacy, yet set them aside. Try as I might, however, her answer just didn't fit for me. I wanted it to, but I was convinced the quasi-legalization of marijuana under a medical necessity pretense would continue the mythology that had historically obscured the truth about this drug. Ultimately, the public would not be well served, I thought. To be honest, I also rankled at the image of a healthy kid smirking because he was able to stick it to the man by getting an authorization letter.

I felt stuck. Stuck and discouraged.

38

ALISON'S INVITATION

SEATTLE
13 MAY 2011

Tat's, an East Coast style deli located in the heart of Seattle's historic Pioneer Square, typically sees lines stretching half a block from the door at lunchtime. There's even a webcam, an early warning system used by downtown workers to check out how busy the place is before leaving their offices.

As a newcomer, the experience was a bit overwhelming, with a cacophony of conversations from the fifty or so people who had snagged seating and the crowd waiting in a line that snaked through the room, the shouting from the kitchen when each order was ready for pickup, and a menu that brimmed over with various options of Philly Steaks, Hoagies, deli sandwiches, soups, salads, and sides. So many choices! If a Philly Steak, which one of four kinds, and would I want onions, mushrooms, peppers? If yes on peppers, would they be sweet, hot, or fried? What kind of bread? What about cheese? Whiz, provolone, Swiss, cheddar, American, pepper jack, mozzarella? It looked like there were at least three options for pastrami, the description of each more mouth-watering than the last. Then there were the posted instructions on precisely how a customer should convey their order when they finally made it to the counter. Indeed, a sign gave an ominous warning: If you make a mistake, don't worry, just return to the end of the line. Yikes.

I looked around to see what people were eating, hoping to be inspired or at least to narrow the list of possibilities. When we arrived, Alison spotted a table just being cleared and quickly grabbed it. I'd need to get her order by phone so as to not lose either my place in line or our coveted table.

When we finally had our lunches, we laughed at the relief in successfully getting through the ordeal. Alison had the Philly Cheese Steak with provolone, grilled onions, and fried peppers. I chose the Tatstrami, a pastrami cheesesteak with cole slaw, melted Swiss cheese, and Russian dressing. The sandwiches were enormous, more than either of us could finish.

Today's conversation over lunch was a continuation of a dialogue Alison and I had been having since we first met in 2007 as members of Seattle's Marijuana Policy Review Panel. Several years after it began its work, I was appointed to fill a vacant seat on this committee that had been established when Seattle voters passed Initiative 75 in 2003.

That initiative had required Seattle to give lowest enforcement priority to adult personal possession of marijuana. It was a creative alternative to decriminalizing possession, which, after Seattle's 1974 decriminalization ordinance was nullified by a 1989 state law, would still remain a criminal offense. Another provision was the creation of a panel to evaluate this new policy's impact. Was public safety endangered as a consequence? Were more young people using pot? What was the fiscal impact on the courts, prosecutors and public defenders, the police, the jails?

Alison looked a bit like Liza Minnelli, with a short pixie hairstyle, dimples, and bright expressive eyes. Both on the city panel and in other public presentations, it was evident she was as masterful in compellingly laying out a complex argument as Liza was in belting out a song. I also came to know how passionate she was about social justice.

At different times while a student, she had set her sights on careers in business, architecture, anthropology, or sports medicine. Her father, noting how much Alison liked to debate, encouraged her to study law. He had been right; she loved the challenges in the courtroom.

She came to hold strong opinions about the drug war's undermining of civil liberties such as protections against unlawful searches and seizures. Those opinions later evolved into an intense commitment to reforming the drug laws. She told me when the turning point had occurred. She defended a man with no criminal record who faced a fifteen-year mandatory minimum sentence. He had been paid to be a "mule," that is, to transport cocaine from one supplier to another. The case containing the drug was placed into his car and he was told where to deliver it. In need of the money, he asked no questions. Without his being told, that case also contained a gun.

She said, "I sobbed the night I came home from my first visit with him in a Montana detention center. He was just a touch younger than me and absolutely terrified knowing what he faced. He had been blind-sided and he was looking to me for reassurance. I was distraught by knowing there was very little I could give him, and I couldn't make any more sense of the sentence he faced than he could."

I eagerly anticipated each of our lunch conversations. They gave me the chance to learn where the action was in drug law reform both locally and nationally. Three decades had passed since NORML imploded, Ronald Reagan was elected, and the momentum of states passing decriminalization measures stopped dead in its tracks. Now, the train was moving once again.

Man, was it moving. In just the past few years, three different decriminalization and legalization bills had been introduced in the Legislature. Then, there was an initiative filed by a group calling itself Sensible Washington to fully legalize marijuana by essentially repealing all laws that prohibited the drug.

There was more. Seattle's new city attorney announced his office would not prosecute adults charged with simple marijuana possession offenses, the new mayor called for legalization and, in November of 2010, fully 46 per cent of California voters marked their ballots for a legalization proposition.

An astute pundit, Alison shared behind the scenes details about the key players and her own views about the likelihood of success for each reform effort. Would any of these bills make it out of committee? She gave the odds. Would enough signatures be gathered to qualify Sensible Washington's legalization initiative for the ballot? Not a chance, she thought. The voters wouldn't support a wide open unregulated market.

Our conversations were enlightening, a policy seminar over lunch. And they were a clear sign, I thought, of how much of a powerhouse Alison had become in shaping drug law reform directions, helping draft bills, recruiting other activists, and eliciting endorsements. When the *Seattle Times* published an editorial favoring legalization, I suspected that somehow Alison had had a hand in the newspaper deciding to take this groundbreaking step.

Today, however, we mostly talked about her vision, a way she believed legalization could actually be achieved. The public was increasingly positive about finding an alternative to prohibition, she said, but the Legislature would shy away from taking such a controversial step. The answer was to file an initiative with provisions that would reflect what polling indicated the public wanted. That is, there'd need to be tight regulation of growers and sellers, strict restrictions on advertising, and oversight by a state agency with the power to write and enforce the rules to govern the market. Driving under the influence of marijuana would need to be clearly prohibited, as would home growing, and taxes would need to be levied to both undercut the cartels and benefit the taxpayers. A key provision would need to be funding effective drug prevention programs targeting young people.

Alison had asked for my feedback on drafts over the past several weeks, and I'd felt encouraged by the direction in which the proposed law was heading. She was on the right track, I thought, even though I remained skeptical. Regardless of the provisions she and I discussed, I feared legalization would stimulate an explosion of a new marijuana industry and a steep increase in young people using pot. I also worried that just the fact that legalization had been enacted would convey a message that marijuana is safe.

Still, it was a good conversation. When we noticed waiting customers eying our table, we prepared to leave. Just then, however, Alison looked over at me and said she had a question. When the initiative was filed with the Secretary of State, would I consider being a sponsor?

That stopped me in my tracks. It was flattering to be asked and I recognized this was a chance to again be involved in reform activism after more than thirty years. But my underlying fears were real and my inclination was to decline. I held back, though, and both thanked her for asking and said I'd need time to think it over. We agreed to talk again soon, and that day's seminar came to an end.

As I drove back to my office, I worried about being aligned with advocates campaigning for legalization on the premise that marijuana use is harmless. That would be untenable. Three years earlier, Alison and I had sparred over just that issue.

—m—

Early in February of 2008 Alison invited me to attend a preview screening at a downtown auditorium of a just completed documentary titled *Marijuana: It's Time for a Conversation*. It was produced by the Washington State chapter of the ACLU and filmed in Seattle before a studio audience. Glancing around at the crowd that evening, it was evident the invitation list had been selective. This middle-aged group of about 150 people, most in business attire, represented power. I suspected many were among the ACLU's most committed supporters. Alison told us the film was intended for airing on local television stations and we were among the first to view it. Audience members would be asked for their feedback.

In the film, Rick Steves, a popular travel writer and television personality, was the host. Cheryl and I often watched his *Rick Steves Europe* travel programs on the local PBS station. The documentary had been professionally produced with many features that make for entertaining television. The cameras cut frequently between the studio audience, Steves, and several speakers seated on the set. Then there were numerous clips from recorded interviews with scientists, legal historians, a law enforcement officer, and patients who used pot medically. Graphics popped up with statistics on the large numbers being arrested for simple possession, the growing percentage of the public that favored decriminalization, and the huge costs of enforcing the marijuana laws. It was impressive.

The cameras showed people in the studio audience laughing while they watched a clip from the 1930's film *Reefer Madness*. They looked thoughtful while New York City Mayor Fiorello LaGuardia argued for the repeal of Prohibition due to its being unenforceable, a conclusion that seemed also applicable to marijuana. They were talking my talk. But before the 30-minute documentary ended, I became discouraged.

I gradually realized a cornerstone of the decriminalization case in the film was the notion that marijuana was risk-free. A retired judge had said pot was "a relatively harmless substance." A professor of pharmacology had said it was "largely safe" and "the most dangerous thing about marijuana is to be arrested for its possession and use." And then there was a policy analyst who said, "With marijuana, the most damage someone is going to likely do is to a bag of Doritos."

The film ended and the lights came up. The applause was enthusiastic and several audience members quickly voiced their approval. I wondered if I'd be alone in having reservations.

I raised my hand. Alison called on me, taking a moment to say a few words of introduction.

"I'm dazzled by the professionalism," I said. "In many respects, it's a great way of educating the public about why the law should be changed. But I believe this film ought to be taken back to the editing room before being released." I felt my throat beginning to constrict and feared my comments would be met with derision, but pushed on. "Marijuana is not harmless," I said, "yet several speakers in this film say it is. A really compelling case can be made for removing criminal penalties without having to misinform the public by saying pot doesn't have risks.

"I've been a proponent of decriminalizing marijuana for thirty years and led this state's NORML chapter in the mid-1970s. But for the past two decades I've also conducted marijuana dependence counseling studies at the UW with adults and teens. Some people, and this is not just a myth, really get into trouble with compulsive use of marijuana. Let me just say that in its current form, the film is conveying erroneous information and it's also bad political strategy. There'll be a lot of push-back because it won't be seen as even-handed."

I noticed some people were nodding in agreement as I spoke and I began to be hopeful that others would support my perspective. That didn't happen, however, and when one person stood, claimed I was spewing reactionary propaganda that had held sway for fifty years and said it was time for some truth for a change, it stung. As the crowd was leaving, Alison suggested we talk further. A few weeks later we continued the conversation at a local Starbucks.

It was 10:00 in the morning and Seattle's late February weather was living up to its reputation. The sky was dark and the rain relentless as I dashed from my car to the café and stood in line to order. Alison hadn't yet arrived and I used the time to rehearse the points I'd make to convince her to revise the film. Would she listen? I wondered. I waved as she came in the door and pointed to the table I had staked out.

"I'm really glad you were able to come to the screening," Alison said. "We were excited that so many people were there and that the response was so enthusiastic."

"Look, Alison, I want you to know I feel crummy about not being totally onboard with the film. With the exception of the statements about there being no risks, it's great. . . . great television, an effective history lesson, compelling examples of injustice, highly credible experts, an audience full of approving moms, Rick Steves' charming performance as MC, and so much more. It's the strongest reform piece I've ever seen."

She was nodding as I spoke, but clearly had a different point of view. "You know, I went back and watched it again, probably for the twentieth time, and I don't think the film says marijuana is harmless. For that matter, one of the specialists, Dr. John Morgan, a professor of pharmacology, acknowledged there are harms."

She took some notes from her briefcase, found the quote she was looking for, and read it aloud. "He said, 'In areas in which it's dangerous, prohibition is doing us no good.'"

Alison looked up from her notes. "I don't think he could have been clearer. He says that there are dangers, but prohibition doesn't prevent them. Isn't he right about that?"

This discussion wasn't going well. To my hearing, Alison's question seemed like a legalistic ploy to avoid the actual concern I had raised.

"Yes, he's right if you only consider one phrase in one sentence of his remarks," I said, "but he said a lot more. In that clip, acknowledgment that people can be harmed by marijuana is really buried. Listen to what he and others on the documentary said." I ticked off the phrases: most safe psychoactive compound people have ever ingested, largely safe, the most danger is to a bag of Doritos, and relatively harmless. "It seems evident that these are the messages people are going to take from watching the film."

"Okay, I hear your perspective," Alison replied. "What do you think should be done to deal with what you see as the problem?"

I had an answer. For that matter, it was the same point I had tried unsuccessfully to make with Keith Stroup, the founder of NORML, back in the mid-1970s when I first became an activist. "I think clips in the documentary where marijuana is called safe, harmless, or relatively harmless should be taken out. And I'd add in new content on the risks."

I watched her as I spoke, wishing she were taking notes. Unfortunately, she just listened, a doubtful look on her face. I pushed on. "I'd include the risk of dependence. I'd mention the risks of school failure and later psychiatric illness in adolescents, particularly those who start early. I'd speak of the risk for those with a history of psychotic disorder or cardiovascular disease, the potential harm to the lungs, and certainly the risks from driving stoned. Sure, an expert can say that prohibition hasn't prevented these problems and that a public health approach will be far more effective. But at least you'll be giving the viewer an accurate picture."

She paused, thought for a few moments, and then closed the door on the subject. "There are two reasons for not doing what you're suggesting, Roger. First, we're out of money. There just isn't any more funding for this project and the changes you're suggesting would be costly. But another reason, and this is more important, is that we'll risk pushing people's buttons if we emphasize the possible harms. It'll seize the viewer's brain and we'll lose the chance to get across the social injustice messages that are at the heart of this issue."

We parted on a friendly note despite our differences. The film was not re-edited and, when local television stations were asked to sell air time to the ACLU so it could be telecast, I wasn't surprised when only one of the local stations agreed, and then scheduled it for after 1:00 A.M.

Decades earlier I'd been a leader in this movement, but through this experience I felt like an outsider. I hardly wanted to walk away from the cause, but there didn't seem to be a place at the table for reformers who thought as I did.

—❧—

Alison's invitation to be an initiative sponsor, coming three years after we held that discussion about *Marijuana: It's Time for a Conversation*, weighed heavily on my mind. Her expertise in drug law and her exceptional skills as a communicator made me hopeful, more hopeful than I had been for many years, that with her leadership injustices in marijuana policy could be corrected. There were still hundreds of thousands of people labeled criminal each year for possessing pot, billions in illicit profits were being funneled to the cartels despite vast taxpayer sums devoted to stemming the trade, and people of color faced gross inequities in how prohibition actually worked, with African-Americans and Latinos having much higher rates of arrest despite use rates comparable to or lower than whites. It was shameful.

If legalization were some day adopted, a lot of what I thought a sound public health approach to marijuana control should look like was included in her initiative draft. That excited me.

But then there were the allusions in the documentary to marijuana being safe and my inability to convince Alison to see the issue as I did, much less agree with me about re-doing parts of the film. That troubled me. If I became a sponsor, would I be fighting that battle over and over again?

If only it were possible to sort out my reservations with Alan Marlatt, my long-time friend who directed the UW's Addictive Behaviors Research Center. He'd been a willing sounding board for decades. Fifteen years earlier, when I ranted about the Clinton administration's threat to punish doctors who recommended their patients use marijuana, he listened patiently, commiserated with me, and offered some sage advice.

We'd talked often about the drug laws. His frequent international trips made him aware that a number of countries responded more progressively than we did to illicit drug use. In his mind, when outcomes of these policies were examined alongside those from the U.S., our country's approach fared poorly.

I wanted to again have lunch with him at Ivar's Salmon House, sit at his favorite table, and bend his ear. I wanted to tell him about my apprehension concerning how the need for reform was being argued and learn what he thought.

39

A MYTH ENDURES

The news that Alan was dying reached Cheryl and me while we were travelling in Cambodia. It was shocking and we were entirely unprepared because early in that three-week trip, Alan and I had exchanged emails, setting a date to talk with Alison about various marijuana law reform possibilities.

Just ten days later a message from his son, Kit, told us what was happening. Alan's melanoma had advanced, his kidneys were failing, and there were no treatment options remaining. Alan was a devoted student of Zen, and it seemed as if karma led Cheryl and me the next day to the Temple of Angkor Wat where we lit incense and said prayers for him as we stood before a statue of the Buddha. Later we learned that Alan had passed away within hours of those moments.

Kit soon wrote again, giving us a comforting description of his father's last days. It brought me to tears. "He was in no pain, no suffering. He was in his beloved summer home in Warm Beach, Washington looking up through the skylights, watching the eagles soar and the rain gently fall."

Alan was genuine in his caring for the people who came to him for therapy. He was authentic, and over the years what he thought about how people used alcohol and other drugs in trying to meet understandable human needs had a large influence on me. People struggling with dependence could all too readily be stereotyped. Caricatures of the alcoholic or addict, of the narcissistic politician, the street thug, the punk musician, or the intensely driven CEO could easily mask the complexity of what each person sought through their use and how each got tripped up. Alan was non-pejorative and compassionate about the human condition, warts and all.

With regard to drug policy, Alan had long ago made up his mind. He supported marijuana legalization. Had he lived and had Alison invited him to be a sponsor of the initiative, I believe he would have accepted, even though he was more than knowledgeable about the harmful possibilities inherent in drug use.

And his advice for me? If I had had that conversation with him, sharing a meal at his favorite table in that Lake Union restaurant overlooking the Seattle downtown skyline, I suspect he'd have encouraged me to sign on as a sponsor despite my misgivings. I even imagined what he'd have said: "Get aboard and work on changing minds from the inside. We're headed toward legalization and we should be, but no one knows how to do it best. Do what you can to shape it in the form you believe it needs to have."

Alan's death hit hard.

Other memories replayed in my mind as I mulled over Alison's invitation to sponsor the initiative. Among them were the events of a day in early March when I returned to the two places where for me it had begun.

—⁓—

Nothing looked as it once had.

Mr. Truong Van Phong, a former sergeant in the South Vietnamese Army who served as an interpreter for the U.S. military during "the American War," had agreed to be our guide. Now in his early 70s, his full head of hair was completely white, his leathery complexion had a shiny olive patina, and he stood about 5'8' tall with a bit of a paunch. He wore wire-rimmed glasses, a white short-sleeved shirt and black dress pants. He was a handsome man.

Mr. Phong might have been a senior bureaucrat from all appearances, but, as we soon learned, his service in a defeated army and the work he had done for the U.S. military had cost him dearly after the communists took over. He and his family had struggled financially, and Mr. Phong was bitter about the closed doors to good jobs and admission to good schools that he, his wife, and children had faced ever since. He had survived by peddling a cyclo, a three-wheel bicycle taxi, and occasionally serving as a guide for returning Americans who had fought in the war.

With a hired car and driver he met us at our Ho Chi Minh City hotel, and from there we embarked on a day-long journey. Our objective was to first visit the place where Camp Bearcat, the 9th Infantry Division's home base, once existed. Then, we'd drive to the area in Long Binh where the 93rd Evacuation Hospital and the USARV Stockade had been located.

Forty-four years earlier, there had been rice paddies, woodlands, and open country at the outskirts of Saigon, but now the city's population had swelled to nine million and its boundaries had stretched far out into the surrounding region. It took hours just to make it through the heavily congested city traffic. The highway was only slightly less jammed with trucks, motor scooters, and cars the rest of the way. The air was brown with engine exhaust, and dust covered everything, buildings, shops, cafés, and seemingly even the people. Most scooter drivers and pedestrians near the road wore masks. Lung diseases had to be rampant here, I thought.

Mr. Phong knew the approximate location of Bearcat, but needed to stop a few times to ask for specific directions. We eventually found ourselves on a long, heavily rutted, and unpaved road through a plantation of neatly aligned trees. Mr. Phong told us that Camp Bearcat was now a Vietnamese army training center and he wasn't sure how close we'd be permitted to get. Soon, a prominent sign gave a definitive answer. Further passage was prohibited. We were in the middle of the plantation, and not even a glimpse of the base was possible. I was disappointed.

Just then an armored personnel carrier, one of many abandoned by our military when we hastily fled, rumbled up the road. I snapped a few photos before one of the soldiers waved me off. To our relief, they left us alone.

Once the APC was out of sight, we took photos of ourselves next to large concrete gateposts on either side of the dirt road. There were no gates. That was as close as we'd get, and I'd have to be satisfied with having made the effort.

Finding the Long Binh site was easier, yet the visuals as we drove through the area were entirely unfamiliar. Not a tent, a tank, an artillery battery, or sandbagged bunker to be seen. Where once stood a huge military logistics post of many square miles in dimension, there now were broad paved avenues, beautifully landscaped, with modern industrial buildings. The signs made it evident that companies from a number of countries had established these factories in what was now the Long Binh Techno Park.

At this area's outer perimeter we came to a concrete wall topped with concertina wire. Next to it there was an unmanned guard tower, standing perhaps sixty feet tall with a long ladder and window openings on all four sides of the elevated enclosure. Could this have been a stockade guard post? As I thought about it, however, it was more likely part of the Techno Park's security rather than a somehow surviving remnant of the American military presence.

The more difficult part of this day, strangely enough, was the trip back to Ho Chi Minh City. Mr. Phong talked on and on quite adamantly about the U.S. being noble, courageous, and absolutely right in fighting the communists in his country. He bitterly lamented that the American and South Vietnamese generals weren't given the resources they needed to win. He spoke derisively of U.S. war protesters as unworthy of citizenship in their great nation. Listening to him, I suspected that if any returning vets for whom he had served as a guide apologized for our country's actions, they'd have been entirely unprepared for his vehement reaction.

Returning to Bearcat and Long Binh, even though one had been entirely transformed and the other was completely inaccessible, brought to the surface thoughts and feelings, still unsettled, with which I had first grappled four decades earlier. As those memories popped up, Mr. Phong persisted in talking about his views about the war, and it felt as if the choking dust and crushing traffic surrounding us had invaded the car's interior.

On the one hand, I knew he too was reliving a piece of history that day. He obviously was also working very hard to fulfill his idea of a guide's responsibilities. In an earlier letter, responding to my request to spend the day with us, he wrote, "I will assume my duty with all my heart and devotion to serve my comrade and Brother-in-Arms."

Yet on the other hand, at that point in the day I couldn't take in any more of it. I had exhausted my ability to feign interest in his views about the war. Focusing on anything other than the swirling fragments of memory this day's journey had revived was beyond my capacity.

Finally, we were back in our hotel, the luxurious Intercontinental. Cheryl and I were both emotionally drained. She started gathering some clothes to wash before we went out for dinner. I stood at the window, looking out but not really focusing.

"When we set off this morning," I said, "I wasn't sure what emotions I'd feel."

"I wondered how it would be for you," she said.

"It's not so much sadness," I replied, "but rather a sense of being powerless. It's as if I want to run, but can't move because my feet are encased in concrete."

I thought about how else to describe the state I was in. "It's also a kind of cognitive freeze," I said, "as if the cursor on the computer screen won't move. I feel closed down, that nothing's moving in my mind."

"What's on the screen?" Cheryl asked, pointing to one of the chairs and sitting in another, encouraging me with a questioning look. Maybe it'd be a good idea, I thought, so I began.

"I remembered getting pretty depressed in the first few months. I'd assessed a number of young guys who'd been in intense firefights and seen friends get killed or badly injured. Some had threatened suicide. The intensity of their anguish was palpable and I wanted to get them out of there, something that just wasn't going to happen for most who instead were soon sent back to their units. For a while, I skipped breakfast and slept until mid-morning, not wanting to face it. That abruptly stopped when I got a dressing down by our battalion executive officer. I remember feeling a lot of shame, that I was seen as a shirker."

Then something occurred to me. "Just now I'm seeing a connection between my role with some of those soldiers and what that XO said to me."

"I don't understand," Cheryl said. "How were they similar?"

"There wasn't going to be any way out, no escape from that war, not for them and not for me. I got reamed by that XO, and while that certainly wasn't my style when interacting with soldiers, the fact of the matter is that the result was the same. The answer to them, most of them that is, and the answer to me were the same: Get back to your job. So I think that's part of the powerless feeling I've been having today, remembering a kind of despair that set in during those first few months and a realization there was no alternative, for me or for those GIs, but to get through it."

Cheryl listened and nodded. She waited to see if I was ready to reveal others of the memory remnants from that day's experiences.

Another scene popped up, perhaps stimulated by having seen that guard tower in the Long Binh industrial park. "While I was the Stockade social worker, I discovered the guards were using a steel conex container, one of those huge shipping boxes you see on cargo ships, as a disciplinary cell. In prisons, they'd call it 'the hole.' The temperature in there was undoubtedly hot enough to kill someone. This was torture, pure and simple. I went to see the Stockade commander, but he brushed me off, saying the only prisoners ever put in there were guys who'd assaulted guards or other prisoners. He insisted they weren't kept there long and were closely monitored. Eventually, the physician who ran the Stockade's medical clinic joined forces with me and together we got them to stop using it."

"You didn't seem powerless in that situation," Cheryl said quietly. "Do you think you were?"

I thought for a moment. Why had that experience been among the scenes that came to mind? Maybe it wasn't just about the steel box.

"No, I think you're right," I said. "But I think the sense of being powerless really came from realizing a lot of those prisoners had been chewed up and spit out for not cutting it in the Army, many because they just couldn't, I believed, and then acted out, some by going AWOL or getting high. I guess it all comes back to not being able to do a damn thing while seeing what being in the Army and in the war did to so many."

I wondered, with all that we learned in the following decades about the toll that war took, as did the wars in Iraq and Afghanistan, on so many soldiers' mental health, when does the myth crack? When do we begin to question what's normal? How much psychiatric illness needs to occur among those in the military before the belief that young people should be expected to return from war *without* emotional injury is challenged? When does the recruitment poster mentality give way to what's real?

I think I understand, at least in some way, how that myth endures. We turn our gaze away from the true horrors of the soldier's experience in war by lifting our eyes to a waving flag.

During the Vietnam War displaying the American flag came to signify a criterion of true patriotism that excluded me, that is, unquestioningly backing the role the U.S. was playing. Similarly, decals with the words "support our troops," and even the "thank you for your service" often heard from flight crews when men and women in uniform are aboard seem to me to be a double-edged sword. Well-intended? Without question. An expression of caring and of solidarity? Yes, of course. But what of the price we pay from not opening our eyes to what really happens to them, and as a result not having any idea about the ripped fabric of their souls?

I don't display the flag, place patriotic decals on my car, or thank soldiers for their service because were I to do so, in my mind too much of what needs to be said would be left out. A Seattle newspaper columnist had interviewed an Army Airborne Ranger who did four tours, three in Iraq and one in Afghanistan. He told her he hated it when people thanked him for his service. In his mind, while the person doing the thanking may think they're offering a gift, he experiences it as an empty box. "The only thing we may be parting with," the columnist wrote, "is our own sense of guilt."

From my perspective, the American flag has been hijacked. Still, when I see it flapping in the wind, when we're abroad, and at events such as a naturalization ceremony for new citizens, I have a deep sense of belonging to my country. But we don't display it on July 4th from our front porch. It would stand for less than I want it to.

—⁂—

I was startled from my reverie when Cheryl reminded me it was time to get ready for dinner. It was surprising that an hour had passed while I was immersed in thoughts stimulated by that day's visits.

It was difficult to shake off a perception of myself standing on the sidelines, my voice unheard, that this visit had prompted. Neither during the Vietnam War nor in the current wars in Iraq and Afghanistan were we acknowledging, much less preventing, the moral character assault experienced by so many in America's military. The call to patriotism masks an inconvenient truth.

In parallel, I thought of the idealism I felt in the early marijuana reform years of the 1970s, an idealism now drowned out as I observed the financial greed fueling much of the growing momentum of quasi-legalization via medical marijuana. The managing of marijuana's imagery to shape the public's beliefs continues to misrepresent, to hide the shades of gray where truth resides.

During and after my military service in Vietnam, I felt troubled by the power of the same myths that prevailed four decades later. In a month, I would be 69 years old. From our room on the seventeenth floor, we looked down on Saigon's orange-tinted air, a virtual scrim that alternately revealed and hid both the sprawling urban landscape and glimpses of who I once was, in my mid-twenties, in this place in 1967.

40

SIGNPOSTS

Finally, spring was in full flourish. Even dyed-in-the-wool northwesterners, well accustomed to the interminable gray of winter, many actually proclaiming a preference for that dark and gloomy time of year, were more than ready for dry weather and sunshine. So were our lawns and gardens.

Now, on the grounds of this community college campus just a short drive from Seattle, the rhodies were blossoming. After parking in the visitors' lot and looking around to get my bearings, I spotted several people in business attire walking in the same direction. It looked as if one of the men was wearing the club's familiar lapel pin. I followed along.

The program chairman greeted me at the entrance to the meeting room and, as people continued arriving, he introduced me to the current president. A buffet was ready along one side of the room and about a dozen round tables, each set for eight people, were gradually filling up.

Déjà vu. Thirty-four years earlier I had spoken before numerous civic clubs across the state, this one probably among them. It was a bit startling to realize that while I was among the youngest in the room back then, I was now among the oldest. Then as now my topic was marijuana law reform. Might people still be debating the issue thirty four years from now? I wondered.

Recent tries at legalizing marijuana had failed in our state. I had a few thoughts about this and wrote an op-ed piece for the *Seattle Times*. I argued legalization would succeed only when the public was convinced public health and safety would be better served by a tightly regulated market than by one that thrived underground. In my mind that certainly would preclude throwing the doors open to any and all for growing, selling, and possessing pot, unimpeded by licensing requirements and oversight by an agency of state government. It would also preclude unconstrained advertising, permitting use in public or access by minors, or driving while high.

Alison had seemed to be on the same page. The legalization initiative she was drafting included much of what I believed was needed. Indeed, we later learned that the state's Office of Financial Management estimated the earmarked tax revenue from legalized marijuana could, in the first five years of the new law's existence, allocate more than $500 million for evidence-based marijuana prevention, education, and treatment, and more than $20 million for marijuana research, including an evaluation of the new law's impact.

I was excited. For the first time, there was a proposal to end criminalizing pot smokers that not only acknowledged harms but also allocated a large amount of money to prevention or alleviation of marijuana problems.

Yet, I remained unsure. I wondered what this sea change in the law could lead to. There'd surely be economic incentives, just as in the alcohol and tobacco industries, to promote use. Would abuse and dependence increase? I never forgot what I had learned that day from the recovering heroin addicts.

I had another concern. How could we be assured that a legal regulated market, with all of its bells and whistles to protect the young, would push the black market out of existence? What if it continued to exist, catering to teens too young to buy marijuana legally? Might illegal sellers also capture their own market share by being the sole source of more potent pot than the legal outlets would be permitted to sell?

But I could easily lay out the arguments pro and con and I thought I was pretty well prepared for just about any question people in this audience might raise. First, however, it was time for lunch and I found that several people at my table had personal reasons for being interested in the topic.

The man to my left, probably in his late fifties, wearing a jacket and bow tie, his white hair thinning, talked about his son. "My boy, Stephen, probably wouldn't like it very much that I'm going to hear a talk about legalizing pot."

"He has some strong feelings about the issue?" I asked.

"Yes, and I'm grateful that he does. He got in over his head when he was in high school and barely graduated. Thank heavens he turned his life around three years ago. He goes to a Marijuana Anonymous meeting every week. I've got to tell you I'm so glad he did this long before my first grandchild came along last month."

Others at the table were nodding as he spoke. "My brother's kid had the same struggle, Norman," the man next to him said.

Sitting across from me, a man wearing a sport shirt and crew neck sweater, probably a few years younger than Norman, also had a story. He said, "You know, there's another side to this. My aunt got to the point where her back pain was so severe, with none of the medications really helping, that she asked a doctor to approve her to use marijuana. She says it's been just short of a miracle for her, and—believe me—she's no druggie."

I was smiling at that story, but then noticed another man at the table who was frowning. Probably about seventy, he had a dark tan and his face was deeply creased. He saw I was looking in his direction and soon made clear the reason for his apparent displeasure. Shaking his head as if to dismiss the medical pot example, he said, "There's way too much permissiveness in all this talk about marijuana. I'll tell you right now that I don't care a whit who's in favor of making it legal."

He looked over at the man who had just talked about his aunt. "You know, if it helps some people to use it medically, why don't they approve it like any of the prescription drugs we take? Why haven't they put it in pharmacies? Maybe there are valid reasons for this we should be talking about.

"In my mind, the *Seattle Times* editorial board veered way off course when they came out for legalizing pot. I tell you," he said, shaking his head, "we're headed in the wrong direction on this."

His forcefulness got my attention. He wasn't finished, though.

"There's a guy I know, I won't mention his name although you'd recognize it if I did, who has been very outspoken that marijuana should be legal. Actually, I'm really not surprised. This guy runs a successful business, but on July 4th and Veterans Day and Memorial Day, do you think he displays our American flag, just like every other businessman in this town? No, he does not! Not ever. These things say something about his values, don't you think?"

He maintained unblinking eye contact with me as he spoke, as if he hoped I'd dare to disagree. This sarcastic maligning of a man, and the inference about his values I had just heard, threw me for a loop. He found it consistent that someone who supported legalization refused to display the flag. I was pretty sure I knew who this fellow was talking about. It was someone I admired. There wasn't time to respond, however, because the program chairman was calling the meeting to order. I was relieved.

Following some announcements and the presentation of an award by the district governor, I was introduced. After my twenty minute talk, someone asked if marijuana is addictive, and another wondered if it was true that there are shops in Amsterdam where pot can be bought right out in the open. A man in the back identified himself as a physician and said he had helped decide which medical conditions marijuana could be authorized for in our state.

We were winding up when another person shouted, a hint of sarcasm in his voice, "Of course, the prospect of the state filling its totally empty coffers with hundreds of millions in new revenue wouldn't have anything to do with our sudden interest in getting into the pot business, would it?"

I laughed, and so did many in the audience. It was time to stop and I was soon on my way back to the University.

During that short car trip, I replayed what that fellow had said just before I began my talk. As I did so, my stomach felt increasingly acidic. "These things say something about his values, don't you think?" he'd asked. Perhaps he intended this as a rhetorical question, yet I found an answer was welling up forcefully in my thoughts as the miles passed.

On the way to my office I realized I was no longer on the fence. I'd sign on as a sponsor and lend my voice to those calling for regulating and taxing marijuana.

Looking back, it seemed evident I didn't need much of a push. As I'd read drafts of the proposed law and offered recommendations to Alison, I'd been looking for a way to justify taking this action. It would be in step with what I imagined my friend Alan would have encouraged, working from the inside to influence the form this new approach would take.

What tipped the scales for me was a visceral reaction to what that man with the creased face had said and to what he inferred. I recalled his look of disdain and the scorn in his voice. I didn't doubt he had legitimate fears. It's what he did with them that troubled me, his inference that the businessman was failing a test of patriotism and realizing he'd think the same of me.

Those few minutes with him during lunch had served as an important catalyst. There's altogether far too much, I thought, of his kind of toxic posturing over issues such as illegal immigration, abortion, gay rights, global warming, Muslims, gun control, and health care policy, let alone marijuana. Culture wars "fought with splenetic bile," wrote a columnist with the *Miami Herald*.

But that's what maintaining this war has required. Closed minds, forbidden topics, and excoriating those who disagree rather than looking for common ground. A war over a pig had been avoided back in 1859 because an admiral saw it would close off other ways of seeking resolution to the American-British boundary dispute. Dr. Jocelyn Elders, on the other hand, was summarily fired from her role as Surgeon General of the United States just for proposing we talk about alternatives to how we were dealing with drugs and teen sex.

When I was a kid, one of my favorite toys was a battery-operated View-Master. You inserted a round disk with seven pairs of slides into a slot. While looking through the two eye pieces, you pushed a lever to make the disk rotate so one image changed to the next. This was stereoscopic vision, the 3-D of the time. I felt as if I were actually in the scene, seeing it all around me and getting the full picture.

I'd come to appreciate that war prevents just that. We take a side and then filter information that comes our way as either backing up what we stand for or so egregiously flawed that it's of no relevance. We focus on fragments of truth and unquestioned myths to sustain our belief that our cause deserves victory and those on the other side must be defeated. All else, the inevitable shades of gray, the uncertainties and ambiguities, are obscured from our vision, with far too many of us willingly letting it happen, perhaps needing it to happen to cloak us in certainty, to avoid being sidelined by an issue's complexity.

Several months earlier while revisiting Vietnam, I'd found myself wondering what it would take for us to question our beliefs about what happens to young people when they are turned into warriors. It had occurred to me that displaying the flag and thanking troops for their service are well-intended, but likely are also how we avoid acknowledging the toll that war actually takes.

The marijuana war is also maintained by fragments of truth and unquestioned myths. Drug education emphasizes the kinds of harms users risk, but rarely acknowledges the benefits at all. We count how many enter treatment for marijuana problems, but not the numbers of users who are free of harm. We argue that protecting young people and the general public justifies prohibition, but are unwilling to honestly evaluate the extent to which it accomplishes its health and safety goals. We choose not to put on the table, even to ponder, what might possibly be a more effective marijuana policy so as not to risk losing face or attracting the ire of others.

Now, Alison's invitation had plopped into my lap the need to make a decision in the midst of powerful pushes and pulls, major uncertainties, and a realization that a perfect choice, one that comes with no risks, is unavailable. Weighing the options brought to the foreground signposts I had followed for much of my adult life. When I looked back and then forward, reaching for synthesis if it indeed could be found, a number of threads became apparent.

One joined the 12-year-old's plight while being bullied with that of the 25-year-old who could not send enough people home from war. Refuge. I'd known the longing for a safe haven from danger. Eventually I saw how getting high could serve as a portal to shelter.

Another began with a court martial board's prison sentence for pot possession, continued with a senator's effort to blame a war atrocity on drugs, and knotted off with wild claims that marijuana was either an insidious evil or merely an innocuous herb. That thread wended its way through one professor's challenge to ask who benefits when certain groups are oppressed, and another's tracing of the parallel prohibition histories of absinthe and marijuana. This thread was about myth. I'd come to realize that the erroneous beliefs many held about marijuana's effects, either of risks or their absence, were not solely based on lack of scientific evidence or ignorance but rather were often the result of an intentional misrepresentation of what's true to serve some political purpose.

A third thread stitched together patches that included a time when my own marijuana dependence was both eroding my marriage and keeping me stuck, my choosing to develop and test marijuana counseling approaches, and lessons learned from being a therapist. This thread was about human vulnerability to being wounded in the pursuit of happiness or relief. I found a niche, a focus for trying to make a difference in the field and in the lives of marijuana-dependent adults and adolescents with whom I worked.

Better understanding what I had cared about in my twenties and thirties was clearly important now. Those signposts alerted me to question what appear to be commonly accepted truths. They eventually prepared me for the decision I made that early day in June when the rhodies were in bloom and it was spring in Seattle.

It's not as if I'd resolved all of my doubts. I knew there'd be a risk for me in stepping into an advocacy role once again. Inevitably, some of my fellow activists would argue that marijuana should be legal because it's harmless. Being misperceived as agreeing with that conclusion because of the company I'd be keeping came with the territory. I'd deal with it.

On the day I made my decision, I realized a leap of faith would be needed, faith that once the new law had been passed, the regulated market would be implemented with public safety in mind and have strong enforcement, the profit motive would somehow be kept in check, and we would find a way as a society to shape norms favoring responsible decisions and behaviors. None of this was certain.

And then there were the uncertainties about doing nothing.

When I first became active in marijuana law reform I was spurred on by the story of an 18-year-old kid who'd been caught at the Canadian border possessing half a joint, the consequence of that youthful indiscretion being jail time and a criminal record that would potentially close doors for him for years to come. More recently, the plight faced by the many parents who seek my advice about their kids who are using marijuana also has been in my thoughts. Their challenge in helping their children navigate a world in which pot is readily available, but effective drug prevention, accurate information, and ready access to treatment are not, is formidable. They and their families deserve better.

Along the way, my own struggle with marijuana dependence and my brother's death from an opiate overdose have kept permeable the membrane that separates what's personal, the realities of life I've experienced first-hand, and what's hypothetical. I'm grateful for that, even if it withholds the comfort of certainty. And here's the deal: We now have a whole culture stuck in a stockade because of marijuana prohibition.

It's time. We need to come home from this war.

EPILOGUE

C heryl and I flew east to be with my family for Thanksgiving this year. The following day was crisp and sunny, and we walked along the Freedom Trail in the Charlestown section of Boston on our way to the Bunker Hill Monument.

The 221-foot granite obelisk stands on sacred ground, commemorating the first major battle of the American War of Independence on June 17, 1775. Exhibits in the adjacent museum jogged our memories of what we had first learned as schoolchildren.

When Great Britain's Parliament imposed the Stamp Act of 1765, the colonists formed a Continental Congress. But when they destroyed shiploads of taxed British tea in an act of defiance, the gauntlet was thrown. London dissolved the colonists' self-government, the Americans began to gather weapons, and British troops were sent to seize them. War ensued.

We found an unoccupied bench on the monument grounds. Basking in the sunshine, we watched scores of tourists lining up to climb the 294 steps to the top. Many stopped to read the outside educational displays that provided period maps of the area and recounted the three main assaults by British troops on the colonists' fortifications. A National Park Service brochure quoted an observer of the carnage: "In the evening the streets were filled with the wounded and the dying; the sight of which, with the lamentations of the women and children over their husbands and fathers, pierced one to the soul."

Defiance. Bunker Hill had been one of the resounding shouts of "no" in our country's history, and there were many of them. The Union said no to the attempted secession of southern states that led to the Civil War. Rosa Parks refused to move to the back of the bus and sparked the civil rights movement. And during the war in Vietnam, hundreds and thousands of young people had protested in a massive show of opposition, saying no.

As we sat there, my thoughts drifted to the recent 2012 election. In another act of defiance, although of an entirely different order of magnitude, Washington state voters approved the marijuana legalization initiative that Alison Holcomb had drafted and so effectively championed. Because federal law prohibits the sale and possession of marijuana and ostensibly preempts the states from taking an alternative policy stance, many expected our state, as well as Colorado which also had legalized marijuana, would be sued to prevent these new laws from going into effect.

When the possibility of preemption was raised, the campaign's activists replied by quoting U.S. Supreme Court Justice Louis Brandeis. He once wrote, "It is one of the happy incidents of the federal system that a single courageous State may, if its citizens choose, serve as a laboratory, and try novel social and economic experiments without risk to the rest of the country."

The Obama administration agreed to not stand in the way of Washington and Colorado legalizing marijuana so long as certain conditions were met, e.g., preventing distribution to youth, out of state diversion, and marijuana growing or possession on public lands. So Washington was about to be a laboratory. But the experiment wouldn't really begin for a year. During that time, the Washington State Liquor Control Board would write rules and regulations concerning the licensing of marijuana growers, processors, and sellers. Then, the first licenses would be issued and a legal commercial marijuana market would be in place.

One aspect of the timing concerned me. Only after the state began to collect new tax revenues from marijuana sales would the earmarked funding for drug education and prevention begin to flow. I looked forward to the day when the public would be far more informed about the drug than it has ever been. Until then, however, I had a worry. The approval of legalization likely would be taken by some young people as a message that marijuana is harmless.

I wrote an op-ed column for the *Seattle Times* several days after the election in which I described my conversation with the father of a 15-year-old boy. The son had tried pot, telling his dad that lots of kids get high and it is no big deal. Noting his own knowledge about pot is dated, the dad asked me for an update.

I steered him to the National Institute on Drug Abuse website where booklets about pot, one for teens and another for parents, can be downloaded at no cost. I also emphasized the importance of parents talking with their children about marijuana and told him about a booklet written for parents to help them prepare for those conversations. Authored by Dr. Marsha Rosenbaum, it's titled "Safety First: A Reality-Based Approach to Teens and Drugs" and can be downloaded free in a number of languages from the Drug Policy Alliance website.

Watching the many visiting families posing for photos at Bunker Hill, I found myself remembering the personal importance of that fateful battle's date. June 17 also was Bryan's birthday. If he had lived he would have turned 57 this year. This Thanksgiving had marked the seventh year of his being missed at our family dinner. With Bryan's wife, Christina, and their now 14-year-old son, Bailey, sitting at the table, I felt his absence all the more. As Bailey excitedly told me about basketball tryouts on the following Monday, hoping he'd make the cut, I had a thought. Maybe there was something I could do for Bryan.

While the dishes were being cleared, I took my nephew aside. We walked together into another room.

"Hey, Bailey. Let's talk about pot."

POSTSCRIPT

T he clock is ticking.

Early in 2014, two states were rapidly moving to fully implement what their voters had endorsed in November of 2012: replacing prohibition with a regulated and taxed system, in which licensed retailers sell limited amounts of marijuana or marijuana-infused products, grown and produced by licensed businesses, to adult consumers.

Colorado's marijuana retail stores opened for business on New Year's Day of 2014, with thousands of customers purchasing an estimated $5 million of marijuana products in the first week. When they open their doors sometime in the spring of 2014, 334 licensed marijuana retailers in the state of Washington will follow suit.

An unprecedented détente underlies this sea change in the two states' laws. Notwithstanding the 2012 elections, a legal marijuana economy is in direct conflict with federal law. Indeed it also remains prohibited under the provisions of international treaties to which the U.S. is a signatory. Technically, what Colorado and Washington are doing should not be possible. Had they gone "by the book," the federal government would have challenged the two states in court just after the 2012 elections.

Nonetheless, the Department of Justice stood down, making a distinction between criminal matters that ought to be given priority by federal law enforcement authorities and those that properly remain in the province of the states. In August 2013, the Deputy Attorney General wrote to all U. S. Attorneys, instructing them that the new state legalization policies were to be permitted to move forward. However, the Justice Department pointedly retained the right to intervene if a state's regulatory scheme broke down.

In brief, Colorado and Washington would be under close scrutiny. Almost immediately, perceiving the Attorney General's memorandum as a green light, legalization proponents in a number of other states began their own campaigns. Alaska, California, Oregon, and Arizona may consider legalization in 2014. More states are likely to follow in 2016.

But, what does intense scrutiny mean? In essence, to avoid a later federal challenge and/or subsequent prosecution by federal authorities, the states will need to demonstrate that they are indeed succeeding in preventing: distribution to minors, revenues from legal sales ending up in the hands of criminal gangs or cartels, diversion of marijuana across state borders, licensed retailers offering "cover" for the sale of other illicit drugs, violence in the production or sale of marijuana, drugged driving and other adverse public health consequences due to marijuana use, and growing or possessing marijuana on federal lands.

So, as their regulatory schemes were finalized, licenses were issued, and a new marijuana retail industry was launched, the clock was ticking as many people in the rest of the country watched to see if these two states could succeed in meeting the requirements the feds had laid out. Skeptics voiced their doubts, particularly focusing on the likelihood of diversion to youth, increased drugged driving, and more users becoming dependent or otherwise requiring care for adverse health consequences. Others, noting the enormity of the estimated $2.34 billion legal marijuana market in 2014, saw the large infusion of new tax revenues for state and local governments as essentially a guarantee that there'd be no turning back.

A key question, therefore, is whether a proverbial red line, the line that must not be crossed without triggering a reprisal, will be heeded. Then again, even if these federal requirements are met, the next few years will also see elections, with the potential for a shift in the power balance in the nation's capital being yet another factor in determining whether this new approach gets stopped in its tracks. If the country politically veers to the right in 2016, might a new occupant in the White House or a conservative Congress pull the plug on legal marijuana? Three and a half decades earlier, that's precisely what happened. The rapidly increasing momentum of that era's marijuana policy reform movement, at that time one state after another decriminalizing possession of the drug, ground to a halt when Ronald Reagan was elected to the White House. Might we see history repeat itself?

Another question looms. Will the illicit marijuana economy in Washington and Colorado, the gangs and cartels that have fed consumer demand all these years, lose out when forced to compete with the legal retail system? Or will it continue to thrive, perhaps undercutting the prices charged in the licensed outlets or further exploiting the youth market by catering to underage consumers? Pulling the rug out from under illicit sellers is likely to require both a pricing and taxing policy that reinforces the consumer's motivation to purchase from legal purveyors, and focused efforts by the police and the courts to force illegal sellers out of business.

From my point of view, only part of the battle had been won when a legal regulated marijuana market replaced prohibition. The egregiously unjust racial inequities in how marijuana criminal penalties were metered out would end in Colorado and Washington. And burdening the many thousands of otherwise law-abiding people with life-long criminal records for marijuana possession offenses would also end. Third, millions of dollars in new tax revenues from this heretofore untaxed market would now be headed to state and local governments. All well and good.

Today, we're witnessing what Bruce Barcott, a *Rolling Stone* writer, referred to as "a political movement giving birth to an economic awakening." He sees marijuana legalization as "one of the greatest business opportunities of the 21st century." But there is much more than a "green rush" that I hope for as a co-sponsor of Initiative 502.

Washington's initiative provides for the earmarking of substantial excise tax revenues to science-based public education about marijuana, to funding effective prevention programs tailored for children and adolescents, to providing a state-wide marijuana help line, to paying for treatment for young people who struggle with marijuana dependence, to research on marijuana, and to evaluating the new law's impact on health and safety.

These provisions are key. Recognizing that criminal prohibition, while well intended, has not sufficiently protected the public from marijuana's risks, I believe that this package of public health activities will stand us in a better position to make a difference in protecting public health and public safety. For our roads to be safer, for consumers to be more accurately informed about marijuana, for those who are vulnerable (e.g., youth, individuals with a history of schizophrenia, individuals with heart disease) to be protected, and for young people to be supported in adopting pro-social norms about marijuana decisions, a solid public health alternative to prohibition is necessary.

Only time will tell, however, whether state authorities use these new revenues well in serving the Initiative's intent, and, if they do, whether the emphases on education, prevention, treatment, and research will indeed have the positive impacts I anticipate.

As we wait and watch, here are some very helpful online resources:

FOR PARENTS

A Parent's Guide to Preventing Underage Marijuana Use. This booklet, produced in 2013 by Seattle Children's Hospital and the University of Washington Social Development Research Group, offers information, resources, and practical advice for parents about:

- The effects of marijuana on adolescent health,
- Techniques for talking to your child about marijuana,
- What to do and how to help if your child is using marijuana,
- The basics of the law in Washington state.

http://learnaboutmarijuanawa.org/parentpreventionbooklet2013.pdf

FOR TEENS

Marijuana: Facts for Teens. Presented in question-and-answer format and targeted to teens. Provides facts about marijuana and its potential effects.

http://www.drugabuse.gov/publications/marijuana-facts-teens

FOR ADULT MARIJUANA CONSUMERS

Information for the Adult Consumer. A flyer that summarizes current knowledge concerning cannabinoids, percentages of THC and CBD, memory, driving, mental health, lungs, dependence, teens, and pregnancy. (http://learnaboutmarijuanawa.org/consumers.htm)

FOR GENERAL INFORMATION

The National Cannabis Prevention and Information Centre at the University of New South Wales in Australia. (http://ncpic.org.au/)

The University of Washington Alcohol and Drug Abuse Institute. (http://LearnAboutMarijuanaWa.org)

FOR INDIVIDUALS SEEKING SUPPORT IN QUITTING OR CUTTING BACK

"Reduce Your Use." A free online program that offers support, advice, and a six-week step-by-step guide. (https://reduceyouruse.org.au/sign-up/)

Marijuana Anonymous. In-person and online. "A fellowship of men and women who share our experiences, strength and hope with each other that we may solve our common problem and help others to recover from marijuana addiction." (https://www.marijuana-anonymous.org/)

ADVOCACY ORGANIZATIONS WORKING TO LEGALIZE MARIJUANA

The National Organization for the Reform of Marijuana Laws. (http://norml.org/)

The Marijuana Policy Project. (http://www.mpp.org/)

The Drug Policy Alliance. (http://www.drugpolicy.org/)

ADVOCACY ORGANIZATION WORKING TO OPPOSE LEGALIZED MARIJUANA

Project SAM. (http://learnaboutsam.com/)

ACKNOWLEDGMENTS

"Writing is a team sport," Max Regan said during one of his annual writers' retreats in Boulder, Colorado. While working on *Marijuana Nation* over a seven year period, that truth became more and more evident.

For their superb pedagogy as teachers of creative non-fiction writing, I'm grateful to Max, Sara Mansfield Taber, and Theo Pauline Nestor. Their workshops and classes, exercises they invented, readings they assigned, their lectures and demonstrations, group conversations they guided, and the feedback they offered, always with encouragement, introduced me to the craft and stimulated a keen desire to learn.

With Dorothy Van Soest and Mary Kabrich, in twice monthly writers' group sessions, we learn vicariously from one another's evolving work just how a narrative arc might be molded, characters made to emerge from mere outline into the full color spectrum, and the texture of place be captured in the written word. I savor the many sections of *Marijuana Nation* where their suggestions made all the difference and eagerly anticipate the conversations we'll continue to have about each new chapter and each new book. A huge and heartfelt thank you, Dorothy and Mary.

Former Army colleagues helped reconstruct bits and pieces of our shared history. Particular thanks to Jacob Romo and Paul d'Oronzio, Army social work officers who first taught me the ropes 47 years ago in Long Binh, Vietnam. William Baker, Spencer Bloch, Norman (Mike) Camp, Ely Sapol, and John Talbott each helped by reading a draft and/or discussing memories of long-ago experiences. Tom Corpora, back then a combat reporter for United Press International, was similarly generous with his comments.

I'm indebted to other friends and colleagues who gave me the opportunity to check the accuracy of my memories, filling in the blanks with their recollections from thirty, forty, even fifty years ago: Evi Adams, Gordon Brownell, David Droppa, Paul Elliott, Clark Elster, Tim Ford, Alison Holcomb, Ron Jackson, Vic Larsen, Marilyn Dexheimer Lawrence, Alan Marlatt, Henry Miller, Vidmantas Raisys, Irene Spencer, and Alan Thompson.

Bob Stephens, now professor and chair of Virginia Tech's Department of Psychology, was a wet-behind-the-ears post-doc fresh from Alan Marlatt's lab when he and I first began to explore ways of helping adults struggling with marijuana dependence in the mid-1980s. A great many budding researchers have benefitted from his skillful mentorship in the decades of our collaboration. Dr. Denise Walker joined us twelve years ago. Now ably carrying the University of Washington team's baton for our substance use disorder studies, Denise is an enthusiastic behavioral scientist who proficiently bridges the gap in "town/gown" research partnerships. Bob, Denise, and I have had the extraordinary good fortune to work with Devon Bushnell, the administrator of the Innovative Programs Research Group. I treasure my friendship with each of them.

When a full draft had been completed, several friends gave me the gift of their critical thinking, not just about what they liked, but more importantly telling me where my writing needed further work. I must extend my deepest thanks to Richard Dancer, Pauline Erera, Rich Furman, Jerry Gillmore, and Richard Weatherley.

I'm grateful to Greg Urban (Ideas Unfold, Inc.) who created an appealing website for the book along with a brief video, and took the photograph of Cheryl, Teddy, and me. Thanks, as well, to Dana Drake at Panda Lab in Seattle for his superb work in restoring old snapshots and slides.

I'm indebted to Peter Riva, literary agent who in 1975 founded International Transactions, Inc. with Sandra Riva, for representing me and for his wise counsel. Thank you, as well, to Associate Editor JoAnn Collins for her enthusiasm about the book.

Jessica Case, Associate Publisher of Pegasus Books, is a keenly astute editor whose queries and suggestions, wisdom and wealth of expertise, enhanced the story I wanted to tell. Thank you, Jessica, for "getting" this book. My deep thanks, as well, to Claiborne Hancock, Publisher, for having selected *Marijuana Nation*.

Memoir is profoundly personal, so much so that at times avoidance is tempting. Along the way, my sisters, Arlyn Roffman and Sherry Blodgett, took to heart what I was trying to do, opening themselves to discussions of difficult memories, recalling what I sometimes had closed off, and helping me more fully understand what each of our experiences had been "at home."

Last and most, all of my love to Cheryl Richey who was invariably in my corner, reliably authentic in her reactions to my drafts. When her comments weren't quite what I'd hoped for, I occasionally needed a bit of time to recognize the wisdom in what she was saying. I never stopped asking, though, because she so helpfully kept me on course. I'm inspired in so many ways by our walks across the sands, on beaches near and far, holding hands.

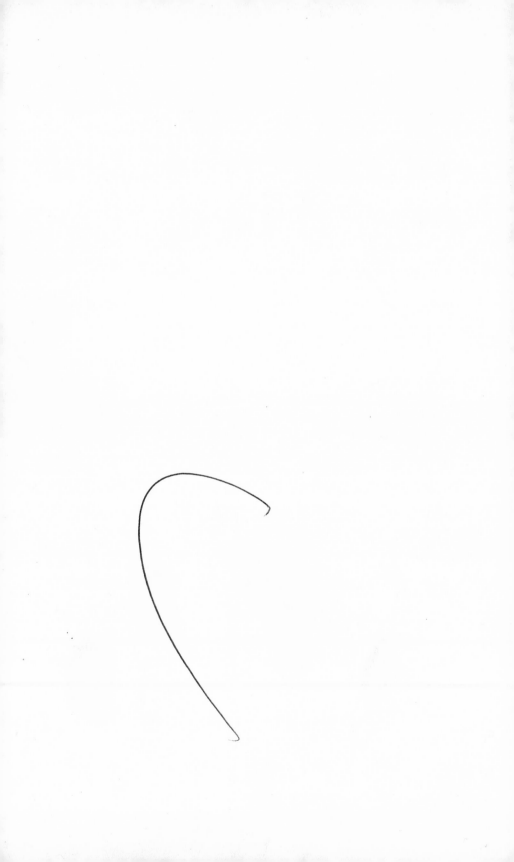